G C S E

A-Z

BIOLOGY

handbook

Steve Potter

Hodder & Stoug'

A MEMBER OF THE HODDER HEADL

D1382594

British Library Cataloguing in Publication Data
A catalogue entry for this title is available from the British Library

ISBN 0–340–75357–9

First published 1999
Impression number 10 9 8 7 6 5 4 3 2
Year   2003 2002

Typeset by GreenGate Publishing Services, Tonbridge, Kent.
Printed and bound in Great Britain for Hodder and Stoughton Educational, a division of Hodder Headline Plc, 338 Euston Road, London NW1 3BH by The Bath Press, Bath.

HOW TO USE THIS BOOK

The *GCSE A–Z Biology Handbook* is a textbook which explains all the main terms used in GCSE Biology syllabuses by all the examining boards. It covers all the terms contained in the core Biology syllabus as well as those contained in the different extension topics in all the major GCSE Biology syllabuses.

Some terms naturally relate to others and an extensive cross-referencing system is used. Italics refer you to a topic covered elsewhere in the book that may help you in your understanding of the term you are looking up.

Understanding is the keynote to success and every effort has been made to ensure that all the terms are presented in as user friendly a manner as possible.

Each term begins with a simple, one sentence definition. There is then a more detailed explanation of the term including, where relevant, links with other areas of Biology.

Coursework is an important part of any Biology syllabus and an appendix has been included specifically to help you get the best marks possible for your coursework.

Three other appendices deal with examiners' terms, revision terms and hints for exam success.

An appreciation of examiners' terms is essential to avoid wasting time in an examination. Each year many candidates waste time and lose marks by giving detailed descriptions when explanations have been asked for. They lose marks by drawing bar charts when they should draw line graphs. You should use this section of the book from the start of your course. Whenever you have a homework which is a past examination question, get into the habit of checking precisely what the question is asking and how you should go about answering it.

The lists of revision terms have been specifically designed to help you to revise key areas of your Biology syllabus. Each list identifies the most important terms for that area of the syllabus and you should make sure you understand these first. The cross-referencing will refer you to other, related terms. The lists are arranged according to syllabus content and so to use this section effectively, you must make quite certain of the syllabus you are following.

Hints for exam success suggests strategies you can adopt from the very first day of your Biology course, through to the moment you walk into the examination room. It shows you some of the commonest ways marks are lost in an examination and suggests a way of approaching the final written examination which will help you to score as many marks as possible.

The *GCSE A–Z Biology Handbook* is a book to use throughout your course to help you with homeworks, coursework assessments, revision for tests, clarifying today's lesson notes or quite simply just to browse through to gain some further understanding. At the end of your course you can use the revision lists as a focus for your revision.

I hope that you get some of the enjoyment from reading the book that I have found in writing it and I wish you every success in your Biology course.

Steve Potter

ACKNOWLEDGEMENTS

I am grateful to Margaret Heritage, Subject Officer for Biology at the Southern Examining Group, for suggesting my name as author of this book. I would like to thank Tim Gregson-Williams and Greig Aitken of Hodder and Stoughton for their help and support during its production

I would also like to thank my wife, Vivienne, for understanding the hours of isolation and for providing a constant supply of caffeine (look it up under 'drug'). Finally, I would like to thank my two daughters, Elizabeth and Hannah, for giving me the real reason (poverty) for completing the book.

Steve Potter

abdomen: the body cavity of a mammal below the *diaphragm*.
The abdomen contains:
- the organs of the *digestive system* except the oesophagus
- the liver, spleen and pancreas
- the kidneys, ureters and bladder
- in females, the ovaries, Fallopian tubes and uterus

as well as the blood vessels and nerves which supply these organs and the
parts of the spine and spinal cord which run through the abdomen.

abiotic: non-living!
Biologists often use the term abiotic to describe a feature of an *ecosystem*
which is non-living. Abiotic features include:
- rainfall
- soil pH
- temperature
- light intensity.

Abiotic features help to determine the types and numbers of organisms
which can survive in an area. If the soil is very acidic, only plants adapted to
those conditions can survive. If a farmer adds too much lime and the soil
becomes more alkaline, these plants may die out and others take their place.
This can then affect the types of animals which can survive with the new
plants as their food source.

absorption: taking substances into cells.
Substances enter cells by one of three processes:
- *osmosis* – only water enters cells by osmosis
- *diffusion* – particles move down a *concentration gradient*, e.g. gas
  exchange in the alveoli
- *active transport* – particles move against a *concentration gradient*, e.g. root
  hair cells absorb mineral ions by active transport.

The surface area of a *cell* plays a big part in determining how effective it can
be in absorbing substances. The *microvilli* on cells lining the gut and the
'hairs' on root hair cells give these cells a large surface area for absorption.

accommodation: the ability of the *eye* to change focus between near and more distant objects so that an object at any distance can be seen clearly. Humans do this by making the lens fatter (more convex) to focus on near objects or thinner (less convex) to focus on distant objects.
Hint: Look at an object which is very close for a few seconds and you can feel the strain of the ciliary muscles contracting.

acetylcholine: a substance which transmits a nerve impulse across a *synapse*.
Substances which do this are called *neurotransmitters*. Acetylcholine is the most common of these.

acid: a substance which lowers the pH of a solution by releasing hydrogen ions (H^+) when it dissolves.
- If the pH of a solution is less than 7, it is an acidic solution.
- Indicators are substances which show a change in the pH of a solution by changing colour as the pH changes.
- Hydrochloric acid (HCl), nitric acid (HNO_3) and sulphuric acids (H_2SO_4) are strong acids because they release a great many hydrogen ions when they dissolve in water.
- Ethanoic acid and citric acid are weak acids because they release relatively few hydrogen ions when they dissolve in water.
- Acids react with alkalis to neutralise them.

acid rain: rain which is significantly more acidic than normal because gases such as sulphur dioxide and nitrogen oxides are dissolved in the rain.
Rain is often naturally slightly acidic because carbon dioxide dissolves in the rain. This creates a weak solution of carbonic acid.

FORMATION

- Most of the sulphur dioxide and nitrogen oxides are formed when power stations burn fossil fuels such as coal and oil. A smaller amount of sulphur dioxide is released naturally during volcanic eruptions. Small amounts of nitrogen oxides are released during lightning storms.
- Air currents may carry the gases hundreds of miles.
- The gases dissolve in moisture to produce sulphuric acid, nitric acid and other acids.
- The acids fall with the rain, forming acid rain.

EFFECTS

- Some conifers (such as red spruce) are killed directly because the acid rain damages their needle-like leaves.
- Soil is made more acidic causing:metal ions, such as aluminium ions, to be leached from the soil into lakes; these ions are often toxic to fish.
- Acidic soil causes *root hairs* to be less effective in absorbing some mineral ions from the soil, so slowing the growth of trees.
- Lakes and rivers become more acidic causing death of *bacteria, algae,* and the eggs of fish and amphibians.
- The increased acidity in lakes and rivers causes a change in the ecosystem, because many species cannot tolerate the acidic conditions.

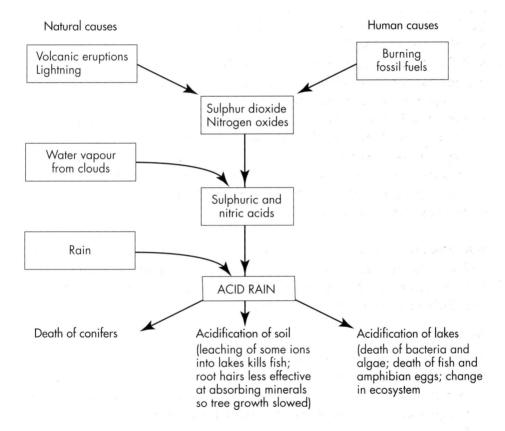

activated sludge method: a method of sewage treatment in which the liquid sewage is broken down by aerobic **microorganisms** in a sewage treatment tank.

When the sewage enters the **treatment tank:**

- bacteria and protozoa **are added to it**
- these microorganisms **digest the organic material in the sewage**

● oxygen is bubbled through the tank to allow the microorganisms to work effectively.

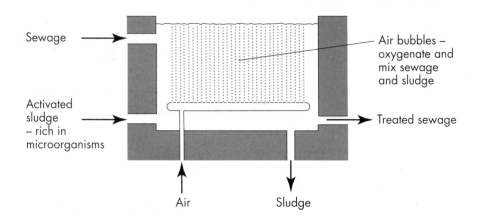

activation energy: the minimum amount of extra energy which must be supplied to particles before they will react.

A piece of paper does not burst into flames just because there is oxygen surrounding it; the particles do not have enough energy to react. But, if you supply more energy by striking a match and holding it to the paper, it will burn. The burning match gives the particles their activation energy. *Enzymes* speed up many biological reactions because they lower the activation energy of the reaction.

Hint: Think of the activation energy for a reaction like a high jump bar. If the bar is set too high, none of the particles have the energy to 'jump' it and so cannot react. If it can be lowered, most of the particles will have the energy to 'jump' the activation energy bar and so the reaction takes place quickly.

active site: the part of an *enzyme* molecule which is shaped so that only molecules which will fit the shape can react together (see *lock and key hypothesis*).

● The active site of an enzyme brings the reacting molecules much closer together than they would normally be and so lowers the *activation energy* of the reaction.
● The very precise shape of an active site means that it can bind with certain molecules only and so enzymes are very specific in the reactions they can catalyse.
● The shape of the active site is changed by too high a temperature and a pH which is too acidic or alkaline.

- Changes in the shape of the active site make the enzyme less able to catalyse the reaction as the reacting molecules will not fit the active site properly; this is called denaturation.

active transport: moving particles into or out of a cell against a concentration gradient, i.e. from a region of low concentration to a region of high concentration.

Particles tend to move from a high concentration to a low one by *diffusion* – with the concentration gradient. To move them against the gradient, cells must use energy from respiration.

Active transport is used to:
- absorb mineral ions from the soil into root hair cells
- absorb glucose molecules from the small intestine.

Cells which carry out active transport often contain many *mitochondria* to supply the necessary energy.

adaptation: a feature or modification which improves the survival chances, in a particular environment, of the organism which possesses it.

Examples of adaptations include:
- plants living in a dry environment may have an extensive root system which can absorb water from a wide area (e.g. *cacti* in the desert)
- mammals with thick fur can retain body heat and withstand freezing environments better (e.g. polar bears in the arctic).

addiction: a craving for and a dependence on a particular *drug*; the dependence may be psychological or physical.

In psychological dependence:
- there are no physiological changes (no changes in the way the body actually works)
- the user becomes emotionally dependent on the drug
- when the drug has been metabolised (used up) by the body, the user craves the sense of elation it produced
- withdrawal (not taking the drug any more) produces emotional distress.

In physical dependence:
- there are physiological changes – for example, there may be more neuro-transmitters released in the brain or more adrenaline secreted into the bloodstream
- the body quickly adapts to functioning in the new physiological state
- when the drug has been metabolised by the body the changes it produced vanish and the body does not function as well; withdrawal symptoms begin to appear

- withdrawal can produce mental distress and physical pain (sometimes including vomiting, cramps, fits and coma).

The two most socially acceptable drugs, nicotine and alcohol, can both produce physical dependence as well as causing damage to a range of body organs. (See *alcohol abuse*.)

adenosine triphosphate: see *ATP*.

ADH: anti-diuretic hormone; a hormone released by the *pituitary gland* which causes less water to be lost in the urine.

When we lose too much water (e.g. during exercise when we sweat a lot):

- our blood plasma becomes more concentrated than usual
- this triggers the pituitary gland to release ADH into the blood plasma
- ADH travels to the kidneys where it causes the collecting ducts to reabsorb more water
- less water is lost in the urine as a result.

When you have a drink and the water balance returns to normal, the pituitary stops releasing ADH.

adolescence: the period of life between childhood and adulthood.

Adolescence commences with the physical changes of *puberty* (the development of the sex organs and secondary sex characteristics).

In adolescence, typically:

- the young person wants to be independent but still needs to rely heavily on parents for emotional and financial support
- there are family conflicts because the young person demands more independence than parents feel they can give
- the young person relies less on parents and teachers as role models and more on other adult figures
- the young person experiments with views, opinions appearance and general behaviour before developing an adult identity.

Adolescence is a period of complex emotional development which goes hand in glove with the physical changes of puberty. It is not just sex and spots!

adrenal glands: a pair of *endocrine glands,* one located just above each kidney (see *endocrine system*).

- They produce a number of hormones which are secreted directly into the blood plasma.
- The main hormone is *adrenaline* which helps the body react to a stressful situation.

adrenaline: a hormone produced by the *adrenal glands*.
It is secreted into the blood plasma in response to stress and is sometimes called the hormone of fright and flight.
Adrenaline causes:

- dilation of the *arterioles* leading to muscles and the brain
- constriction of arterioles leading to the gut, skin and kidneys
- increased cardiac output by increasing the heart rate and the amount of blood pumped per beat
- an increase in the conversion of glycogen to glucose
- more nerve impulses to be allowed into the brain.

Most of these changes cause more blood with more oxygen and glucose to enter the muscles. The muscles can therefore respire faster and for longer without suffering *fatigue*. More nerve impulses entering the brain makes us more alert and better able to deal with the stressful situation.

aerobic respiration: an oxygen-requiring process which releases energy from glucose molecules; the energy released is stored in molecules of *ATP*. The equation summarises the process:

$$\text{glucose} + \text{oxygen} \longrightarrow \text{carbon dioxide} + \text{water} + \text{energy released}$$
$$C_6H_{12}O_6 + 6O_2 \longrightarrow 6CO_2 + 6H_2O + 38ATP$$

The energy released is used to:

- maintain a constant, high body temperature in mammals and birds
- contract muscles so that we can move, breathe, the heart can beat and *peristalsis* can take place
- build large molecules from small ones; e.g. join amino acids to form a protein or join glucose molecules to form starch (in plants) or glycogen (in animals)
- absorb substances against a concentration gradient by *active transport*; e.g. to absorb glucose from the gut.

Aerobic respiration takes place in the *mitochondria*. Very active cells, such as muscle cells, contain many mitochondria to release the energy they need.

afferent: leading or carrying towards a structure, the opposite of efferent.
Afferent neurones carry nerve impulses into the central nervous system.
Afferent arterioles in the kidney carry blood to the capillaries of the *glomerulus*.

afterbirth: the name given to the structures forced out of the *uterus* after the birth of a baby.

The afterbirth consists largely of the *placenta* and the membranes which surrounded the baby inside the uterus.

agar: a powder containing a mixture of two polysaccharides produced by some algae.

Agar is used to culture bacteria and fungi in the laboratory.
- The powder is boiled with water and then poured into petri dishes.
- When cool, it forms a gel on which the bacteria can grow.
- The petri dish containing the agar is sterilised before use.

Scientists can make a range of agars by adding different nutrients, to culture particular bacteria and fungi.

Agar is also used as a stabiliser in the food industry and as a laxative.

air: the mixture of gases which makes up the earth's atmosphere.

The composition of normal, dry air is:

Gas	Percentage (by volume)
oxygen	20.94
nitrogen	78.08
argon	0.93
carbon dioxide	0.03
other gases	0.02

albinism: a rare inherited condition which results in the inability to make the pigment *melanin*. Albinism occurs in many animal species.

Melanin is the main pigment in the skin, hair and irises of the eyes and gives them their colour. Without this pigment, at birth, the skin and hair are almost white and the irises are a pinkish colour (because of the blood flowing through them).

The *allele* which causes albinism is recessive.

Albinism has two serious consequences:
- cancers form more readily on exposed areas, especially in regions where sunlight is intense (there is no melanin to protect the surface cells from the ultraviolet rays in the sunlight)
- eyesight is often poor and individuals cannot stand bright light (there is no melanin in the iris to limit the amount of light entering the eye).

albino: an individual who suffers from *albinism*.

albustix: a card strip with a reagent at one end which can be used to test urine for the presence of protein.
To carry out the test:
- dip the reagent end of the strip in fresh urine for 10 seconds
- remove the strip and tap off any excess liquid
- look for a colour change.

If the reagent changes colour from brown to purple/violet, protein is present in the urine.

alcohol: a substance produced by the *fermentation* of sugars by *yeast*.
There are many different alcohols; the one produced in fermentation is called ethanol.

alcohol abuse: drinking alcoholic drinks to excess over a long period.
Alcohol is a drug and repeated heavy drinking can lead to dependence. It is a *depressant* and has short-term effects on the *central nervous system* as well as long-term effects on a range of organs.

SHORT-TERM EFFECTS

Concentration in blood (mg per 100 ml)	Effects
0–50	increased confidence, more talkative, reactions slower
50–150	co-ordination markedly reduced, self control reduced, irresponsible behaviour
150–250	confusion, slurred speech, unsteady, may exhibit emotional outbusts/aggression
250–400	extreme confusion, disorientation, cannot stand, incoherent speech, may fall into a coma
400–500	coma, risk of death due to stopping breathing

alcoholic fermentation: see *anaerobic respiration*.

algae: a group of mainly aquatic organisms which are not plants, yet which can photosynthesise.
The size and shape of the algae varies enormously and includes:
- tiny one-celled organisms
- filaments (strings of cells) several centimetres long
- seaweeds several metres long.

Some have *flagella* and can move; others are fixed. Some form symbiotic associations with fungi and some with animals.

Some algae are important economically and commercially.

- Alginates and carrageenin (chemicals produced by some algae) are used as stabilisers in the food and pharmaceutical industries (although these products are now often produced by genetically engineered bacteria).
- Agar (for culturing bacteria) can be produced from algae.
- Some are important foods and are considered delicacies in Japan and China in particular.
- Algal blooms (rapid growths of algae in rivers and ponds) can lead to oxygen depletion in the water and death of fish and other animals.

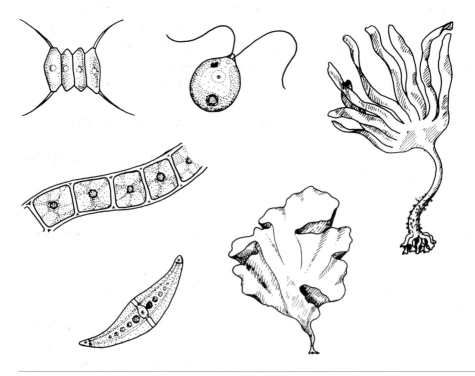

alimentary canal: the gut of an animal; it extends from the mouth to the anus.

The main regions of the alimentary canal are the mouth, stomach, small intestine and large intestine. The alimentary canal carries out four basic processes:

- ingestion of food
- *digestion* of food
- absorption of digested food
- *egestion* of indigestible materials.

alkali: a soluble, metal hydroxide (e.g. hydroxide of sodium, potassium, lithium). Ammonium hydroxide is also an alkali.

When alkalis dissolve in water they:

- release hydroxide ions (OH^-) into it
- the hydroxide ions react with some of the hydrogen ions (H^+) present to form water molecules
- this lowers the concentration of hydrogen ions in the solution and raises the pH. If the pH rises above pH 7, we say that the solution is **alkaline**.

Other substances can also form alkaline solutions but, because they are not soluble metal hydroxides, they are called bases not alkalis.

---

all or nothing: a term which describes the nature of a *nerve impulse*.

Neurones (nerve cells) transmit impulses (not messages or signals!) when they are stimulated by either a sense cell or another neurone.

A nerve impulse is said to be 'all or nothing' because:

- a nerve impulse is triggered only if the stimulation from the other cell reaches a certain threshold (if it is strong enough)
- no nerve impulse is triggered if the stimulation does not reach the threshold
- there are no weak or strong nerve impulses – there is just a nerve impulse or no nerve impulse – 'all or nothing'.

So how can the brain distinguish between a bright orange light and a dim orange light if all nerve impulses are the same? This is possible because the bright light triggers more nerve impulses per second than the dim one. The brain interprets these as a more intense colour.

---

allele: one of the forms of a *gene* controlling a particular feature.

For example:

- in humans, the gene for melanin production has two alleles – normal and albino
- in pea plants, the gene for height has two alleles – tall and dwarf
- in guinea pigs, the gene for hair length has two alleles – short and long (Angora).

All individuals inherit two alleles of each gene: one from each parent. The alleles they inherit may be the same (they will be *homozygous)* or different (they will be *heterozygous)*. In this case one of the alleles is often *dominant* over the other, which is *recessive*. In all the examples above, the first allele is the dominant one.

---

alveolus (plural alveoli): a small air sac at the end of one of the finest *bronchioles* in the *lungs*.

The alveoli are the places where gas exchange between air and blood takes place. Oxygen diffuses from the air in the alveoli into the bloodstream and carbon dioxide diffuses in the opposite direction.

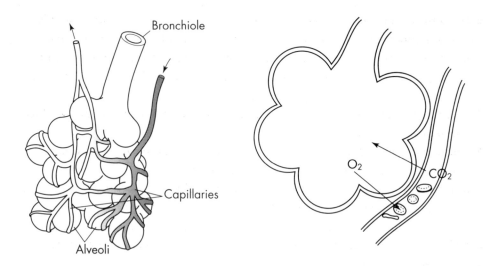

Note: oxygen is carried around the body by haemoglobin in the red blood cells. Carbon dioxide is carried in the blood plasma.

Gas exchange is extremely efficient because:

- each alveolus is surrounded by a dense network of capillaries
- there are many alveoli creating a very large surface area in contact with the capillaries
- the walls of the alveoli are very thin (only one cell thick) so the gases can pass easily through them
- the walls of the alveoli are moist.

---

amino acid: an organic compound containing the elements carbon, hydrogen, oxygen and nitrogen.

Amino acids can be linked together to form large molecules called proteins. The way in which the amino acids are joined determines the type of protein which is produced.

Plants and animals obtain their amino acids in different ways.

- Plants make amino acids by combining nitrogen from nitrates from the soil with carbohydrates produced in *photosynthesis.*
- Animals digest proteins in their food using enzymes called *proteases* to release the individual amino acids which are then absorbed into the bloodstream.

The amino acids are used to make proteins for the plant or animal. Humans need about twenty amino acids to make all the proteins in their bodies. Some of these can be made in the liver by converting one amino acid into another. Those which cannot be made in this way must be obtained from our food and are called essential amino acids.

ammonium compound: a compound containing the ammonium ion (NH_4^+). The ammonium ion contains nitrogen and so ammonium compounds are used in many *fertilisers* to supply the nitrogen plants need to make proteins. Ammonium nitrate (NH_4NO_3) is a particularly effective fertiliser because it contains nitrogen in two different forms:

- nitrate ions (NO_3^-) – these are taken up immediately by plants and produce immediate growth
- ammonium ions (NH_4^+) – these are slowly converted to nitrate by *nitrifying bacteria* in the soil and are taken up later.

Ammonium ions are formed naturally from proteins and amino acids in dead organisms when they are decomposed by bacteria and fungi.

amnion: one of the membranes which surrounds the *embryo / fetus* in the *uterus* (see *pregnancy*).

The amnion produces a clear liquid called *amniotic fluid* (or, commonly, 'the waters') which surrounds the fetus and cushions it against pressure from the internal organs.

When birth is imminent, the amnion breaks and the amniotic fluid is lost through the vagina.

amniotic fluid: the clear liquid produced by the *amnion* which cushions the embryo/fetus and protects it from physical damage before birth.

Amoeba: a one-celled organism which uses *pseudopodia* for movement. Most species of *Amoeba* are free-living and are often found on the mud at the bottom of still water (e.g. a pond). A few are *parasites*: one species can live in the human gut and cause severe diarrhoea.

amphibians: a group of *vertebrates* with a slimy skin; adults can live on land but return to water to breed.

Amphibians:
- are vertebrates with slimy, non-scaly skin
- produce eggs with no shells
- reproduce sexually in water using external fertilisation
- breathe using gills when living in water
- breathe using lungs and skin when living on land.

Most amphibians have a distinct aquatic larval and land-dwelling adult stage in their life cycle (the familiar tadpole is the larval stage of the adult frog). The change from larva to adult is called *metamorphosis*. A few amphibians (such as some salamanders) do not metamorphose fully and reproduce while still in the larval form.

amylase: a *digestive enzyme* which breaks down *starch* into maltose. Starch is a polysaccharide which consists of hundreds of glucose molecules joined together in a chain.
Amylase:
- breaks this long chain molecule into pairs of glucose molecules (each pair is called maltose) by a process called hydrolysis
- is produced in the salivary glands and the pancreas of humans, by germinating seeds and by many microorganisms

Amylases have many commercial applications, such as brewing, production of baby foods, production of some digestive aids and production of agents to strip wallpaper!

anabolic reaction: any biological reaction which links smaller molecules to form larger ones.
Examples include:
- joining amino acids to form proteins
- joining glucose molecules to form glycogen
- producing glucose from carbon dioxide and water in *photosynthesis*.

Anabolic reactions always need an input of energy.

anabolic steroid: a *drug* which increases muscle mass, strength, endurance and aggression.

These drugs are called anabolic steroids because they promote protein synthesis and, therefore, can increase muscle mass.

Most anabolic steroids:

- are synthetic (man-made)
- resemble the male sex hormone, testosterone
- need to be injected, although a few can be swallowed.

They are used in medicine to treat:

- injuries involving severe muscle damage
- some types of anaemia
- occasionally, older women suffering from osteoporosis.

Some athletes abuse anabolic steroids in an attempt to improve their perfomance. This is illegal and may also have serious side-effects including damage to the liver and adrenal glands, infertility and impotence in men. Women who abuse anabolic steroids risk altering their body shape to become more like that of a man.

---

anaemia: a condition in which concentration of *haemoglobin* in the bloodstream is lower than normal.

There are many types of anaemia, but there are three main categories:

- too few *red blood cells* are produced
- each red blood cell has too little haemoglobin
- red blood cells do not survive as long as is usual.

The commonest type of anaemia is caused by a lack of iron (which is needed to make haemoglobin) and results in each red cell having too little haemoglobin. The underlying cause of a lack of iron can be:

- a poor diet
- heavy bleeding (e.g. from heavier than usual menstruation)
- poor absorption of iron from the gut.

People suffering from anaemia may have a pale skin and tire easily.

---

anaerobic respiration: a process which releases energy from glucose without needing oxygen to do so; the energy released is stored in molecules of ATP.

In anaerobic respiration:

- the glucose molecules are only partly broken down
- very little of the energy stored in the molecule is released
- in humans the process forms lactic acid as a by-product
- in yeast the by-product is alcohol (ethanol) and the process is also called alcoholic fermentation.

The equations summarise the process:

glucose $\longrightarrow$ lactic acid + little energy released (humans)

$C_6H_{12}O_6 \longrightarrow 2C_3H_6O_3 +$ 2ATP

glucose $\longrightarrow$ ethanol + carbon dioxide + little energy released (yeast)

$C_6H_{12}O_6 \longrightarrow 2C_2H_5OH + 2CO_2 +$ 2ATP

When we exercise:
- anaerobic respiration provides extra energy if the aerobic process cannot supply all that we need
- lactic acid is produced; it builds up in the muscles and causes the familiar 'stitch' or 'cramp'
- we must then stop or slow down to allow us to oxidise the lactic acid; the amount of oxygen we need to do this is called the *oxygen debt*
- the time we take after exercise to oxidise the lactic acid is called the *recovery period*.

analgesic: any treatment which reduces the sensation of pain.
Commonly used analgesic drugs include aspirin, ibuprofen and paracetamol.
When we injure ourselves, chemicals called prostaglandins are released at the site of injury and these trigger nerve impulses to the brain. The brain interprets these impulses as 'pain'.
Analgesics work in one of two ways:
- they prevent the formation of prostaglandins at the site of injury – aspirin and ibuprofen work in this way
- they block the nerve impulses in the brain – paracetamol works in this way.
If you use analgesics to relieve pain, you should do so strictly according to the manufacturer's instructions. If the pain persists, you should see a doctor.

androgens: male sex hormones like testosterone produced by specialised cells in the *testes*.
Androgens are produced throughout life, but production is raised before birth and again at *puberty*.
Before birth androgens control:
- initial development of sex organs
- descent of testes into the scrotum.
At puberty androgens control:
- further development of the sex organs
- production of sperm by the testes
- the *secondary sexual characteristics* (growth of facial hair, deepening of voice, broadening of shoulders, etc.)

- adolescent growth spurt.

The effects of androgens at puberty are maintained into adult life.

angiosperms: seed-bearing plants which have true *flowers*.
The group has a huge range of forms. Angiosperms include daisies, dandelions, horse chestnut trees and water-lilies. There are more than 230 000 known species of angiosperms, and many scientists think that there may be nearer one million!
They all share these two features:
- their reproductive structures (stamens and carpels) are found inside flowers
- seeds are formed following fertilisation.

animals: one of the five kingdoms in modern classification systems.
All animals:
- are multicellular
- have cells with no cell walls
- must ingest their food into a digestive system
- develop from a hollow ball of cells (called a blastula) which forms from the zygote after fertilisation.

You must take care not to confuse organisms like *Amoeba* with animals. These one-celled organisms used to be classified as animals, but they are now placed in a separate kingdom – the *protoctista*.

annelids: a phylum of invertebrate animals with segmented bodies and no limbs.

Annelids are soft-bodied animals with a fluid-filled body cavity. Examples include earthworms and leeches.

annual: a plant which completes its life cycle in one year.
During the year, the plant:
- germinates from seed as soon as conditions are favourable
- grows
- flowers and produces seeds
- dies.

Poppies and marigolds are examples of annuals.

antagonistic muscles: a pair of muscles which produce the opposite effect when they contract.

The biceps and triceps muscles in the arm form an antagonistic pair. When the biceps contracts, it pulls the forearm up and bends the arm at the elbow. When the triceps contracts, it pulls the forearm down and straightens the arm.

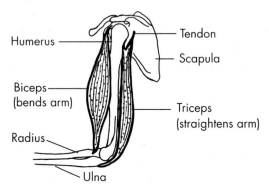

Muscles must be arranged in pairs because each muscle can only move a bone by pulling it when it contracts. When the muscle relaxes, it does not exert any force and so cannot push the bone back into its original position. Another muscle must contract and pull it back.

Muscles do not just move bones; three antagonistic pairs of muscles co-operate to move each eyeball up, down, sideways and even round and round!

antenna: a jointed structure on the head of some *arthropods*.
Antennae are nearly always sensitive to either touch or smell, but a few *crustaceans* have antennae adapted for attachment or swimming.

anterior: a term which means towards the head end of an animal; opposite of posterior.

For example, the anterior vena cava returns blood to the heart from the head and neck, that is the regions anterior to the heart.

anther: the part of the *flower* where the pollen grains are produced.
The anther:
- is part of the stamen which is the male reproductive organ in flowering plants
- contains four pollen sacs which form pollen grains by *meiosis*
- releases the pollen grains from the pollen sacs when they are fully developed.

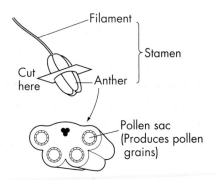

antibiotic: any substance produced by one type of microorganism which kills or prevents the growth of another microorganism.

Antibiotics:

- are used to treat infections caused by *bacteria*
- act by disturbing bacterial cell wall formation, protein synthesis or DNA replication
- may kill bacteria (bactericidal antibiotics) or just prevent their reproduction (bacteriostatic antibiotics)
- are ineffective against viruses because viruses only become active inside other cells
- can be effective against many bacteria (broad spectrum antibiotics) or against just a few.

When antibiotics were first used to treat diseases, they were nearly always successful. Now, more and more bacteria are becoming resistant to the antibiotics and scientists are continually developing new ones to counter this.

antibody: a type of protein which can act against and destroy *antigens*. Antibodies are produced and secreted by white blood cells called *lymphocytes* in response to a specific antigen which is usually on the surface of an invading microorganism. This is an example of our *immune response* in action.

antigen: any substance foreign to the body which provokes an *immune response* by the *lymphocytes*.

Antigens are usually:

- complex molecules like proteins or polysaccharides which are not part of the body's natural 'set' of chemicals
- found on the surfaces of cells
- recognised as foreign by the lymphocytes.

antiseptic: a substance which can be used on the surface of the body to kill or inactivate harmful bacteria.

Antiseptics do not kill all bacteria, but do kill or inactivate most harmful bacteria.

Their effectiveness often depends on their concentration. Many antiseptics are bactericidal (kill bacteria) when concentrated, but are only bacteriostatic (stop bacteria reproducing) when more dilute. Very few have any effect at all on bacterial spores.

Dettol and iodine solution are examples of antiseptics.

antitoxin: a specialised *antibody* produced by *lymphocytes* in response to bacterial toxins (poisons).

Almost all harmful bacteria produce toxins, but most just release them into the tissues where they are multiplying. The tetanus and diphtheria bacteria release toxins into the bloodstream which are highly damaging to nerve cells. The toxins are *antigens* and provoke an *immune response* by the lymphocytes. Tetanus antitoxins are produced commercially by injecting horses with a small dose of the toxin and then extracting the antitoxins formed. These can then be used to treat patients with tetanus who cannot manufacture their own antitoxins quickly enough.

anus: the last part of the *alimentary canal*.

The anus is normally kept closed by two sphincter or circular muscles and opened only to allow the egestion of faeces.

aorta: the main artery of the body. In humans it passes over the heart from the left ventricle and runs down in front of the backbone. The aorta:
- carries oxygenated blood from the left ventricle of the *heart*
- is thicker-walled than any other artery to withstand the high pressure generated by the left ventricle
- leads to arteries which carry oxygenated blood to all parts of the body, except the lungs
- has a valve, called the aortic valve, where blood enters from the ventricle to prevent backflow of blood when the ventricle relaxes.

aortic valve: the valve at the base of the aorta where blood enters from the left ventricle of the *heart*.

The aortic valve:
- is made from three flaps of tough tissue
- is a one-way valve, allowing blood from the left ventricle into the aorta, but not back again
- is opened and closed by the difference in pressure between the blood in the ventricle and that in the aorta.

A similar valve, the pulmonary valve, is found at the base of the *pulmonary artery*.

apex: the tip of some structure, such as a stem or root.

apical growth: growth at the *apex*. Many plant stems and roots grow longer by cell division and cell elongation at the apex.

appendix: a small tube which extends from the *caecum* at the junction of the small intestine and large intestine.

The appendix has no function in humans, but in some herbivores such as the rabbit, both caecum and appendix contain bacteria which can digest cellulose into sugars. These are absorbed into the bloodstream.

---

aqueous humour: one of the liquids found in the *eye*.

The aqueous humour is:
- a transparent watery liquid containing no cells
- found between the lens and the cornea
- produced continually by the ciliary body
- reabsorbed into the bloodstream.

The aqueous humour has two main functions:
- to help to maintain the shape of the eyeball
- to transport nutrients to the cells in the cornea and lens.

---

arachnids: *arthropods* with two body sections and four pairs of legs.

Like all arthropods, they have an exoskeleton and jointed legs. Spiders, mites and scorpions are all arachnids.

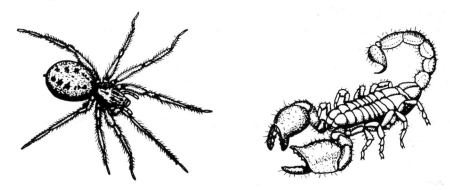

---

arteriole: a small branch off an *artery* which carries blood to a capillary network inside an organ.

The diameter of an arteriole can be altered by contracting or relaxing the muscle in its wall.

- Narrowing the arterioles (*vasoconstriction*) reduces the amount of blood passing into the capillaries
- Making the arterioles wider (*vasodilation*) increases the amount of blood passing into the capillaries.

By narrowing the arterioles in some organs and making those in others wider, blood can be diverted to those organs which need it most urgently.

---

arteriosclerosis: loss of elasticity of the walls of the arteries; literally 'hardening of the arteries'.

Arteriosclerosis does not have a single cause; it can result from several different but related conditions.

Arteriosclerosis can be caused by:

- *atherosclerosis* – a condition in which fatty deposits are laid down on the inner lining of arteries, reducing their elasticity
- fibrosis – a condition in which the muscle and elastic fibres in the walls of arteries are replaced by inelastic fibres
- calcification – occasionally, calcium ions are deposited in the linings of arteries.

Often, all three contribute to the development of arteriosclerosis.

---

artery: a blood vessel which carries blood away from the *heart*.

All arteries have:

- thicker walls than similar sized veins
- more muscle fibres and elastic tissue in their walls than veins
- a narrower lumen (or central space) than similar sized veins.

Because of the muscle and elastic tissue in their walls arteries can:

- be stretched when blood is pumped into them under high pressure by the ventricles of the heart and then
- recoil back to their normal diameter when the ventricles relax.

This alternate stretching and recoiling helps to smooth out the peaks and troughs of pressure caused by the ventricles contracting and relaxing.

---

arthritis: inflammation of one or more *joints* giving pain, swelling and stiffness.

Arthritis is not a single disorder, but a name for a collection of conditions producing similar effects. Arthritis can range in its effects from a mild ache to a chronic (ongoing) condition where joints become painful and difficult to move.

Types of arthritis include:

- osteoarthritis – cartilage at the joint becomes damaged by wear and tear
- rheumatoid arthritis – the body's own immune system attacks the cartilage at the joint
- gout – a metabolic disorder which results in uric acid crystals being deposited in the joints.

Arthritis can sometimes be treated using drugs to reduce the swelling and pain. In severe cases joint replacement may be necessary. Once this has been carried out it may have to be repeated after a number of years, as securing artificial joints in bones also places serious stress on the bone.

arthropods: invertebrates with an exoskeleton, segmented bodies, and jointed limbs.

The group:

- includes the *insects, crustaceans, arachnids* and *myriapods*
- is the most successful in terms of number of species and habitats colonised.

All arthropods must moult (shed their exoskeleton) in order to grow.

artificial insemination: introducing sperm into the vagina of a female without intercourse – by artificial methods.

In humans, artificial insemination falls into two broad categories:

- insemination with sperm from the woman's husband – suitable for couples who are unable, for some reason, to have intercourse
- insemination with sperm from an anonymous donor – suitable for couples where the male is infertile or for single women who wish to become pregnant but who do not wish to have a partner.

In other animals, artificial insemination is used to fertilise eggs in many females using sperm from a male with desired features. It is a form of *selective breeding* used a great deal in farm animals such as cows, sheep and pigs to improve meat and milk yields. It is also used in breeding programmes in zoos to help conserve endangered species.

artificial selection: producing new strains of animals and plants by selective breeding.

Human needs, not environmental factors, determine which features will be passed on to future generations.

Examples include:

- linseed oil plants selected for a high oil content of the seed
- Jersey cows selected for a high cream content of their milk.

These features clearly benefit humans, but natural selection probably would not have produced them – unless the features also gave the linseed oil plants and the Jersey cattle some advantage.

asbestosis: a serious lung condition caused by inhaling asbestos fibres; asbestosis is one form of pneumoconiosis.

Asbestos fibres irritate the delicate lung tissue and cause fibrous scars to form. These scars:

- seriously affect the air flow and gas exchange in the lungs
- continue to spread throughout the lungs even after exposure to asbestos ends.

Because of the scarring, people suffering from asbestosis often have a dry cough and are very short of breath. This can lead to severe disability and even death. Asbestosis also makes smokers and non-smokers five times more likely to develop lung cancer.

ascorbic acid: the chemical name for vitamin C; formula $C_6H_8O_6$.
Ascorbic acid is essential for the formation of collagen, bone and teeth. It is also important in allowing wounds to heal.

asexual reproduction: reproduction which does not involve fusion of sex cells.
Asexual reproduction:
- often involves part of an organism enlarging by *mitosis*, breaking away and developing into an independent organism
- is most common among plants and bacteria
- produces *clones* – groups of offspring which are genetically identical to each other and to the parent organism
- is important commercially in producing, quickly, large numbers of plants which all possess the same desired features.

Examples of asexual reproduction include:
- budding in *Hydra* (a small freshwater animal)
- production of bulbs by daffodils
- production of runners by strawberry plants.

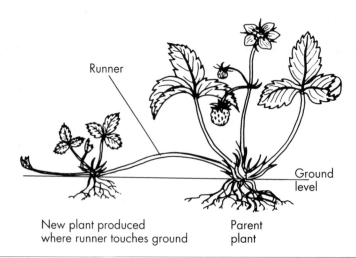

Runner

Ground level

New plant produced where runner touches ground

Parent plant

assimilation: the process by which molecules in our food become part of our body.
We might assimilate protein in the following way. After digesting it to amino acids and absorbing the amino acids:

- the amino acids are carried to a muscle
- they are re-built into a new protein to be part of the muscle.

---

asthma: recurring attacks of breathlessness and wheezing caused by narrowing of the bronchi and bronchioles in the *lungs*.
In an attack of asthma:
- some factor irritates the linings of the bronchi and bronchioles
- the smooth muscle around the bronchi and bronchioles contracts making them narrower
- because of the narrowing, it is difficult to remove mucus from these airways and a blockage results
- the linings of the bronchi and bronchioles become inflamed and swell
- these three changes seriously restrict the flow of air in and out of the lungs.

Treatment usually involves the use of an inhaler which delivers a bronchodilator drug. This relaxes the muscle around the bronchi and bronchioles and so widens the airways.

---

astigmatism: a defect of the eye in which curvature of the cornea is irregular. People with astigmatism find it difficult to focus on vertical and horizontal lines at the same time.

---

atheroma: fatty deposits in the inner lining of an artery.
The fatty substances often include cholesterol and other animal fats.

---

atherosclerosis: a condition in which fatty deposits (atheroma) are laid down in the inner linings of arteries.
Atherosclerosis narrows the lumen of the arteries which may become completely blocked, either:
- by the atheroma itself, or
- by a thrombus (blood clot) travelling to the artery and becoming lodged in a narrowed region.

When this happens in a *coronary artery*, it causes the following to happen:
- the blood supply to part of the heart muscle is cut off
- the heart muscle receives little or no oxygen
- the heart muscle cannot respire effectively and so
- it cannot contract.

If a large enough area of heart muscle is involved, then the heart will stop beating and the person will suffer a heart attack.
Atherosclerosis occurs slowly in most adults, but it is accelerated by:
- smoking

- a diet containing too much cholesterol and animal fat
- lack of exercise
- being overweight
- high blood pressure.

Atherosclerosis is one factor which can lead to *arteriosclerosis*.

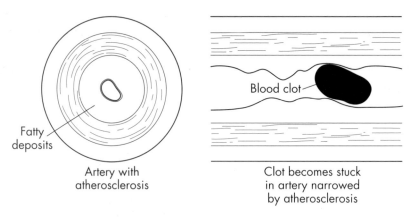

| Artery with atherosclerosis | Clot becomes stuck in artery narrowed by atherosclerosis |

Fatty deposits

Blood clot

---

atmosphere: the layer of gases surrounding the earth.

Without the atmosphere, life on earth would be almost non-existent. This is because of:

- the supply of oxygen and carbon dioxide held in the atmosphere
- the *greenhouse effect* of our atmosphere – without it, the earth would be as cold as the moon
- the *ozone layer* – high in the atmosphere molecules of ozone reflect much of the sun's high energy ultraviolet radiation from reaching the earth's surface.

The atmosphere today is very different from that present when the earth was first formed. That atmosphere contained water vapour, hydrogen, carbon dioxide, carbon monoxide and ammonia. All the oxygen now present in the atmosphere has been put there by *photosynthesis*. This was initially due to bacteria and, later, to algae and plants.

---

atom: the smallest part of an element which can take part in a chemical reaction.

Atoms are made of smaller particles called protons, neutrons and electrons.

- The protons and neutrons are found at the centre of an atom in the nucleus (don't confuse this with the nucleus of a cell).
- The much lighter electrons 'spin' around the nucleus.

In chemical reactions, atoms gain, lose or share electrons. When atoms join together, they form larger **particles called molecules.**

ATP: adenosine triphosphate; the chemical which transfers energy released in respiration to drive energy-requiring processes.

atrio-ventricular valve: a one-way valve found between an atrium and ventricle in the *heart*.
- The valve between the left atrium and left ventricle is the bicuspid valve.
- The valve between the right atrium and right ventricle is the tricuspid valve.
- Both valves prevent blood from returning to the atrium when the ventricle contracts.

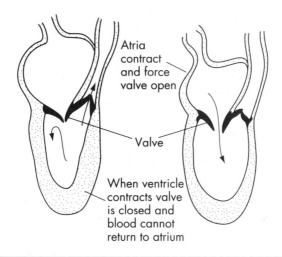

Atria contract and force valve open

Valve

When ventricle contracts valve is closed and blood cannot return to atrium

atrium (plural atria): one of the upper chambers of the *heart*.
Each atrium:
- receives blood returning from the organs of the body
- contracts and forces the blood through an atrio-ventricular valve into a ventricle
- has only a thin wall to force blood into the ventricles.

autosome: a *chromosome* which is not involved in gender (sex) determination. Human body cells contain 46 chromosomes; two of these are sex chromosomes, the remainder are autosomes.

autotroph: an organism which shows *autotrophic nutrition*.
Most autotrophs are plants, algae, or bacteria.
Compare this with *heterotrophic nutrition*.

autotrophic nutrition: a method of feeding which involves producing complex food molecules from simpler ones using energy from the environment.

By far the commonest form of autotrophic nutrition is *photosynthesis*, which:
- uses light energy to drive reactions which manufacture carbohydrates
- is carried out by plants, algae and some bacteria.

A few bacteria can use energy from chemicals to drive similar reactions. Because autotrophs can make their own food molecules, they are always at the start of a food chain; they are the producers.

Compare this with *heterotrophic nutrition*.

auxin: a type of plant hormone which causes cell elongation in shoots. Auxins are produced at the tips of shoots and roots, and help produce tropic responses such as *phototropism* and *geotropism*.

Auxins, or auxin-like substances are used commercially:
- as rooting powders – dipping new stem cuttings in these powders helps them to form roots
- in some herbicides (weedkillers) – the high concentrations of auxins in herbicides interfere with the normal growth pattern of the weeds
- to prevent fruit trees losing too many of their fruits before they are properly ripe
- in combination with other plant growth substances, to produce seedless fruits.

axon: a long extension of a *neurone* (nerve cell) which carries nerve impulses away from the cell body to another cell. (See *motor neurone* and *sensory neurone*.)

bacillus: a term used to describe any rod-shaped bacterium.

Bacillus is also the name of a genus of *bacteria* which includes:

- *Bacillus anthracis*, which causes the disease anthrax in farm animals
- *Bacillus subtilis*, which is used in *genetic engineering* because it can take up DNA from other bacteria easily.

---

backbone: the *spine* or vertebral column.

---

backcross (test cross): a breeding experiment between an organism showing a *dominant* feature, whose *genotype* is unknown, and one showing the *recessive* feature.

For example, in pea plants the *allele* for tallness is dominant to that for dwarfness, so a tall pea plant could be either *homozygous* or *heterozygous*. If we use the symbols **T** for the tall allele and **t** for the dwarf allele, then it could have the genotype **TT** or **Tt**.

In the backcross we:

- predict possible outcomes of the breeding experiment (this is possible because the dwarf allele is recessive and so the dwarf plant must have the genotype **tt**)
- breed this tall plant with a dwarf one
- collect the seeds and grow them
- analyse the results to see if they fit either of the predictions below.

	If the unknown tall plant was homozygous		If the unknown tall plant was heterozygous	
parent genotypes	TT × tt		Tt × tt	
gametes	T t		T t t t	
offspring genotypes	Tt		Tt	tt
offspring	all tall		50% tall	50% dwarf

So, if we get a ratio which is approximately 50% tall and 50% dwarf (ratios are never exact), we know that the original unknown tall plant was heterozygous. If all the offspring are tall, we know it was homozygous.

bacteria (singular bacterium): single-celled organisms which lack a true nucleus, *mitochondria* and *chloroplasts*.
Bacterial cells vary in shape; they can be spherical (cocci), rod-like (bacilli), spiral shaped (spirilla) or comma shaped (vibrios). The diagram shows the shapes and some of the arrangements of bacterial cells.

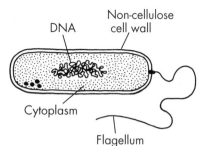

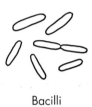

Bacilli

Cocci

Spirilla

Vibrio

Bacteria are important because some:
- cause disease
- cause food spoilage
- cause decay and so release nutrients from dead organic material
- modify and recycle the nutrients released in decay
- are used in *biotechnology* and *genetic engineering*.

bacterial growth: a slightly misleading term since it refers to the growth of numbers (= reproduction) of bacteria not growth in size.
Bacteria generally reproduce asexually in the following way:
- their cells grow to full size and then split into two
- under favourable conditions, this is repeated every twenty minutes
- soon, a cluster of thousands of bacterial cells is formed
- this cluster is called a colony
- as more bacteria are formed, the colony grows in size.

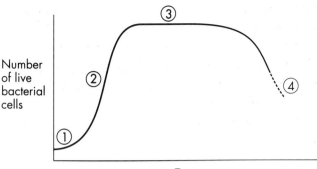

① Bacteria adapting to new conditions
② Bacteria reproducing rapidly
③ Bacterial numbers remain stationary; number of bacteria produced equals the number dying
④ Bacterial numbers reduce; bacteria have used up the available resources

bactericidal: a term used to describe the action of a chemical or a process which kills bacteria.

All bacteria are killed in an autoclave – a sort of pressure cooker where steam, under pressure, can reach temperatures of 130°C.

Sodium hypochlorite (found in household bleach) kills all harmful bacteria.

bacteriostatic: a term used to describe the action of a chemical or process which prevents the reproduction of bacteria, but does not necessarily kill them.

Many chemicals which are *bactericidal* in high concentrations are only bacteriostatic when diluted. *Antibiotics* are frequently bacteriostatic.

baking: the process by which bread is made.

- Yeast, sugar, water and flour are combined to make a dough which is then left in a warm place.
- The yeast ferments the sugar and produces carbon dioxide gas.
- The carbon dioxide gas is trapped inside the dough and as more is made it expands the dough, making it rise.
- The dough is heated in an oven which kills the yeast and expands the carbon dioxide still more, producing the spongy texture of the bread.

balance: our sense of balance allows us to remain upright and stable, even when moving.

The *receptors* involved in our sense of balance are located in the inner *ear* and are surrounded by fluid.

When we move:
- movement of the fluid disturbs the receptors
- *nerve impulses* are sent to the brain
- the brain interprets these impulses and decides what we must do to remain upright and balanced.

balanced diet: a diet which supplies proteins, carbohydrates, fats, vitamins, minerals, fibre and water in amounts which meet, but do not exceed, a person's requirements.
- Proteins are essential for making new cells in growth and repair as well as for making enzymes, some hormones and other chemicals such as haemoglobin.
- Carbohydrates are the body's primary energy source.
- Fats are needed for insulation, making cells and as a secondary energy source.
- Vitamins often help the body to make proper use of the other nutrients.
- Minerals have no overall function; different minerals are needed for different purposes.
- Fibre is essential to add bulk to the food so that it can be moved effectively through the alimentary canal. It is thought to prevent colon cancer and some kinds of fibre may help to reduce heart disease.
- Water is needed for almost every body function; we would die very quickly without water.

barbiturate: a type of sedative drug.
Barbiturates work by slowing down the activity of the brain and so making us feel sleepy. They are used much less now than they used to be because they have been found to be habit forming. An overdose of barbiturates can be fatal, especially if taken with alcohol.
One barbiturate in particular, phenobarbitone, also reduces the likelihood of epileptic fits.

beer: an alcoholic drink produced by fermenting sugar produced from the starch in barley grains. (See *brewing* for details.)

Benedict's test: a biochemical test used to show the presence or absence of reducing sugars such as glucose.
(See *food tests*.)

beriberi: a metabolic disorder caused by a lack of vitamin B$_1$ (thiamine). Beriberi affects the working of the nervous system and the muscles. In severe cases, the patient becomes emaciated, paralysed and bed-ridden. A balanced diet which includes nuts, green vegetables, meat and wholemeal cereals will supply sufficient thiamine.

biceps: the muscle which bends the arm.
(See *antagonistic muscles* for details.)

bicuspid valve: the *atrio-ventricular valve* between the left atrium and left ventricle of the *heart*.
It is called bicuspid because it is made from two sections or 'cusps'.

biennial: a plant which takes two years to complete its life cycle.
In the first year:
● it germinates from seed
● it produces roots, stem and leaves but no flowers
● it stores the products of *photosynthesis* in underground storage organs, such as roots which become swollen with the stored food
● at the end of the year, the stem and leaves die.
In the second year:
● new stems and leaves grow using the products stored during the first year
● flowers are formed
● seeds are produced and dispersed
● the plant dies.
Carrots and parsnips are examples of biennials.

bile: a yellow/green liquid containing waste products which are produced in the *liver*.
Bile is produced by the cells in the liver, stored in the *gall bladder* and then periodically released into the duodenum.
Bile contains:
● bile salts – these emulsify fats in the small intestine which gives them a larger surface area and makes it easier for lipase enzymes to digest them
● bile pigments – these are formed by breaking down the haemoglobin in worn out red blood cells
● sodium hydrogencarbonate – which makes bile alkaline

binary fission: a form of *asexual reproduction* in which a unicell such as *Amoeba* or a bacterium divides equally into two daughter cells (see the diagram on page 34).

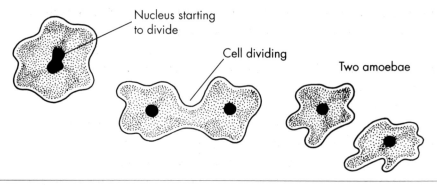

Nucleus starting to divide

Cell dividing

Two amoebae

biodegradable: a substance which is biodegradable can be broken down by the action of *decomposers*. Biodegradable materials will decay!

- Nearly all biological materials are biodegradable – the substances in living organisms are constantly being recycled by decomposers.
- Materials such as paper and cotton fabrics are made from biological substances and are biodegradable.
- Materials made from non-biological substances are usually non-biodegradable and will not decay. These materials accumulate in the environment and may be harmful to wildlife. Glass and most plastics are non-biodegradable, although plastics are now being developed which will decay.
- Most *herbicides* (weedkillers) are biodegradable, although some are not and these accumulate in the environment.
- Some *insecticides* are also non-biodegradable and accumulate in the environment. Because they persist in the environment, levels may increase along a food chain producing toxic effects in animals they were never intended to harm.

biological control: the control of populations of pests using living organisms rather than chemical (pesticides) or mechanical methods.
Methods of biological control include:

- introducing a predator – ladybirds have been introduced to orange groves to control the aphids which reduce the crop yields
- introducing a herbivore – a moth from South America was introduced to Australia to control the prickly pear cactus which was a serious weed in grazing land
- introducing a parasite – a parasitic wasp is used to control whitefly populations on tomato plants in large glasshouses
- introducing a pathogen – the myxomatosis virus was deliberately released in Australia to control the rabbit population
- introducing sterile males – when the females breed with the sterile males, no offspring are produced

- using pheromones – these are natural hormones which can be used to attract male pests which are than destroyed.

---

biomass: the mass of living organisms in a particular area.
Scientists can use biomass to measure:

- the amount of each species in the area, individually
- the amount of groups of organisms in the area, for example the biomass of the *producers, consumers* and *decomposers* in the area
- the amount of all the organisms in the area – the total biomass.

We measure biomass in grams (or kilograms) per square metre (or per square kilometre). The amount of water in plants and animals varies from day to day – and so biomass is sometimes measured in grams of dry mass (the mass after all water has been removed).

Pyramids of biomass show the amounts of living material at each stage in a *food chain* or *food web*.

---

bioreactor: a reaction vessel in which cells, usually microorganisms, are cultivated in large numbers, under ideal conditions to produce a useful product. Sometimes called **fermenters**.

Modern bioreactors:

- are made from stainless steel to minimise any contamination and reaction with the contents
- have many sensors to monitor the conditions inside the reactor
- are computer controlled to maintain the optimum (ideal) conditions for the production process.

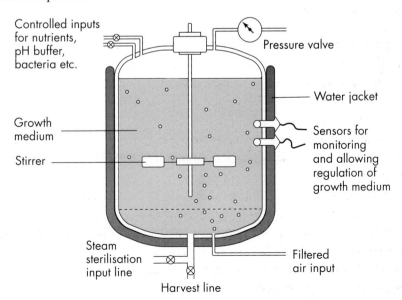

Many of the products of *biotechnology* such as insulin, antibiotics and enzymes for detergents are produced in bulk in bioreactors.

biosphere: that part of the earth's surface which supports life.
The biosphere includes:
- the surface layers of the earth's crust
- the oceans of the earth, particularly the surface layers
- the part of the atmosphere which contains breathable air – up to a height of about 35 kilometres.

The biosphere has maintained itself for millions of years by:
- constantly recycling the materials which make up living things
- maintaining the conditions for life on earth more or less constant.

Human activities may upset the natural regulating abilities of the biosphere by:
- adding greenhouse gases and other pollutants to the biosphere too quickly (see *greenhouse effect*).
- upsetting the balance of the biosphere by disrupting *ecosystems* – for example, felling areas of the rain forests.

biotechnology: using living organisms or biological systems to make or modify substances or to carry out processes which are important to us.
The organisms used are nearly always microorganisms of some kind, some of which have been known and used for thousands of years. More recently, biotechnologists are making use of genetically engineered microorganisms to produce a whole range of valuable products.
Biotechnology falls into two broad categories:
- traditional biotechnology
- modern biotechnology.

Some examples of traditional biotechnology:

Product or process	Type of microorganism used	Way in which microorganism is used
wine/beer	yeast	ferments sugar into alcohol
bread	yeast	produces CO_2 to make dough rise
yoghurt and cheese	lactic acid bacteria	produce lactic acid from the lactose (sugar) in milk
vinegar	bacteria	convert ethanol (alcohol) into ethanoic acid
sewage treatment	protozoa, aerobic bacteria and fungi (biological filter method)	digest and oxidise organic materials in the sewage

Biotechnology is a rapidly expanding area of research and development which will have an increasing impact on our daily lives.

Some examples of modern biotechnology:

Product or process	Microorganism or biological system is used	Way in which micro-organism or biological system is used
biosensor for detecting heroin	enzymes from bacteria which can digest heroin	enzymes immobilised on a strip with a dye which changes colour when they digest heroin
biosensor for pregnancy testing	monoclonal antibodies	antibodies bind to an embryonic hormone present in the urine and produce a colour change
human growth hormone	genetically engineered bacteria	human growth hormone gene is introduced to the bacterium which then produces the growth hormone
insulin	genetically engineered bacteria	human insulin gene is introduced into the bacterium which then produces insulin
biodegradable plastic	bacteria	bacteria modify glucose and an organic acid and polymerise them into the plastic

biotic: from life.

A biotic factor of an *ecosystem* is one where living things influence the numbers of other living things.

Biotic factors include:

- predators
- parasites and pathogens
- competition with other members of the same species for food and space
- competition with other species for food and space.

birds: *vertebrate* animals with *feathers* and beaks.

Everyone can recognise an animal as a bird because of these two features, but birds have many other adaptations too.

The main features of birds are:

- a four-chambered heart similar to that in mammals
- forelimbs modified as wings
- powerful breast muscles attached to a keel (an extension of the sternum)

- laying eggs with a shell made largely from calcium carbonate
- maintaining a constant internal temperature.

birth: the process by which live young move from inside the body of a female to the outside.

In humans birth has three distinct stages.

- Dilation of the cervix – In this stage the *uterus* starts to contract strongly and regularly. These contractions rupture the *amnion* and the *amniotic fluid* escapes ('the breaking of the waters'). The contractions also soften and stretch the cervix so that it pulls up and merges with the wall of the uterus. This stage may last up to twelve hours for a first baby.
- Delivery of the baby – More contractions force the baby's head through the dilated (widened) cervix and then through the vagina. The shoulders and the rest of the body follow.
- Delivery of the afterbirth – The afterbirth (placenta and membranes) are forced out within 10 minutes of birth of the baby.

Stage 1

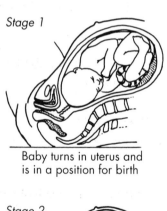

Baby turns in uterus and is in a position for birth

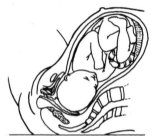

The baby's head pushes the cervix; a plug of mucous is released and 'waters break'

Stage 2

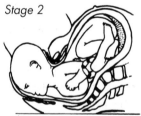

The uterus contracts and the baby is pushed out through the vagina

Stage 3

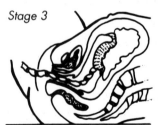

The placenta becomes detached from the wall of the uterus

Birth does not just happen in mammals. Many other species produce live young, and in some cases the male gives birth! Female sea-horses lay fertilised eggs in brood pouches in the male's body where they are incubated and from where they are 'born'.

birth control: controlling the number of children born.

For *pregnancy* to occur, a sperm must fertilise an ovum and then implant (embed) in the wall of the uterus.

Couples may decide how many children they wish to have and when they wish to have them. They may use one or more methods of *contraception* to help them achieve this.

birth rate: the number of live births per 1000 of population per year.

biuret test: a biochemical test for proteins.
(See *food tests*.)

bladder: a hollow organ with a muscular wall which holds urine.
The bladder:
● receives urine from the kidneys through the *ureters*
● releases urine to the urethra through a sphincter muscle.
Contraction of the sphincter muscle keeps urine in the bladder. When it is relaxed, urine can pass out into the urethra.

blind spot: a point in the retina of the *eye* where there are no light sensitive cells. Light rays falling on this point cannot be detected.

blinking: closing and then re-opening the eyelids rapidly.
Blinking is normally a *reflex action*, although we can blink voluntarily if we choose to.
Blinking can be triggered by:
● a speck of dust or a build up of tears on the *cornea*: this is called the corneal reflex
● a threat approaching the eye (e.g. someone trying to poke you in the eye): this is called the blink reflex.
Unlike most other reflex actions you will learn about, the brain is involved in both these reflexes, but not consciously. The *synapses* between the sensory and motor neurones in the *reflex arcs* are found the brain.

blood: the fluid found in the blood vessels of a vertebrate.
● Blood has two main components: the liquid *blood plasma* and the *blood cells*.
● It is important in our defence against infection through *blood clotting*, *phagocytosis* and producing *antibodies*.
● It is our main transport fluid.

The table below shows how some substances are transported by the blood.

Substance	Transported as	Transported by	Transported from	Transported to
oxygen	oxyhaemoglobin	red blood cells	lungs	organs
carbon dioxide	hydrogen-carbonate ions	plasma	organs	lungs
urea	in solution	plasma	liver	kidney
soluble food	in solution	plasma	small intestine	organs
hormones	in solution	plasma	endocrine glands	target organs

blood cells: the cells which are carried by the *blood plasma*.

There are three main types of blood cells.

- *Red blood cells* – these cells contain haemoglobin and carry oxygen combined with the haemoglobin as oxyhaemoglobin.
- *White blood cells* – cells involved in defending our bodies against disease-causing microorganisms. Some defend our bodies by engulfing the microorganisms (these white cells are called *phagocytes*). Others (called *lymphocytes*) produce *antibodies* to destroy the microorganisms.
- *Platelets* – these are actually fragments of cells, but they play an important role in *blood clotting*.

blood circulation: movement of blood from the *heart*, through a system of *blood vessels* and back to the heart again.

(See *circulatory system*.)

blood clotting: the solidification of blood.

Blood clotting has only one function: to plug a damaged blood vessel and stop blood escaping. When we damage a blood vessel a series of reactions occur which result in the formation of a clot.

The main stages are as follows.

- The damaged tissue releases a number of chemicals which make the platelets stick together and become active.
- The active platelets release calcium ions and other substances.
- The substances released by the platelets change the plasma protein pro-thrombin into thrombin.
- Thrombin changes another plasma protein, fibrinogen into fibrin.
- The fibres of fibrin form a tangled mesh at the site of the injury and blood cells become trapped in the mesh to form a clot.
- The clot plugs the wound and prevents blood from escaping.

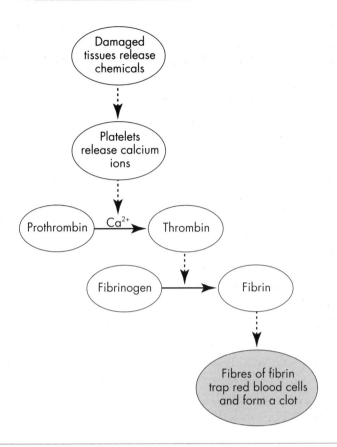

blood group: the type of blood a person has.

Red blood cells have *antigens* on their surface which are used to classify blood into groups. There are many systems of blood grouping but the commonest is called the ABO system.

In the ABO system:

- there are two antigens, **A** and **B**, on the red blood cells
- there are two antibodies; **a** (which will react with antigen **A**) and **b** (which will react with antigen **B**), in the plasma
- a person's blood group depends on the combination of antigens and antibodies in the blood.

Blood group	Antigens present on the red blood cells	Antibodies present in the plasma
A	A	b
B	B	a
AB	A and B	none
O	none	a and b

If you needed a *blood transfusion*, the doctor would find out your blood group so that you could be given the same type of blood. If you were given the wrong type, it could be fatal.

blood plasma: the liquid part of the blood; plasma is a pale straw-coloured liquid.
- Plasma is 90% water and 10% dissolved substances.
- Plasma proteins, such as albumin, fibrinogen and prothrombin make up most of the dissolved substances.
- Other substances in the plasma include soluble foods, hormones and hydrogencarbonate ions.
- The main functions of plasma are transporting materials around the body and *blood clotting*.

blood pressure: the pressure due to the flow of blood through the *blood vessels*.
The pressure is generated by the *heart*.
- When the left ventricle contracts (systole), it raises the pressure of the blood in the aorta and all the arteries which branch off the aorta. This is called systolic blood pressure.
- When it relaxes again (diastole), the blood pressure in these arteries falls. This is called diastolic blood pressure.
- When you feel your pulse, you are feeling the systolic pressure wave caused by the contraction of the left ventricle.

As blood gets further away from the heart and passes into smaller and smaller arteries, two things happen to the blood pressure:
- it is smoothed out – the difference between systolic and diastolic pressure is reduced
- it gets lower overall due to resistance from the walls of the blood vessels.

When blood enters the capillaries, the pressure falls even more – because they are leaky – and you know what happens to water pressure in a leaky hosepipe! Blood returns to the heart at very low pressure in veins. Veins are adapted to carrying low pressure blood and have:
- valves to prevent the low pressure blood flowing the wrong way
- a large lumen (central space) to lower the resistance of the wall (it is easier for a liquid to flow down a wide tube rather than a narrow one).

blood transfusion: transferring large amounts of blood (usually of another person) directly into the bloodstream.
Doctors give blood transfusions when someone has lost a large amount of blood, for example in an accident or during an operation. It is important to

tranfuse blood of **either the same type**, or of a type which is compatible with the patient's blood **and will not cause a reaction.**

If blood of the wrong type is given:

- *antibodies* in the patient's plasma react with *antigens* on the red blood cells of the donated blood **causing these red blood cells to burst or stick together**
- kidney failure and death may result.

The table shows safe and unsafe transfusions.

	Patient's blood group (and antibodies in plasma)			
	A(b)	**B(a)**	**AB(none)**	**O(ab)**
A(b)	safe	unsafe	safe	unsafe
B(a)	unsafe	safe	safe	unsafe
AB(none)	unsafe	unsafe	safe	unsafe
O(ab)	safe	safe	safe	safe

Donor's blood group (and antibodies in plasma)

People with blood group O can give blood to anyone in an emergency; they are called universal donors.

People with blood group AB can receive blood from anybody in an emergency; they are called universal recipients.

blood vessels: tubes in which blood is pumped around the body.

The table compares the structure and functions of the three main types of blood vessel: *arteries, veins* and *capillaries*.

Feature of blood vessel	Artery	Vein	Capillary
thickness of wall	thick, with much elastic tissue	thin, with little elastic tissue	one cell thick
type of blood transported	oxygenated (except pulmonary artery)	de-oxygenated (except pulmonary vein)	blood loses its oxygen as it flows through capillaries (except in lungs)
direction of blood flow	away from heart	towards heart	through organs
valves	absent	present	absent
pressure	high	low	low

bone: the main supporting tissue in the skeletons of most vertebrates.
It is easy to think of bones as almost non-living material – but remember:
- bones grow
- bones bleed
- bones hurt when you hit them hard so, they are obviously very much alive!

The three main components of bone are:
- collagen – a fibrous protein with the tensile strength of steel; collagen acts like the steel rods in reinforced concrete and also gives bone some elasticity;
- calcium salts – mainly a complex calcium phosphate – which make the bone extremely hard
- bone cells – these enable the bone to grow and repair itself by producing more cells and collagen when needed.

Bone also contains *nerves* and *blood vessels*.

bone marrow: a soft, fatty tissue found in the central cavities of bones which produces red *blood cells, white blood cells* and *platelets*.
Healthy bone marrow can be transplanted into a person with bone marrow which is not producing red and white cells properly.

Bowman's capsule: the first part of the *nephron* in the *kidney*.

brain: the organ which controls the activity of the *nervous system* and through this, the activity of the body.

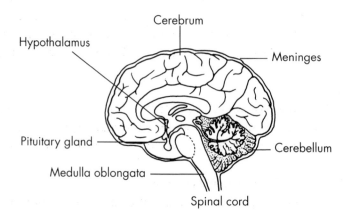

The main areas of the brain and their functions are summarised in the table.

Region of brain	Description and location	Function
cerebral hemispheres (cerebrum)	the uppermost and largest area of the brain; in two halves (right and left hemispheres)	conscious thought, action, interpretation of sensory impulses, speech, language, memory, etc.
cerebellum	second largest area of the brain; underneath the cerebrum to the rear	coordination of skilled movements, controls balance and posture
medulla oblongata	the part of the brain that attaches to the spinal cord	reflex control of heartbeat and breathing and other body functions
hypothalamus	small area of brain (7 g) found under the cerebrum, in the middle of the head	regulates body temperature and water balance and controls release of some hormones

breasts: in mammals, paired structures consisting of 15–20 lobes of milk-secreting glands enclosed in fatty tissue.

Human female breasts are *secondary sex characteristics* as well as producing milk to feed newborn babies.

breastbone: common name for the sternum: a flat bone found, centrally, at the front of the *thorax*.

The ribs attach to the breastbone at the front and to the spine at the back.

The breastbone contains red *bone marrow* and manufactures *blood cells*.

breathing: in humans, a coordinated sequence of movements of the ribcage and diaphragm which move air into the lungs (inhaling) and out of the lungs (exhaling).

When you inhale:
- your intercostal muscles contract and lift the ribs upward and outwards
- your diaphragm muscle contracts and pulls the diaphragm down
- these movements enlarge the *thorax* and so reduce the air pressure in the lungs
- air enters from outside to equalise the pressure.

While the air is in your lungs, gas exchange takes place in the alveoli.

When you exhale:
- your intercostal muscles relax and the ribs fall back to their resting position
- your diaphragm muscle relaxes and the diaphragm returns to its domed position

- these movements make the thorax smaller and so increase the **air pres-**
  sure in the lungs
- air is forced out of your lungs by the increased pressure.

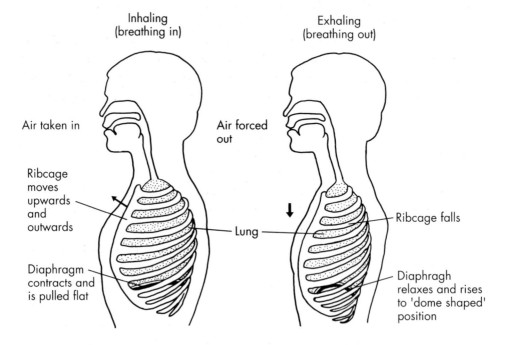

Note: take care not to confuse breathing with *respiration*.

---

breathing system: the structures which are involved in breathing.
(See *breathing* and *lungs*.)

---

breeding: literally – reproduction, but usually used to mean controlled or
selective breeding where humans select individuals to reproduce.

---

breeding true: showing the same feature generation after generation when
self-fertilised.
The tall pea plants which *Mendel* used in his breeding experiments were
true breeding plants. Individuals which breed true for a particular feature
are usually *homozygous* for the gene which controls that feature.

---

brewing: producing beer, lager and similar alcoholic drinks from cereals,
usually from barley.
The main stages in brewing are as follows.
- Barley grains (seeds) are allowed to germinate; *enzymes* in the grain
  change stored starch into sugars.

- The partly germinated grain (now called malt) is heated to stop further germination, ground and mixed with hot water.
- The liquid (called wort) containing the sugars is extracted and boiled with hops (flower heads from the hop plant) to give it a bitter taste.
- The wort is now transferred to a fermenter and yeast is added.
- The yeast ferments the sugars in the wort and forms alcohol (ethanol) and carbon dioxide. Other reactions take place which develop flavour.
- The beer is allowed to mature in casks or smaller containers. The beer in smaller containers is usually pasteurised (heat treated to kill harmful bacteria).

bronchiole: a tiny air passage found in the lungs.
- Bronchioles are branches from the larger *bronchi*.
- The smallest bronchioles (called terminal bronchioles) end in *alveoli*.
- The cartilage rings which support them are more irregularly spaced and the terminal bronchioles have none.
- Cells lining the larger bronchioles secrete mucus to trap dirt and dust particles.
- Cilia on some cells lining the bronchioles then waft these particles towards the *trachea*.

bronchitis: inflammation of the bronchi and bronchioles.
There are two main kinds of bronchitis, acute bronchitis and chronic bronchitis.
The two forms are compared in the table.

Type	Duration	Possible causes	Symptoms
acute	sudden onset, lasts a few days	infection by viruses or bacteria, or atmospheric pollution; the old, very young and smokers at highest risk; most attacks in winter	difficulty in breathing, persistent cough, pain behind the sternum and raised temperature
chronic	ongoing, may last years	smoking, heavy smoking in particular	as above, but may also lead to emphysema, raised blood pressure and sometimes heart failure

bronchus: (plural bronchi): a large air passage branching off the *trachea* and leading to a *lung*.
Inside the lung, each bronchus branches repeatedly, the branches (bronchioles) becoming smaller and smaller.

Each bronchus:
- is surrounded by rings of cartilage to hold it open
- has a layer of muscle underneath the cartilage
- is lined with an epithelium whose cells produce mucus to trap dirt and dust particles and have cilia to waft the dust towards the trachea.

buccal cavity: the mouth.

bud: an undeveloped region of a shoot which may develop into a shoot, leaf or flower.

budding (1): a type of *asexual reproduction* in which a small part of an adult organism separates from the rest and develops into a new individual. Some animals (*Hydra* and some jellyfish) reproduce by budding. (The diagram opposite shows budding in *Hydra*.)

Yeast is a unicell which reproduces by budding.

budding (2): a method of grafting – joining parts of two different plants together into one plant.
- A bud is cut from one plant together with some surrounding tissue.
- A slit is cut in the bark of the stem of another plant.
- The bud is placed in the slit and fastened in place.
- All the original stem above the new bud is cut away.
- The bud grows into a new stem.

Plants formed in this way have the roots from one variety and the stem of another.

Budding is carried out to give a plant with a desirable stem feature better roots than it would have normally.

cactus (plural cacti): flowering plants adapted to survive in hot dry deserts. Cacti can survive in hot areas with little regular rainfall because they have:

- extensive root systems and so can absorb water from a wide area
- leaves reduced to spines to minimise water loss by transpiration
- stems with cells containing chlorophyll so that they can *photosynthesise*
- tissue which can store water.

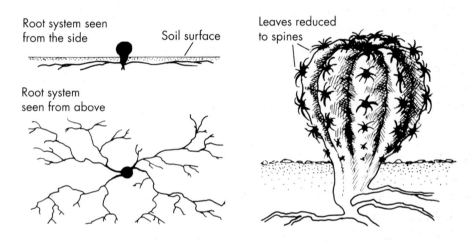

caecum: the first part of the *large intestine.*

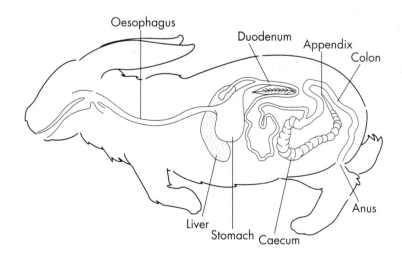

The caecum is a pouch which is joined to the small intestine and leads into the colon. In humans it is only a few centimetres long and has no particular function. The *appendix* projects from the caecum.

In rabbits and hares, the caecum and appendix contain billions of bacteria which digest the cellulose in the cell walls of the grass which they eat. The products of digestion are then egested with the faeces. The rabbit must eat the faeces to absorb the sugars formed by the bacteria in the caecum digesting the cellulose (see page 49).

calcium: a mineral ion needed by both plants and animals.

Calcium ions are needed by animals:

- for *muscle* contraction
- to produce healthy *bones* and *teeth*
- for *blood clotting*
- to transmit nerve impulses across *synapses*.

Calcium ions are needed by plants:

- to produce *cell walls*
- to activate *enzymes*.

calcium chloride: a chemical with the formula $CaCl_2$ used to absorb water and so create a dry environment.

One way to find out if a particular process needs water is to see if it will carry on without water. For example, to see if pea seeds need water to germinate, you could try to germinate some in a sealed test tube containing the seeds and some calcium chloride. The calcium chloride would absorb any water present and, after a few days, you would be able to see if the seeds had germinated.

Of course, you would need a control tube, which had water present, for comparison.

calorimeter: a piece of apparatus which is used to determine the energy content of a substance.

In biology, you usually use calorimeters to find the energy content of foods. To do this, you:

- weigh the food
- set the food alight
- use the heat it releases as it burns to raise the **temperature of a known** mass of water
- record the highest temperature reached by the water.

The energy content of the food (in joules per gram) is calculated from the formula:

$$\text{energy content of food} = \frac{\text{mass of water (g)} \times \text{temperature increase (°C)} \times 4.2}{\text{mass of food (g)}}$$

The diagrams show two kinds of calorimeters.

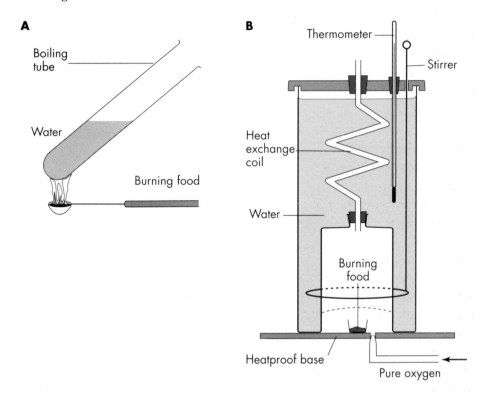

A

Boiling tube

Water

Burning food

B

Thermometer

Stirrer

Heat exchange coil

Water

Burning food

Heatproof base

Pure oxygen

You have probably found the energy of a peanut or other food using apparatus very similar to that shown in diagram A. The calorimeter shown in B gives a more reliable estimate of the energy content of foods because:
- more heat from the burning food actually heats the water – in A, a lot escapes to the air
- the food is burned in pure oxygen, which means it burns more efficiently and releases more of the energy in the food.

cancer: a type of tumour, or growth of abnormal cells, that has the ability to spread to other parts of the body.
Cancers form because:
- the *genes* which control the normal growth and cell division of cells mutate
- the affected cells begin to divide without proper control.
You run more risk of developing a cancer if you expose parts of your body to conditions which increase the rate of mutation. This includes:

- high energy radiation, such as ultraviolet light and X-rays
- many of the chemicals in cigarette smoke
- certain chemicals used and made in some industrial processes.

capillary: a microscopic *blood vessel* which carries blood around the individual cells inside an organ.

Capillaries are so small that over one million capillaries would fit into the aorta at the point where it leaves the heart. Red blood cells can only just pass through capillaries.

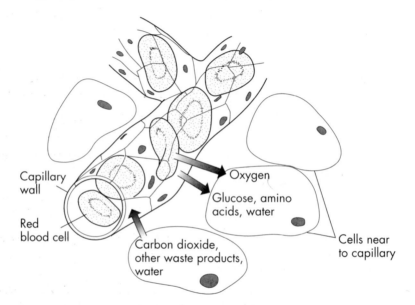

Capillary wall

Oxygen

Glucose, amino acids, water

Red blood cell

Carbon dioxide, other waste products, water

Cells near to capillary

Their main function is to allow substances to pass into and out of the cells as the blood flows past. Capillaries are effective because:

- their walls are only one cell thick so materials can diffuse through them easily in both directions
- their walls are leaky: this means that liquid can escape and carry dissolved food materials to the cells
- the blood flows slowly through capillaries so there is time for exchange between blood and surrounding cells.

carbohydrase: any *enzyme* which can break down a carbohydrate.

Examples of carbohydrases include:

- *amylase* – which breaks down starch into maltose
- maltase – which breaks down maltose into glucose.

carbohydrate: a compound which contains only carbon, hydrogen and oxygen. We need carbohydrates in our diet to supply energy.

There are three principal types of carbohydrate:

- monosaccharides (mono = one, saccharide = sugar) – these are compounds whose molecules are single sugar molecules
- disaccharides (di = two) – the molecules of these carbohydrates are made from two sugar molecules joined together
- polysaccharides (poly = many) – the molecules of these carbohydrates are made from many sugar molecules joined together.

There are many different carbohydrates, but there are five in particular that you should know about. The table gives details of these.

Carbohydrate	Type	Normal function	Source in our diet	What happens to it in our bodies
glucose	mono-saccharide	respiration	widespread in plant tissue	respired to release energy
maltose	disaccharide	no specific function – is only a product of starch digestion	part of starch molecule	digested to glucose
starch	poly-saccharide	storage carbohydrate in plants	potatoes, rice, pasta	digested to maltose
cellulose	poly-saccharide	used to make plant cells' walls	cereals, bran, vegetables	not digested, helps peristalsis and prevents colon cancer
glycogen	poly-saccharide	Storage carbohydrate in animals	red meat and liver	digested to glucose

carbon: the element which is the basis of life on earth.

All biological molecules, such as carbohydrates, lipids, proteins and DNA, contain carbon. It would be difficult to imagine life without these molecules.

carbon cycle: the recycling of carbon atoms on planet earth.

Carbon atoms are contained in many compounds in rocks and are released from the rocks by chemical reactions. The part of the carbon cycle you must know and understand is the biological carbon cycle.

The diagram on page 54 shows the main stages in the biological carbon cycle.

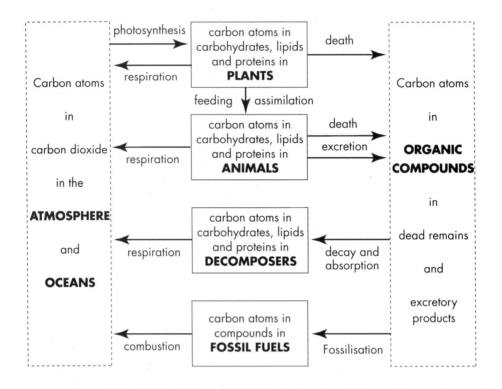

carbon dioxide: a colourless gas with the formula CO_2, which is heavier than air and does not allow things to burn in it.

Carbon dioxide is one of the most biologically important gases. Plants, algae and some bacteria can use carbon dioxide to photosynthesise. Carbon dioxide is produced by all organisms when they respire.

You can show that your breath contains carbon dioxide by blowing through a straw into a test tube of limewater. The carbon dioxide turns the clear limewater cloudy.

(See *photosynthesis* and *respiration*.)

carbon monoxide: a colourless, odourless gas with the formula CO, which burns with a pale blue flame.

Although carbon monoxide does not directly kill living cells, many people die each year as a result of inhaling it.

Carbon monoxide is dangerous because:

- it is odourless so people can inhale small amounts over a long period without being aware of it
- it binds with *haemoglobin* in the *red blood cells* and stops them from carrying oxygen around the body

- the effect is progressive: as more and more haemoglobin becomes bound to carbon monoxide, less and less oxygen can be carried, leading to unconsciousness
- the lack of oxygen can cause brain damage and even death.

cardiac muscle: the type of muscle found in the heart.
Cardiac muscle is very special; it is the only muscle in your body which contracts continuously all your life. If you have a pulse rate of just over 60 beats per minute, and live to be 75, the cardiac

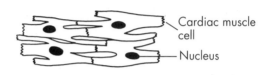

muscle in your heart must contract 2.5 billion times! (See *muscle (1)*.)

carnivore: an organism which eats only (or very largely) meat.
Carnivorous animals have specially adapted teeth and digestive systems.
They have:

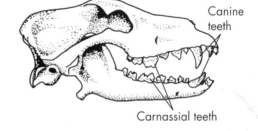

- canines which are pointed and large in relation to the jaw to pierce flesh
- strong, pointed carnassial teeth to crush bones
- a jaw action which is straight up and down to allow the molars and pre-molars to cut through flesh
- shorter digestive systems than similar sized herbivores as their food is easier to digest – there are no tough plant cell walls to break down.

carpals: the bones in the wrist.

carpel: the female reproductive structure in a *flower*.
There are three parts to a carpel:

- the *stigma* – this is the part which catches the pollen grains carried by the wind or an insect
- the *style* – this tube holds the stigma in a position where it can catch the pollen
- the *ovary* – this contains the ovules which, when fertilised will form the seeds.

carrier: a person who can pass on a disease but does not suffer themselves. There are two types of diseases which can be passed on by carriers – infectious diseases and inherited diseases.

INFECTIOUS DISEASES

- Some people can carry in their bodies the microorganisms which cause diseases such as *tuberculosis* and *hepatitis*.
- They do not develop the disease because they have some immunity.
- They can, however, pass the microorganisms to healthy people who then contract the disease.

INHERITED DISEASES

- Some inherited diseases are caused by recessive *alleles*.
- If a person inherits only one of a pair of recessive alleles, he or she will not suffer from the disease.
- If this carrier marries another carrier (or someone who is affected), then it is possible for some of their children to inherit two recessive alleles.
- The children with two recessive alleles will suffer from the disease.

An example of an inherited disease caused by a recessive allele is *cystic fibrosis*.

- **C** is the dominant allele which causes normal development.
- **c** is the recessive allele which causes production of excess mucus in the lungs.
- A carrier would have both alleles – **Cc**.

If two carriers married, there would be a 25% chance that children would be affected.

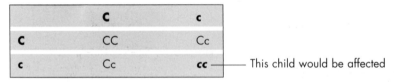

	C	**c**
c	CC	Cc
c	Cc	**cc** ——— This child would be affected

---

cartilage: a fibrous supporting tissue.

Cartilage is found in many places in our bodies and varies from being extremely hard and tough to quite flexible. Cartilage is found:

- in the discs between the *vertebrae* to act as a shock absorber: this cartilage is extremely tough
- in the epiglottis and the ear lobes: this cartilage is quite elastic
- in the tip of the nose and covering bones at *joints*: this cartilage is in between the other two in toughness and elasticity; it acts as a shock absorber and reduces friction between the bones of a joint.

catalase: an enzyme which catalyses the breakdown of hydrogen peroxide to water and oxygen.

Hydrogen peroxide is toxic. It is produced in large amounts by active cells (e.g. liver cells) which also produce a lot of catalase.

catalyst: a substance which speeds up the rate of a chemical reaction. Biological catalysts are called *enzymes*.

cell: the basic unit of all living things.

The table and the diagrams compare the structure of plant, animal and bacterial cells.

Component	Animal cell	Plant cell	Bacterial cell
genetic material	DNA in chromosomes in a nucleus	DNA in chromosomes in a nucleus	DNA not enclosed in a nucleus
cell wall	absent	cellulose cell wall	non-cellulose cell wall
cell membrane	present	present	present
mitochondria	present	present	absent
ribosomes	present	present	present, but smaller
vacuole	sometimes contains a few small vacuoles	large central storage vacuole	absent
chloroplasts	absent	present	absent, but some do contain *chlorophyll*

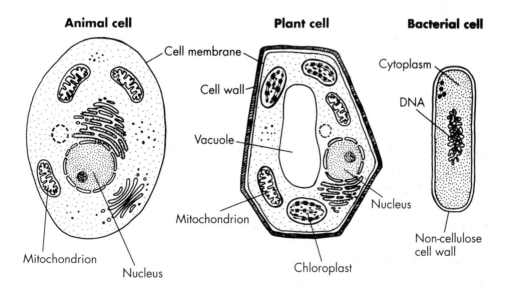

Animal cell **Plant cell** **Bacterial cell**

Cell membrane — Cytoplasm

Cell wall

DNA

Vacuole

Mitochondrion — Nucleus

Mitochondrion — Nucleus — Chloroplast — Non-cellulose cell wall

All cells contain genetic material (usually DNA), ribosomes and a cell membrane.

Cells are grouped together in *tissues*.

cell division: a process by which one cell divides to make two, or more, cells. There are two types of cell division:
- *mitosis* – this occurs whenever cell replacement or growth is taking place.
- *meiosis* – this occurs only when sex cells are being formed.

Feature	Mitosis	Meiosis
number of cells formed	2	4
when it occurs	cell replacement/ growth of body	formation of sex cells
genetic variation in cells formed	no variation – cells formed are genetically identical	genetic variation in cells formed
number of chromosomes in cells formed	same as number in original cell	half the number in original cell

cell membrane: the membrane which surrounds the *cytoplasm*, often called the cell surface membrane.

The cell (surface) membrane:
- is made from *protein* and *lipid* molecules
- is partially permeable and so controls the passage of molecules into and out of the cell
- can be specialised to carry out specific functions – the membrane of a nerve cell is specialised to allow nerve impulses to pass.

Do not confuse it with the *cell wall*; the cell membrane has no supportive function.

cell sap: the solution found in the central *vacuole* of plant cells.

The cell sap is a solution of sugars and mineral ions. It has two main functions:
- it acts as a store for the sugars and ions
- the concentration of the cell sap determines whether water will enter or leave the cell by *osmosis*.

cell wall: the structure which contains the *cytoplasm* and *cell membrane* of plant and bacterial cells.

Plant cell walls:
- are made of cellulose

- give some rigidity to the cells: they help to keep them in shape
- are totally permeable: they will allow any molecules to enter or leave.

cellulose: a polysaccharide found in plant cell walls.
Cellulose molecules:

- are made from chains of hundreds of glucose molecules
- link together to form fibres which make up the *cell walls* of plant cells
- form an important part of dietary fibre – we have no enzymes to digest cellulose, but the fibres help our intestines to move food along by *peristalsis.*

central nervous system (CNS): in *vertebrates,* the *brain* and the *spinal cord.*
The CNS coordinates the activities of the body by:

- receiving impulses from sense organs
- originating impulses which cause a response in the muscles and glands.

These impulses are carried into and out of the CNS by nerve cells (*neurones*) in nerves which connect to the brain or spinal cord.
Coordination by the CNS is possible because of:

- *reflex arcs* – a reflex arc is a nervous pathway which always produces the same automatic response to the same stimulus
- association by the brain of information from different sense organs and of information from the past with the present situation.

Most *synapses* occur within the CNS.

cereals: crop plants which produce edible grains; nearly all cereals are grasses which have undergone *selective breeding.*

- The cereals most cultivated are wheat, maize (corn) and rice; together they make up about 75% of the cereals eaten.
- Cereals make up a high proportion of the diet of many people in the world.
- They contain carbohydrates and protein, although the protein does not supply enough of all the essential *amino acids.*

cerebellum: a part of the *brain* concerned with coordinating control of skeletal muscles.

cerebrum (cerebral hemispheres): the area of the *brain* concerned with consciousness, memory, emotions, sensory perception and initiating responses.

CFCs (chlorofluorocarbons): chemicals used in aerosols (as propellants) and in refrigerators (as coolants).

CFCs have been affecting the *ozone layer* high in the atmosphere. The ozone layer is important as it prevents too much of the sun's harmful ultraviolet radiation reaching the earth. Ultraviolet radiation can cause sunburn and skin cancer.

When CFCs are released into the air:

- the sun's energy breaks them down and they release chlorine which is very reactive
- the chlorine atoms react with the ozone, forming oxygen and a chlorine–oxygen substance
- this chlorine–oxygen then breaks down, regenerating the reactive chlorine; so one chlorine atom can break down many molecules of ozone.

The use of CFCs is now banned because of the damage they cause to the ozone layer.

Chain, Ernst: a microbiologist who worked with Howard Florey, following up Alexander Fleming's discovery of *penicillin*.

---

characteristic: a feature of an organism.

Some characteristics you inherit from your parents, others are acquired (learned during your lifetime).

- Eye colour, height and blood group are inherited characteristics: they are determined by your *genes*.
- Ability to play an instrument, to speak a language or to paint are acquired characteristics. There is no gene which makes you able to play the guitar – you must learn how.

---

cheese: a dairy product made from the solid components (curds) of milk.

To make cheese:

- lactic acid bacteria are added to the milk: they turn the sugar (lactose) in the milk into lactic acid, which sours the milk
- the enzyme rennin is added to the milk: this makes the proteins in the milk curdle and become solid
- the solids (curds) are separated from the liquid (whey), pressed and allowed to mature.

Maturing is a complicated process and varies greatly with the cheese being made.

Scientists are currently using *genetic engineering* to produce improved strains of the lactic acid bacteria so that the process can be more efficient.

---

chlorine: a greenish toxic gas.

Chlorine is a halogen: it belongs to the same family of elements as fluorine and iodine. All of these elements have antibacterial properties.

Because of these properties, chlorine is used:

- as a *disinfectant* in swimming pools
- as the active ingredient in household bleaches
- to kill bacteria in water treatment plants.

chlorination: the process in which chlorine is added to water at water treatment plants.

At a water treatment plant, water is filtered to remove suspended solids and this process removes most bacteria also.

To ensure that the water is completely free from microorganisms, enough chlorine is then added to:

- kill any *bacteria* and inactivate any *viruses* which may remain after filtration
- kill any bacteria which may enter the water after it leaves the water treatment plant.

chlorophyll: the chemical found in *plants*, *algae* and some *bacteria* which absorbs light energy.

Organisms which contain chlorophyll:

- can photosynthesise because the light energy it absorbs is converted to chemical energy and can drive the reactions of *photosynthesis*
- often appear green because chlorophyll absorbs the blue and red components of white light, but reflects the green component.

chloroplast: an *organelle* (structure within a cell) which contains *chlorophyll*.

Chloroplasts are found in the cells of any green part of a plant, but mainly in the leaves. They contain chlorophyll and are the sites where *photosynthesis* occurs.

cholera: an infection of the small intestine caused by the bacterium *Vibrio cholerae*.

Transmission – cholera is nearly always transmitted by contaminated water or food.

Symptoms – severe diarrhoea and vomiting within one to five days of infection.

Treatment – rehydration by drinking a solution containing the correct proportions of sugars and salts. If this fails to rehydrate the patient, then an intravenous drip may be necessary. Doctors may prescribe antibiotics if the symptoms persist.

Prevention – worldwide improvement of sanitation will reduce the incidence of cholera; if in an area where cholera is common, drink only boiled or bottled water.

cholesterol: a fatty substance found in most animal tissues.
We need cholesterol in our diet to produce:
- cell membranes
- bile salts
- some hormones, including male and female sex hormones and some of the hormones released by the *adrenal glands*.

Too much cholesterol in our bloodstream can lead to *atherosclerosis* which is a major cause of heart attacks and strokes.

chromatography: a method of separating substances based on how far they can be carried through special paper by a solvent.
You can use chromatography as follows to show that cells from a green leaf do not just contain one pigment.
- Cut the leaf into small pieces and grind to a pulp with sand using a mortar and pestle.
- Shake the pulp with propanone in a test tube and allow to stand for a few minutes (this extracts the pigments from the broken cells)

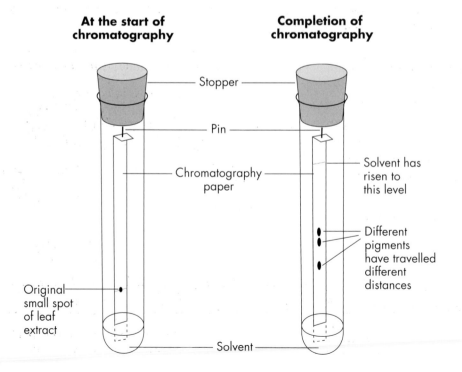

At the start of chromatography

Completion of chromatography

Stopper

Pin

Chromatography paper

Solvent has risen to this level

Different pigments have travelled different distances

Original small spot of leaf extract

Solvent

- Place a small spot of the extract about 1 cm from the end of a strip of chromatography paper.
- Allow to dry thoroughly then place another spot in the same place.
- Similarly, add more spots to the same place until a small, concentrated spot has been produced.
- Suspend the chromatography paper in a test tube as shown in the diagram and leave.
- As the solvent rises, it carries the different pigments different distances.

Note: you must take care not to let the solvent reach the top of the paper.

You can also use chromatography to find out which amino acids are present in a protein.

---

chromosome: a thread-like structure found in the nucleus of a cell, made from *DNA* and protein.

Chromosomes are found in almost all plant and animal cells (red blood cells are an exception) and are:

- the structures which contain the genetic information in the DNA molecule to determine inherited *characteristics*
- usually present in pairs: these pairs carry alleles of genes for the same features in the same sequence
- only present in half the normal number in the sex cells (*gametes*): these cells contain one chromosome from each of the pairs present in other cells
- copied exactly before a cell divides.

---

cilia (singular cilium): a microscopic, hair-like projection from the surface of a cell, capable of rhythmic movement.

Only a few cells have cilia; some *unicellular* organisms use cilia to move (see the diagram opposite), and the cells lining the *bronchioles* use their cilia to move mucus upwards towards the trachea.

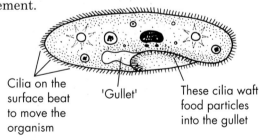

Cilia on the surface beat to move the organism

'Gullet'

These cilia waft food particles into the gullet

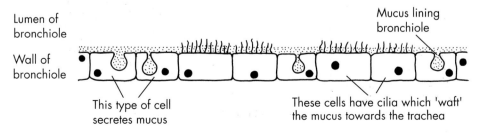

Lumen of bronchiole

Wall of bronchiole

Mucus lining bronchiole

This type of cell secretes mucus

These cells have cilia which 'waft' the mucus towards the trachea

Smoking can damage the cilia lining the bronchioles and reduce the removal of mucus resulting in 'smoker's cough'.

ciliary muscles: the muscles in the ciliary body in the *eye* which allow focusing to take place by altering the shape of the lens *(accommodation)*. The ciliary muscles:
- are involuntary muscles (not under conscious control)
- are circular muscles: the muscle fibres form a ring outside the edge of the lens
- are attached to the lens by suspensory ligaments
- alter the shape of the lens by contracting or relaxing.

(See *eye, accommodation*.)

circulation: the movement of *blood* through the *circulatory system*. Blood is circulated by the pumping action of the *heart*.

circulatory system: the system which moves *blood* to and from all parts of the body.

There are two distinct parts to the human circulatory system:
- the pulmonary circulation – blood is circulated through the *lungs* to be oxygenated
- the systemic circulation – oxygenated blood is circulated through all other organs.

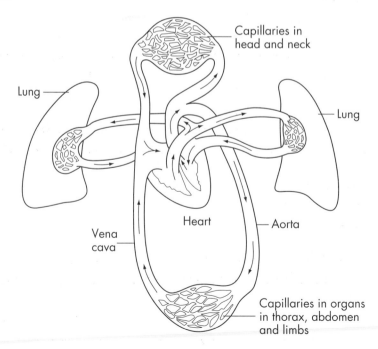

The *heart* provides the force to pump the blood through both parts of the system. Each part contains *arteries* (carrying the blood to the organs), *capillaries* (carrying the blood inside the organs) and *veins* (carrying the blood from the organs, back to the heart).

The diagram on page 64 shows the main components of the circulatory system.

Because blood must flow through the heart twice in one complete circulation, our circulatory system is called a double circulation. A fish has a single circulation because the blood passes through the heart only once per circulation.

classification: a method of placing organisms in a hierarchy of groups. The smallest groups may contain only a very few similar and closely related *species*. The largest groups contain many organisms, but the number of features common to them all may be relatively small.

Biologists now use evolutionary history as well as observable features to decide which group an organism belongs to. This produces a more natural system of classification than one based only on structural features.

clone: a group of genetically identical individuals or cells formed asexually from one organism or cell.

A clone is formed when some parts break away from, or are taken from, an individual and develop into new organisms. The members of a clone are genetically identical because:

- they are all derived from the same parent organism
- *fertilisation* was not involved
- they produced all their new cells by *mitosis* – copying the genes that came from the parent organism.

cloning: any method of producing a clone.

Asexual reproduction produces clones, but there are many artificial techniques which also produce groups of genetically identical offspring. These include:

- taking stem and leaf cuttings from plants
- *tissue culture*
- *embryo transplants*.

clot: blood which has solidified.

Clots normally form at the site of injury to the skin, but may form inside blood vessels.

(See *blood clotting*.)

cobalt chloride: a chemical with the formula $CoCl_2$ used to test for the presence of water.

Filter paper is soaked with cobalt chloride paper and allowed to dry. The dry paper is pink/white. If water touches it, the cobalt chloride paper turns blue.

colostrum: the thick, yellow liquid secreted by the mammary glands for the first few days after birth.

Colostrum differs from milk because it contains:

- less fat and sugar
- more mineral ions and protein
- a high level of the mother's *lymphocytes* and *antibodies*.

The lymphocytes and antibodies provide the baby with short-lived *passive immunity*.

combustion: rapid, high temperature oxidation of a fuel. Burning!

Combustion is a chemical reaction in which:

- the fuel reacts with oxygen
- carbon dioxide and water are produced
- energy is released as heat and light
- a flame can be seen.

community: all the organisms which live in a specific area.

A community will:

- consist of all the plants, animals and decomposers in the area
- be interdependent to some extent and will form a *food web*
- interact with the physical environment to recycle materials in the area.

competition: a struggle between organisms for a resource.

The struggle may be between individuals of the same species or between individuals of different species.

Competition within a species results in the best able to obtain the resource surviving whilst the others die. Charles Darwin called this the 'struggle for survival' and it was a key feature in his theory of *natural selection*.

Competition between species for exactly the same resource usually results in one species becoming extinct in that area as the other can compete more strongly for the resource.

Plants may compete for:

- water – for support, *photosynthesis* and manufacture of new cells
- light – for photosynthesis
- mineral ions

- carbon dioxide – for photosynthesis.

Animals may compete for:

- food
- water
- breeding sites
- mates.

---

compound: a substance in which the particles of two or more elements are chemically bonded together.

Most biological compounds are molecular – the particles of which they are made are not ions (charged particles) but molecules.

---

concentration gradient: the difference in the concentration of a substance between two places.

For example, the difference between the concentration of oxygen in the air in the alveoli and that in the blood is the concentration gradient of oxygen in this situation.

Substances tend to move down a concentration gradient – from a higher concentration to a lower one (Y to X in the diagram) – by *diffusion*. The rate of diffusion depends partly on the difference in concentrations: a large difference will produce faster diffusion than a small difference.

To move substances against a concentration gradient – from a lower concentration to a higher one – energy must be used; there must be *active transport*.

---

condensation reaction: a reaction in which two or more molecules combine, with the net loss of a small molecule. In biological systems, the small molecule is nearly always water.

glucose + glucose $\longrightarrow$ maltose + water
$$C_6H_{12}O_6 + C_6H_{12}O_6 \longrightarrow C_{12}H_{22}O_{11} + H_2O$$

Many hundreds of glucose molecules combine to form starch. Each time a new glucose molecule is added to the chain by a condensation reaction, a molecule of water is lost.

Similar reactions occur when:
- amino acids join together to form proteins
- fatty acids and glycerol join to form fats.

conditioning: a process involved in learning in which animals associate two unrelated stimuli.

The Russian scientist Pavlov carried out some classical conditioning experiments on dogs. He used the salivation response to the sight and smell of food as the basis for these experiments.
- He fed the dogs at the same time each day.
- After establishing the routine, he rang a bell each time he was about to feed the dogs.
- After several days of both ringing the bell and feeding, he sometimes just rang the bell at feeding time. The dogs salivated – they had become conditioned to associate the ringing of the bell with being fed.
- Pavlov also demonstrated that these 'conditioned reflexes' could be lost. If he just continued to ring the bell, the dogs quickly learned that there was no food to follow and no longer salivated.

conduction (heat): the process by which heat is transferred from particle to particle without the particles needing to move: it is the main process by which heat is transferred through solids.

We lose heat by conduction:
- when we touch something which is cooler than the surface of our *skin*
- when particles of the gases in the air collide with our skin (if they are cooler than the skin).

cones: light sensitive cells found in the *retina* of the *eye*.

Cones are sensitive to:
- bright light – they do not respond to the low intensities of light at night (*rods* allow us to see at night)
- a particular range of wavelengths of light – these broadly correspond with either red light, green light or blue light.

Because different cones are sensitive to different colours, we can perceive colour – but only when the light is bright enough to stimulate the cones. Cones also allow us to perceive objects in greater detail than rods. The greatest concentration of cones is found at the centre of the retina (the yellow spot). To perceive maximum detail we must look straight at an object so that rays of light from the object are focused onto this high concentration of cones.

conjunctiva: a membrane which lines the eyelids and covers the cornea and sclera at the front of the *eye*.

Cells in the conjunctiva produce a fluid which is similar to tears: this fluid lubricates the eyelids and the cornea. Where it covers the cornea, the conjunctiva is transparent to allow vision.

conjunctivitis: an inflammation of the *conjunctiva*.

Conjunctivitis is easily recognisable: the front of the eye becomes pink/red except for the region where the conjunctiva covers the cornea. The front of the eye itches and becomes sore. Sometimes the sufferer cannot stand bright light.

Conjunctivitis can be caused by:
- *bacteria* spread by contact between the eye and a contaminated source (e.g. handkerchief, towel)
- the *viruses* causing a cold, sore throat or measles.

conservation: protecting the earth's natural resources so that they will be able to meet the needs of future generations as well as our own.

Conservation does not mean that we should not use a resource; it means that we should use it carefully, with respect for the environment and for future generations.

The table on the following page shows some aspects of conservation you should be aware of.

There are other areas for consideration, and many other aspects to the ones mentioned in the table.

constrict: get narrower.

Arterioles can constrict because of the muscle in their walls. When nerve impulses cause these muscles to contract, the arterioles constrict and so they can carry less blood. This means that blood supply to the area is reduced. When we are too cold, the arterioles in the skin constrict to allow less blood into the *capillaries* near the surface of the skin. As a result, we lose less heat by radiation.

consumer: an organism which eats other organisms.

All animals are consumers, but many other organisms are consumers also. Animals which feed on plants are called *primary consumers* or *herbivores*. Animals which feed on herbivores are called secondary consumers or *carnivores*. Animals which feed on carnivores are also called carnivores; the carnivore at the end of a food chain is the top carnivore.

conservation

Area for conservation	Some problem(s)	Possible solution(s)
energy	• fossil fuel reserves are running out yet we still depend on them and are using increasing amounts; this produces more *pollution* (such as *acid rain*) as well as contributing to the greenhouse effect	• burn less fossil fuels • develop new, sustainable energy sources – e.g. nuclear fusion • increase the efficiency of energy generation from wind, tides, sun
wildlife	• pollution is killing wildlife • increased development and new farming methods remove breeding sites and food sources • *pesticides* kill wildlife as well as pests	• anti-pollution legislation • encourage the conservation of hedgerows, make best use of existing housing • research *biological control* methods
materials	• many plastics are made from oil, which is running out • increased demand for paper and wood results in felling of many trees	• use less oil as an energy source (there is much more coal left) • research new plastics • encourage recycling of materials • encourage the replanting of trees when any are felled for timber
food	• there are food surpluses in the developed world while millions starve elsewhere • the population in developing countries is growing faster than in the developed world • one-third of the crops grown are destroyed by pests	• encourage subsidised export of food surpluses • encourage more effective food production in developing countries, including support in managing food production following drought • encourage *contraception* in developing countries • research more effective pest control without use of ecologically damaging pesticides

continuous variation: variation which shows a range of values between two extremes.

Height in humans is an example of a characteristic showing continuous variation. There are only a few very tall people and only a few very short people; most of us fall somewhere between the two extremes. The most common heights are those around the average height.

contraception: controlling *fertility* to prevent *pregnancy*.

Any device or behaviour which prevents pregnancy is called a contraceptive. The main methods of contraception are shown in the table.

The effectiveness of a contraceptive is measured by their failure rate: the number of pregnancies per year per 100 women using the device (= pregnancies per 100 woman years).

Type of contraception	Examples	How they work	Effectiveness (pregnancies per 100 woman years)
barrier methods	condom	prevent sperm from penis entering the vagina	2.5
	cap	prevent sperm in the vagina entering the uterus	2.5
	female condom	prevent sperm entering the vagina	no information
natural methods	abstinence	attempt to pinpoint the time of ovulation so that, by avoiding intercourse, a pregnancy will not occur around the time of *ovulation*	10
sterilisation	vasectomy – cutting the tubes carrying sperm from the testes	prevents sperm from reaching the urethra and so cannot be released during intercourse	0.05
	tubal ligation – the *Fallopian tubes* are cut and tied	prevents eggs from reaching uterus and sperm from reaching eggs high in Fallopian tubes	0.05
hormonal methods	contraceptive pill	contains female sex hormones which act to suppress ovulation	0.5
	hormonal implant	a capsule implanted into the arm where it releases female sex hormones for several years	0.5
mechanical methods	intra-uterine device (IUD)	a small piece of moulded plastic inserted in the uterus interferes with implantation of an embryo	2.5
chemical methods	spermicides	chemicals in the form of foams, aerosols, creams and jellies are inserted into the vagina before intercourse to kill sperm	25 (when spermicide is used alone) 2.5 (when used with a condom)

contraction: getting shorter.

When some *muscles* contract they pull a *bone*: this causes the bone to move. When the muscle relaxes back to its original length, it does not exert any force – it cannot push a bone.

Contractions of the uterus are a result of contractions of muscles in the wall of the uterus and are part of the process of *birth*. These contractions push the baby through the cervix and vagina and out of the body.

convection: a method of transferring heat in which hot particles move, carrying their heat with them. Convection occurs in liquids and gases.

We lose heat by convection when we:

- breathe out – the molecules of the gases in the air we exhale carry heat with them out of our bodies
- sweat – the particles in vaporised sweat move away from our bodies carrying body heat with them.

convoluted tubule: a portion of a *nephron* in a kidney.

The convoluted tubules are the regions of the nephron where useful materials from the filtrate formed in the *glomerulus* are reabsorbed into the bloodstream.

coordination: using information from sense organs, memory or both to produce a response.

In humans, the *central nervous system* is the main coordinator.

- In *reflex actions*, the sensory neurones and motor neurones meet at a synapse in the central nervous system and so the response to a certain stimulus is automatic and always the same.
- In voluntary actions, the brain acts as coordinator by receiving information from sense organs and using memory to decide what to do.

cornea: the transparent front part of the wall of the *eye* which allows light to enter the eye.

The cornea plays an important role in focusing rays of light on the retina. Because it is curved, the cornea will always refract (bend) the rays of light by a considerable amount. The lens must just 'finish the job' by refracting the rays sufficiently to focus them on the retina. The cornea is lubricated by a liquid from the conjunctiva and kept free from dust by tears.

coronary artery: an artery which branches off the *aorta* just as it leaves the *heart* and carries oxygenated blood to the wall of the heart itself.

Branches of the coronary arteries carry oxygenated blood to the capillaries which run through the muscle in the heart wall. Oxygen and nutrients diffuse from these capillaries into the muscle fibres, enabling them to contract continuously and the heart to keep beating.

Most of the blood carried in the coronary arteries goes to the muscle in the wall of the left ventricle.

Blockage of a coronary artery results in a heart attack.

coronary thrombosis: blockage of a *coronary artery*, or a branch of a coronary artery, by a blood clot forming in the artery.

When a coronary artery is blocked:

- the area of heart muscle it serves becomes starved of oxygen and nutrients
- muscle fibres in this area die or are damaged
- the area loses the ability to contract and pump blood
- if the area is a large one, the heart may stop beating – this is a heart attack
- if the area is small, the heart may continue to beat, but the person may feel pains in the chest when exercising – these pains are called angina pectoris.

corpus luteum: the part of the *follicle* remaining in the *ovary* after ovulation.

If a pregnancy occurs, the corpus luteum remains in the ovary for about three months, after which it degenerates.

- During this time the corpus luteum releases *progesterone* into the bloodstream which maintains the lining of the *uterus*.
- After three months, the *placenta* takes over the function of manufacturing the progesterone.
- Most miscarriages occur at about three months into a pregnancy because the timing of the 'switch over' may not be precise. This can leave the body with nothing manufacturing progesterone and so the uterine lining breaks down, resulting in a miscarriage.

cotyledons: seed leaves which, in many species, store food materials needed for *germination*.

When *seeds* are formed, they contain an embryo which comprises a shoot, root and one or two cotyledons. The cotyledons store the food materials which will provide the energy and materials necessary to produce new cells until the leaves develop and can *photosynthesise*.

In some species, as germination proceeds, the cotyledons are brought above ground.

Crick, Francis: a biologist who, with *James Watson*, worked out the structure of the *DNA* molecule.

Watson and Crick worked in a laboratory in Cambridge University and used information which had been discovered by other scientists. In particular, they used some X-ray images of the DNA molecule first obtained by Rosalind Franklin working in a laboratory in London University.

Piecing together all the information, Watson and Crick proposed the now famous double helix structure for DNA.

Understanding the structure of the DNA molecule was crucial to understand how it copies itself and controls *protein synthesis*. Without this knowledge, *genetic engineering* would be impossible and many of the products of modern *biotechnology* would not exist.

---

cross-fertilisation: fusion of male and female sex cells which come from different individuals of the same species.

Cross-fertilisation produces more *variation* in the offspring than self-fertilisation because it brings together the genes of two individuals.

In most animals and some plants, individuals are either male or female so cross-fertilisation must occur. Most plants have flowers with both male and female sex organs and many species have evolved mechanisms which ensure that self-fertilisation cannot occur. These include:

- *anthers*, which develop and release their pollen before the *stigma* is receptive
- female sex organs, which develop and are fertilised before the anthers are mature
- pollen grains being unable to grow and penetrate the stigma of the same flower (self-sterility).

---

crustaceans: *arthropods* with two pairs of antennae, a pair of jointed legs on most body segments and, frequently, a hard shell.

Nearly all crustaceans live in water; the woodlouse is an example of a crustacean which lives on land.

Krill are microscopic crustaceans found in the Antarctic oceans which feed on the photosynthetic plankton. The billions of krill are the main food source for many fishes and the baleen whales found in the Antarctic.

Crabs, lobsters and shrimps are also examples of crustaceans.

---

cuticle: a non-cellular layer covering the outside of part or all of an organism.

Cuticles usually protect the organism from physical damage or prevent it from losing too much water. Examples of cuticles include:

- the waxy coating covering the surface of a *leaf* – this prevents the loss of water
- the exoskeleton of *arthropods* – in some cases this prevents physical damage, but the waxy cuticle of *insects* is mainly to reduce water loss.

cutting: a part of a plant removed deliberately for the purpose of growing into a new plant.

When you grow a plant from a cutting, it will be genetically identical to the parent plant. This is because:

- no fusion of sex cells has occurred to introduce new genes
- the cutting develops new cells by *mitosis* which copies the genes exactly, so the genes from the parent plant in the cells of the cutting will be copied into all the cells of the new plant.

You can use most parts of a plant to take cuttings, but not all methods are suitable for all plants.

cystic fibrosis: an inherited condition which affects *lungs, pancreas* and *sweat glands*.

Cystic fibrosis affects the *cell membranes* of all cells, but the most serious effects are on cells which secrete chemicals. The main effects are on:

- the *bronchioles* – cells lining the bronchioles secrete too much mucus which is difficult to remove, making lung infections more likely
- the pancreas – thick secretions block the ducts which carry the pancreatic enzymes into the small intestine, resulting in poor digestion and malnutrition
- the sweat glands – these secrete sweat with a very high concentration of salt, which may lead to heatstroke and collapse in hot climates.

Cystic fibrosis is caused by a recessive *allele* and so, to be affected by the condition, a person must inherit two cystic fibrosis alleles. If the person inherits only one recessive allele and a dominant normal allele, he or she will be a *carrier* but will be unaffected by the condition. The chance of two carriers producing an affected child is 25%.

- **C** is the dominant allele which causes normal development.
- **c** is the recessive allele which causes production of excess mucus in the lungs.
- A carrier would have both alleles – **Cc**.

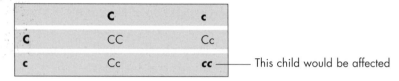

	C	c
C	CC	Cc
c	Cc	**cc** —— This child would be affected

Treatment of cystic fibrosis includes physiotherapy to help remove the mucus in the lungs and *antibiotics* to cure any infections which have already developed. A preparation of pancreatic enzymes is often given with meals to aid digestion.

Scientists are currently researching the use of *gene therapy* to cure affected individuals.

cytoplasm: the region of a *cell* between the nucleus and cell membrane: most of the cell's chemical reactions take place here.

The cytoplasm was once thought to be a simple jelly-like substance. Now, we know it is very complex and consists of:

- a watery solution (called the cytosol)
- a system of membranes
- a number of *organelles*, such as mitochondria, ribosomes, chloroplasts and many others.

The chemical reactions which take place throughout the cytoplasm are controlled by *enzymes*.

cytosine: one of the four building blocks of the *DNA* molecule. Cytosine always pairs with guanine.

Darwin, Charles: an English scientist who put forward the idea of *natural selection*.

Darwin was not the first to suggest that organisms could evolve into new species over long periods of time, but he was the first to propose a mechanism which could be accepted.

Darwin had found much of his evidence on the Galapagos Islands in the Pacific Ocean during a five year voyage aboard the HMS Beagle as ship's naturalist. At about the same time, Alfred Wallace working in the Far East, reached very similar conclusions and sent all his findings to Darwin in England. They presented their ideas jointly to a scientific institution in 1858.

In 1859 Darwin published a book called 'The origin of species by means of Natural Selection'. Many people read the book and it aroused great controversy as it conflicted with the ideas of the creation described in the Bible.

In 1871, Darwin published another book, 'The descent of Man' in which he applied his ideas of natural selection to the origin of mankind.

DDT: an insecticide banned since 1972 because of its effects on wildlife.

DDT is an extremely effective insecticide and was widely used, preventing millions of deaths from *malaria*. However, it became apparent that DDT was being passed along *food chains* and affecting organisms it was never intended to affect.

The problems arose because:
- DDT is very stable: it is non-biodegradable (living things cannot break it down) and it persists in the environment for up to ten years
- it is fat soluble and is stored in fatty tissue.

In the food chain, a consumer eats many of the organisms it feeds on and so receives all the DDT which they have stored in their bodies. The flowcharts show how the concentrations of DDT increase along the food chain.

dead elm leaves $\longrightarrow$ earthworms $\longrightarrow$ robin
(24 ppm DDT)   (86 ppm DDT) (109 ppm DDT)

plankton $\longrightarrow$ crustaceans $\longrightarrow$ small fish $\longrightarrow$ large fish $\longrightarrow$ osprey
(0.000 0003 ppm   (0.04 ppm   (0.5 ppm   (2 ppm   (25 ppm
DDT)   DDT)   DDT)   DDT)   DDT)

High concentrations of DDT in birds can cause them to stop laying eggs or to lay eggs with very thin shells which break easily. Both result in decreased fertility. Very high concentrations of DDT can kill.

deamination: turning *amino acids* into *urea* and carbohydrate.
All amino acids have a group of atoms called the amino group (NH_2) some-where in their molecule.
If amino acids are in surplus in the body, they are deaminated: the amino group is removed and turned into urea. What is left of the amino acid molecule can be turned into the carbohydrate *glycogen* and stored, or it can be respired. Deamination takes place in the *liver*.

decay: see *decomposition*.

decomposers: organisms which bring about the breakdown of the complex organic molecules in excretory products and dead organisms.
Most decomposers are either bacteria or fungi, but earthworms and other invertebrates help to decompose dead materials.
The bacteria and fungi secrete digestive *enzymes* onto the dead matter and then absorb the products of digestion. They release simple inorganic com-pounds like carbon dioxide and ammonia and so help to recycle carbon and nitrogen. See also *saprobionts*.

decomposition: breaking down complex organic molecules in excretory products and dead organisms into simpler ones.
There are three aspects to decomposition:
- leaching of any soluble substances from the dead material into the ground (by rain)
- fragmentation of the remaining dead material into smaller pieces (brought about by the action of weather and the material passing through the guts of soil animals)
- chemical breakdown of the organic molecules (brought about by the release of digestive *enzymes* by *decomposers*).

All three take place more or less at the same time, although the chemical breakdown proceeds faster when the physical fragmentation has taken place. The chemical breakdown takes place best when conditions are warm and moist and there is a good supply of oxygen.

defence mechanisms: systems which help our bodies to resist infection by microorganisms.
Our main defence mechanisms are:
- the *skin* acting as a barrier to infection

- the acid in our *stomach* killing *bacteria* which enter with our food
- the mucus and cilia in the *bronchioles* trapping and removing microorganisms
- our blood being able to *clot* and so prevent entry of microorganisms when we cut ourselves
- our *immune system* killing microorganisms and giving lasting immunity to disease.

deforestation: deliberate felling of forests.

Deforestation is usually carried out so that:

- land can be cleared for agriculture or for buildings
- ores can be mined from the cleared areas
- timber can be obtained for making paper, making charcoal, making furniture or as a building material.

Deforestation is the result of immediate need being seen as more important than long-term considerations. It has been carried out for centuries – much of Europe used to be covered in forest. As the human population has grown, deforestation has spread to new areas and now threatens the tropical rain forests. When tropical rain forest is cleared, a number of effects automatically follow.

- Not just the trees are removed. The animals which lived in and on them are also affected: they must find new habitats or die.
- The relatively nutrient-poor soil of rain forest is exposed and can be easily eroded. The roots of large trees are important in holding the soil in place.
- Less carbon dioxide is removed from the atmosphere. The millions of large trees in the rain forests use large amounts of carbon dioxide each year. If they are removed and it is unused, it must remain in the atmosphere, possibly increasing the *greenhouse effect*.

denature: to permanently alter the structure, shape and properties of a *protein* molecule.

Proteins can be denatured by strong heat and by a pH which is too acid or too alkaline.

When you boil an egg, the heat denatures a protein in the liquid white of the egg (it isn't white at this stage) and turns it to a white solid. If you leave the egg to go cold, the egg white doesn't change back. Denaturing is irreversible. *Enzymes* are proteins and so they too can be denatured. If human enzymes are heated to temperatures above 45°C:

- the structure and shape of the enzyme molecule changes
- this changes the shape of the *active site* of the enzyme
- it cannot 'fit' as well with the reactant molecules

- the reaction the enzyme is catalysing slows down.

At very high temperatures, the change in shape of the active site is so great that the reaction stops altogether. Very high or low pHs usually have the same effect, although the enzyme *pepsin* in the stomach is adapted to work best in acidic conditions.

denitrification: changing nitrate ions (NO^{3-}) into nitrogen gas (N_2) by *denitrifying bacteria* in the soil. It is one of the stages in the *nitrogen cycle*. Denitrification results in a loss of nitrate ions from the soil and means that plants can grow less well as they lose one of their main sources of nitrogen, needed to build *proteins*.

deoxyribonucleic acid: see *DNA*.

depressant: any drug which slows down the working of the *central nervous system*.

Alcohol is the most common depressant drug. The effects of alcohol in slowing down the working of the brain are the basis of the anti drink-drive campaigns. As you drink more alcohol, your reaction times get longer and you may be unable to respond in time to a hazard.

detritivore: an animal which feeds on detritus – the organic debris from dead and decomposing animals and plants.

Earthworms are important detritivores in soils in temperate climates; termites are equally important in the tropics.

Detritivores eat and fragment large amounts of the detritus, but digest and absorb very little. The majority passes out with the faeces. The fragmentation increases the surface area of the detritus and makes it easier for *decomposers* such as bacteria to break it down.

diabetes: under-secretion of *insulin* by the *pancreas*.

Normally, if the level of glucose in the blood plasma rises above a certain limit (90 mg per 100 cm³), the following corrective mechanism is set in action.

- The pancreas secretes insulin into the bloodstream.
- The insulin causes increased uptake of glucose and conversion of glucose to *glycogen* in liver and muscle.
- The blood glucose level returns to normal.
- The pancreas stops secreting insulin.

A diabetic person cannot produce any (or enough) insulin, and so the blood glucose level remains above normal for long periods. This may affect the body in many ways, including:

- glucose normally reabsorbed into the blood in the *kidney* is lost in the urine
- increased amounts of urine are produced
- increased thirst (because of the increased loss of water in the urine)
- coma – there is too much sugar in the blood plasma, but without insulin the brain cells (and all other cells) cannot take it up.

Diabetes is normally treated by controlling diet and/or administering daily injections of insulin.

dialysis: a method of separating substances using a partially permeable membrane.

A partially permeable membrane will allow small molecules to pass through it, but not large ones.

You can see how dialysis works as follows, using a mixture of starch and glucose solutions in visking tubing.

- Place the starch/glucose mixture in a length of visking tubing.
- Place the visking tubing in a boiling tube containing water.
- After 20 minutes, test the water in the boiling tube for the presence of starch and glucose. Only glucose is present as dialysis has taken place: the starch molecules were too large to pass through the visking tubing.

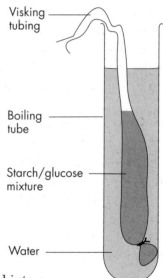

Visking tubing

Boiling tube

Starch/glucose mixture

Water

When a person has *kidney* failure, they have to undergo dialysis. Their blood is passed between a series of partially permeable membranes for several hours. This dialysing membrane:

- allows the waste *urea* to diffuse out of the blood into a special fluid on the other side of the membrane
- large protein molecules and red blood cells stay in the blood.

diaphragm: a sheet of fibrous and muscle tissue which separates the *thorax* from the *abdomen*.

The muscular part of the diaphragm, around the edge, is attached to the spine, lower ribs and the lower end of the sternum. There are openings in the diaphragm where nerves and blood vessels pass through.

The main function of the diaphragm is in *breathing*. It helps to create the changes in pressure in the thorax which either draw air in or force air out of the lungs.

When we breathe in:	When we breathe out:
• the muscular part of the diaphragm contracts	• the muscular part of the diaphragm relaxes
• the diaphragm is pulled downwards – from its resting dome shape	• the diaphragm returns to its dome shape
• this reduces the pressure in the thorax	• this increases the pressure in the thorax
• air is drawn into the lungs	• air is forced out of the lungs

diastole: relaxation of a chamber of the *heart*.
Atrial diastole is relaxation of the atria. Ventricular diastole is relaxation of the ventricles.
During diastole, blood enters the chamber.

diet: see *balanced diet*.

dietary fibre: the part of our food made from indigestible parts of plant material.
Dietary fibre consists largely of the materials such as *cellulose* which make up plant cell walls. We have no enzymes which can digest these materials and so they must pass straight through our gut.
Despite not being digested or absorbed, dietary fibre is an important component of our diet because:
• it helps to give the food bulk and so aids the passage of food through the gut by *peristalsis*
• it appears to reduce the risk of *heart disease* and colon cancer.
All vegetables and fruits contain fibre as do most foods produced from them. Cereals and bran are particularly rich sources.

diffusion: the movement of particles of a fluid from a region of high concentration to one of low concentration (down a concentration gradient).
Diffusion results in an even distribution of particles. If someone sprays some perfume in a room, everyone can smell it after a while. The particles of the perfume diffuse from the highly concentrated area (near the person who sprayed it) to the areas of low concentration (the rest of the room). Diffusion will continue until there is no difference in the concentrations.
Examples of diffusion in living things include:
• the exchange of oxygen and carbon dioxide between the air in the *alveoli* and the blood
• the exchange of oxygen, carbon dioxide, urea and soluble food molecules across the *placenta*

- movement of water vapour out of a leaf, through *stomata*
- movement of water into a root hair cell – this is *osmosis* which is the diffusion of water only.

digestion: breaking down large, insoluble food molecules into small soluble ones.

Organisms need to digest large food molecules otherwise they could not be absorbed into their cells.

Digestion does not just occur in humans.

- All animals with a gut must digest their food to be able to absorb it.
- Plants must be able to digest insoluble starch into glucose so that it can be moved around the plant.
- *Decomposers* must digest the dead material outside their bodies before they can absorb it.

The main food molecules which need digesting are *starch, protein* and *lipids* (fats and oils).

- Starch is broken down into glucose.
- Proteins are broken down into amino acids.
- Lipids are broken down into fatty acids and glycerol.

digestive enzymes: enzymes released to break down large insoluble food molecules into small soluble ones.

The main human digestive enzymes are described in the table.

Enzyme	Produced by	Acts in	Acts on	Produces
amylase	salivary glands	mouth	starch	maltose
	pancreas	small intestine		
protease	stomach wall	stomach	proteins	amino acids
	pancreas	small intestine		
	small intestine wall	small intestine		
lipase	pancreas	small intestine	lipids (fats and oils)	fatty acids and glycerol
maltase	small intestine wall	small intestine	maltose	glucose

digestive system: the *alimentary canal* plus other glands and organs associated with it.

The alimentary canal consists of the various parts of the gut, from mouth through to anus. Other organs, however, are involved in *digestion*. These are the *salivary glands, liver, gall bladder* and *pancreas*. The digestive system is the whole system of alimentary canal plus these other structures.

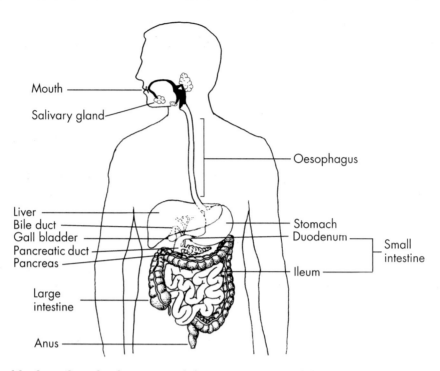

The table describes the functions of the main organs of the digestive system.

Organ	Function(s)
mouth	teeth cut food into smaller pieces; digestion of starch by salivary amylase from salivary glands
oesophagus	moves food from mouth to stomach by *peristalsis*
stomach	produces acid which kills bacteria; produces a protease adapted to the acid conditions
liver	excretory products from liver pass into the gall bladder and form bile
gall bladder	stores bile and releases it periodically into the duodenum
pancreas	produces an amylase, a protease and a lipase which are secreted into the small intestine
small intestine: ● duodenum ● ileum	bile from gall bladder emulsifies fats to form droplets with a large surface area for digestion; pancreatic enzymes digest starch, lipids and proteins here digestion of starch, lipids and proteins continues; digestion of maltose; absorption of soluble products of digestion
large intestine (colon)	reabsorption of water secreted with the enzymes as more and more water is reabsorbed, solid faeces are produced
anus	egestion of faeces

digit: in vertebrates, a finger or a toe.
Digits are made from bones called phalanges. Most vertebrates have five digits on each limb.

dilate: get wider.
Arterioles can dilate because of the muscle in their walls. When nerve impulses cause arterioles to dilate, they can carry more blood and so the blood supply to the area is increased.
When we are too hot, the arterioles in the *skin* dilate to allow more blood into the capillaries near the surface of the skin so that we can lose more heat by radiation.

dinosaurs: a group of *reptiles* which became extinct about 70 million years ago.
Dinosaurs ranged in size from small fast-running carnivores about the size of a dog to gigantic herbivores, some of which may have weighed as much as 100 tons. At nearly 6 metres tall, the gigantic carnivore *Tyrannosaurus* was one of the largest predators ever to have lived.

Although the dinosaurs as a group became extinct, some dinosaurs evolved into animals which are still living today. Crocodiles are descended from dinosaurs called crocodilians. All the modern-day birds are descended from dinosaurs.
People used to think of dinosaurs as slow-moving animals. Recent evidence suggests that, although they were ectotherms (i.e. their body temperature varied with the temperature of the surroundings), they may have been able to keep a fairly constant, high body temperature and were capable of moving very quickly.

diploid: the number of *chromosomes* in a normal body cell.
The diploid number in humans is 46. We have 46 chromosomes in all our cells except the sex cells (and red blood cells which have none).
The 46 chromosomes exist as 23 pairs, with each chromosome in a pair carrying *alleles* of the same *genes* in the same sequence. This is really what diploid means – it is the number of chromosomes in a cell when both members of the pairs are present.
(See *haploid.*)

discontinuous variation: variation where a feature shows only a few categories.

Examples of discontinuous variation include:

- whether or not you can roll your tongue
- whether your ear lobe is attached to the side of your head or hangs free
- whether pea plants are tall or short
- whether or not a bacterium is resistant to the antibiotic penicillin.

Characteristics showing discontinuous variation are usually:

- controlled by one or two genes
- not influenced greatly by the environment.

(See *continuous variation*.)

disease: a condition in which part or all of a body functions less effectively than normal.

All organisms can have diseases. In humans, diseases are of six main types:

- infectious diseases – those caused by parasites, usually microorganisms
- deficiency diseases – those caused by lack of a particular nutrient or group of nutrients
- inherited diseases – those due to our genes
- degenerative diseases – those caused when parts of the body degenerate, often as a result of ageing
- human induced diseases – those caused by the activities of humans
- mental illness – disorders of the mind.

disease, infectious: a disease which is caused by a parasite, usually a microorganism which has infected the body.

Most infectious diseases of humans are caused by either bacteria or viruses. A few are caused by fungi and a few by protozoa (protoctistans).

The table on page 87 gives details of some human infectious diseases.

disease, prevention: activities which can be undertaken to reduce either the transmission of disease or the number of people who are susceptible to a disease.

Transmission of disease can be reduced by a number of commonsense measures, such as:

- washing hands before handling or eating food
- ensuring that food is cooked properly
- hygienic preparation and storage of food
- avoiding drinking water which has not been treated at a water treatment plant
- avoiding unprotected sexual intercourse

- good standards of personal hygiene
- using a handkerchief to trap microorganisms when we sneeze or cough ('Coughs and sneezes spread diseases – trap your germs in a handkerchief' – the 1950's slogan is still valid today).

The number of people who are susceptible to a disease can be reduced by vaccination and by improving standards of living, particularly diet.

disease, transmission of: carrying a disease-causing organism from an infected individual to a healthy one.

Human diseases can be transmitted by contaminated water and food, contact, and by airborne droplets.

water	the bacteria causing cholera and typhoid fever are transmitted in this way; drinking water in some developing countries is not treated and may be polluted by human faeces
food	some bacteria causing food poisoning (e.g. *Salmonella*) are transmitted in contaminated food
contact	the microorganisms causing AIDS and syphilis are transmitted by sexual contact; skin infections are often transmitted by direct contact
airborne	many respiratory diseases (e.g. colds, influenza, pneumonia) are transmitted in airborne droplets

disease, infectious

Type of disease	Example	Symptoms	Method of transmission
viral	chickenpox	slight fever, rash	airborne droplets, direct contact
	common cold	sneezing, aches, runny nose	airborne droplets, hand-to-hand contact
	AIDS	fever, weight loss, fatigue, more likely to contract other diseases	sexual contact, shared hypodermic needles
bacterial	pneumonia	cough, fever, chest pains, short of breath	airborne droplets
	whooping cough	runny nose, fever, coughing spasms	airborne droplets
	tuberculosis (TB)	weight loss, chest pains, cough, shortness of breath	airborne droplets, cows' milk
protozoan	malaria	chills, high fever, sweating, headache, fatigue	bite from infected mosquito
fungal	athlete's foot	itchy skin between toes, skin flakes off	direct contact with infected people or animals

disinfectant: any substance which kills *microorganisms*.
The term is usually used to describe strong chemicals which are unsafe to use on human skin. They are used to prevent the transmission of disease-causing organisms by keeping work surfaces clean, and preventing their build up in toilets and drains.
Household bleach is an example of a disinfectant.

dislocation: displacement of the bones at a *joint* so that they are no longer in contact.
Dislocation is always a serious injury and a force large enough to produce this usually causes other damage also.
- The ligaments holding the joint together are often torn.
- The capsule (the membrane encasing the joint) is often damaged.
- One or more of the bones is often fractured.
Treatment must be carried out by a qualified person who will:
- X-ray the joint to see if a bone has been fractured
- re-align the bones in the joint (surgery may be necessary)
- encase the joint in a plaster cast to allow it to heal without moving.

diversity index: a measure of the species richness of an area.
A diversity index does not just measure how many species there are in an area – you can do that by walking round the area and recording all the different species you see. It also takes into account the success of each species – how abundant each one is.
For example, suppose you studied two areas and found 100 organisms in each area and just five species. Suppose the numbers of each species were the same as those shown in the table:

| Species | Number of organisms in each species | |
	Area 1	Area 2
A	91	20
B	2	20
C	3	20
D	2	20
E	2	20

Although there are the same number of organisms and species, they are clearly very different. Area 1 contains, effectively, just one species, whereas in Area 2, there are five successful species and this area would have a higher diversity index.

DNA (deoxyribonucleic acid): the chemical of which *genes* are made; DNA carries the genetic code which determines how all cells will work and the characterstics an organism will develop.

DNA is made from three main units:

- four special bases called adenine, thymine, cytosine and guanine, usually represented by their initial letters
- a sugar called deoxyribose
- phosphate groups.

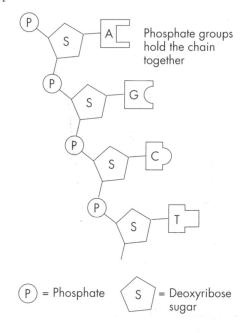

Phosphate groups hold the chain together

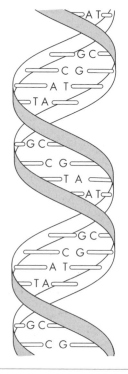

These are arranged into two long strands wound into a double helix as shown in the diagram to the left.

Notice that adenine (A) on one strand is always placed opposite thymine (T) on the other strand. cytosine (C) is always placed opposite guanine (G). This is called the 'base pairing rule'.

dominant: refers to an *allele* which is always expressed, even when an alternative allele is present.

For example, tallness in pea plants is dominant. Any pea plant which inherits the tall allele will be tall, whether it inherits a dwarf allele also or another tall allele.

(See *recessive.*)

double circulation: circulation in which the blood passes through the heart twice.

(See *circulatory system.*)

Down's syndrome: a condition resulting from inheriting an extra chromosome from the mother.

Humans have 46 chromosomes in each body cell, in 23 pairs. The pairs are the same size and shape because they carry *alleles* of the same genes in the same sequence.

There are 23 chromosomes in the sex cells (*gametes*), one from each pair. Sometimes egg cells are formed which contain three chromosome 21s. When these egg cells are fertilised, the zygote will contain 47 chromosomes not 46. All the cells of the individual will therefore have an extra chromosome 21.

Down's syndrome can be mild or very severe, but usually includes the following:

● short hands and feet with stubby digits

● distinctive facial appearance

● retarded mental development

● a higher than usual risk of heart disease.

The risk of Down's syndrome is generally about 1 live birth in 600. After age 35 however, a mother's chance of giving birth to a child with Down's syndrome rises and is 1 in 80 by age 40.

drug: a substance which alters the way in which all or part of the body works. Drugs can be classified in a number of ways:

● chemically – according to the type of chemical they are

● by the disorder they are used to treat – an anti-hypertensive drug is used to treat very high blood pressure

● according to the effect they have on the body.

Different drugs have different effects on the body. For example:

● *stimulants* speed up the working of the *nervous system*

● *depressants* slow down the working of the nervous system

● *sedatives* act on an area of the brain, making us less alert

● diuretics increase the production of urine

● *analgesics* reduce our perception of pain

● *hallucinogens* distort our view of reality.

Some drugs may fall into more than one category. For example, caffeine is a diuretic and a stimulant.

drug abuse: using a drug for a purpose other than the normal one, or using excessive amounts of a drug.

(See *alcohol abuse, anabolic steroid*.)

ear: the sense organ in vertebrates which enables them to hear and maintain balance.

There are three regions to the human ear.

- Outer ear – this consists of the pinna (the 'ear' we can see) and the tube which leads inwards from it to the ear drum.
- Middle ear – a cavity hollowed out in the bone of the skull. Three bones (ossicles) vibrate to transmit sound waves across the middle ear.
- Inner ear – another cavity in the skull, but this is filled with liquid.

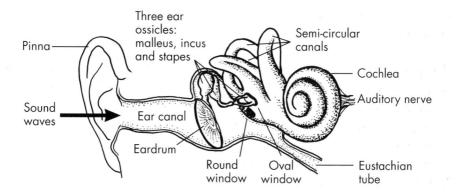

Vibrations of the ossicles cause the liquid in the cochlea to stimulate special sense cells which send *nerve* impulses to the brain – and we 'hear'.

When we run or spin, the liquid in the semi-circular canals stimulates sense cells which send nerve impulses to the brain about any change in our position. The brain uses this information, together with information from our eyes, to maintain our balance.

earth: the third planet from the sun in our solar system.

Because of its distance from the sun and its atmosphere, life (including intelligent life) has evolved on earth. Many scientists believe that, somewhere in the universe, there must be planets with similar conditions and that intelligent life will have evolved there also.

At the moment, earth is the only planet we are certain supports life. This life is found in the *biosphere.*

ecosystem: a self-supporting system of organisms interacting with each other and with their environment.

Interaction between organisms in the ecosystem includes:

* *competition* – for food, mates, territory, nesting sites (animals); for light, carbon dioxide, water, nutrients in the soil (plants)
* feeding relationships – plants, herbivores, carnivores, detritivores and decomposers all pass the same recycled nutrients through *food webs.*

Interaction between the organisms and their environment includes:

* using materials from the environment – carbon dioxide from the air (plants), oxygen from the air (all organisms), water from the soil/waterways
* plants absorbing the sun's energy
* seeds being carried by the wind
* using materials/structures in the environment for nests/homes.

Ecosystems vary enormously in size, from a small garden pond to a tropical rain forest. Both of these are self-supporting ecosystems.

---

ectoparasite: a *parasite* which lives on the surface of its host. A flea is an ectoparasite found on humans and other mammals. Dodder is a plant which is an ectoparasite of nettles.

---

effector: a structure which carries out a *response* to a *stimulus*.

All biological behaviour is triggered by a stimulus and carried out by an effector. Some examples are shown in the table.

Example of behaviour	Stimulus	Response	Effector
reducing amount of light entering eye	bright light shone into eye	pupil is reduced in size to limit light entering	muscles of iris
lowering blood sugar level if too high	blood sugar level rises above threshold	*insulin* is secreted to cause liver to convert glucose to glycogen	insulin-secreting cells in pancreas
growth of plant shoot towards light from window	more light from one side than the other	growth towards brightest light	cells on side of stem away from bright light growing fastest
withdrawing hand from a hot object	hot object touching hand	withdrawing hand	muscles in arm and hand

egestion: the expulsion of *faeces* from the *anus*.

Faeces are formed from the indigestible parts of an animal's diet, dead cells from the gut lining, dead bacteria, mucus, bile and other secretions from the gut.

You must not confuse egestion with *excretion*, which is removing waste products such as carbon dioxide and urea which have been produced by chemical reactions in the body. The faeces have not been produced by the body's reactions: they are just a collection of substances formed as food travels along an animal's gut.

egg: in *vertebrates*, a structure which contains a developing *embryo*.
- Fish eggs have no protective coating.
- Amphibian's eggs are protected by a coating of jelly.
- Reptile's eggs have a leathery shell.
- Bird's eggs have a hard shell.

egg cell: the female sex cell (*gamete*) of animals and plants.
Eggs cells are:
- haploid cells – they only contain half the normal chromosome number (one chromosome from each pair)
- usually bigger than sperm
- usually sessile – they don't move, the sperm move to the eggs
- produced by *meiosis* in the *ovary*.

element: a substance containing only one type of atom.
Each element is represented by a symbol which is often the first letter or letters of its name. Sometimes the first letter(s) of a Latin name are used.
Carbon (C), hydrogen (H), oxygen (O) and nitrogen (N) are the most abundant elements in most organisms.
Calcium (Ca) and magnesium (Mg) are also quite abundant in many animals.

embryo: a young, developing organism formed from the *zygote* by cell division (*mitosis*) and development.
In mammals, when an embryo has developed to the point where we can tell what species it is, we call it a *fetus*. In humans, this is about two months into pregnancy.
Embryos develop in different places, according to the type of organism.
- Mammal embryos develop in the *uterus*.
- Bird embryos develop in hard-shelled eggs.

- Reptile embryos develop in soft-shelled eggs.
- Amphibian embryos develop in unshelled eggs which float in water in groups (like frogspawn).
- Fish embryos develop in unprotected eggs which are laid in great numbers.
- Plant embryos develop in *seeds*.

embryo transplantation: transferring an *embryo* from its natural mother to the *uterus* of a surrogate mother.

There are several situations when embryo transplantation is an advantage.

- Improving the reproductive capacity of a valuable animal. If a farmer wishes to breed from a cow with desirable features, the cow can be injected with reproductive hormones to make it release several ova (egg cells) at the same time. These can be fertilised by artificial insemination and the embryos transferred to other animals.
- Transporting an animal long distances – sheep and goat embryos have been transported long distances in rabbits. When they arrive at their destination, they are transplanted again into an appropriate surrogate mother to complete their development. Transporting the embryos in this way saves a valuable animal from being stressed.
- *Cloning* – an early embryo from a valuable animal can be divided into several genetically identical embryos which can then be transplanted for development.

emphysema: a condition in which the walls of the *alveoli* are damaged, so that several alveoli merge into one larger unit.

Because of the damage to the walls of the alveoli, there is less area for exchanging gases between air and blood. Some people who suffer from mild emphysema can compensate for the less efficient gas exchange by breathing faster than normal. Others may develop raised blood pressure in the *pulmonary artery* and this can lead to heart failure in the right *ventricle*. Emphysema is nearly always caused by smoking or industrial pollution and is often accompanied by *bronchitis*.

emulsify: break down large pieces of fat, or large drops of oil, into small droplets which will mix with water.

Chemicals in the *bile* secreted by the *gall bladder* emulsify fats and oils in our diet. Emulsification has two main effects:

- it allows the small particles of fat/oil to be dispersed in a watery medium
- it increases the surface area of the fat at which lipase enzymes can digest the fat/oil.

endocrine gland: a gland which secretes a *hormone* directly into the blood, rather than through a duct.
Endocrine glands are sometimes called ductless glands.
Examples of endocrine glands include:
- the *adrenal glands*
- the *pituitary gland*
- the *thyroid gland*.

The study of the endocrine glands and the hormones they secrete is called endocrinology.

endocrine system: the system of *endocrine glands* which works closely with the *nervous system* to regulate many processes.
Although invertebrates produce hormones and have some endocrine glands, only vertebrates have a true endocrine system. The diagram shows the human endocrine system, but most vertebrates have similar glands.

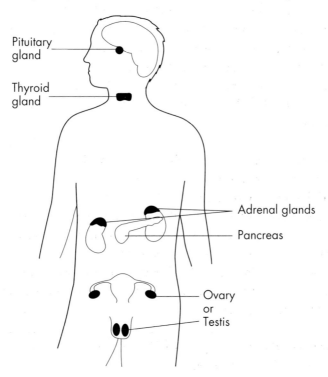

Pituitary gland

Thyroid gland

Adrenal glands

Pancreas

Ovary or Testis

endoparasite: a *parasite* which lives inside another organism.
Tapeworms and *Plasmodium* (the malarial parasite) are examples of endoparasites found in humans.
Some protozoans and thread worms live as parasites in the roots, stems, leaves and flowers of flowering plants.

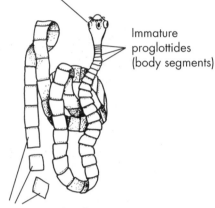

'Head' of tapeworm attaches to lining of small intestine

Immature proglottides (body segments)

Mature proglottides contain thousands of eggs. They break off and pass out with faeces

endothermic reaction: a reaction which takes in energy from its surroundings as it proceeds.

In biological systems, reactions involving synthesis (building large molecules from smaller ones) are endothermic. The energy for the synthesis is supplied by *ATP* molecules formed in *respiration*.

energy: the capability to do work (to make something happen).

Energy can exist in many forms and can be changed from one form to another, but cannot be created or destroyed.

The 'energy currency' of living things is molecules of *ATP*. Some of the energy stored in ATP can be released to make things happen, for example:

- transmit a nerve impulse
- assemble a molecule of starch from glucose molecules
- make a muscle contract
- absorb mineral ions from the soil into a root hair cell against a concentration gradient (*active transport*).

energy flow diagram: a diagram showing the flow of energy through the various levels of a *food chain* or *food web*.

Energy is lost at each link in the food chain. This is because:

- only energy which is used for growth can be passed on to the next link in the chain
- not all the energy in new growth produced will be passed on: some parts will not be eaten and some is indigestible

● energy used for movement, excretion and other processes will be lost to the environment as heat.

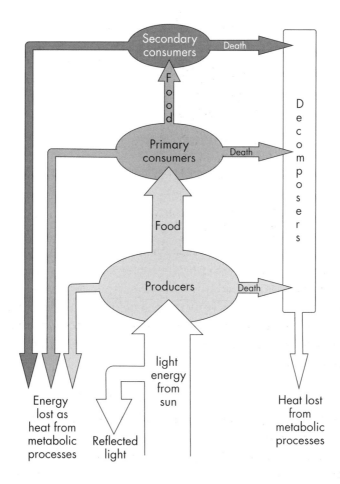

The loss of energy at each link is the reason why food chains rarely have more than four links: there just isn't enough energy for a fifth.

If you think about this idea of loss of energy along food chains, you will see that the earth would be able to feed more people if we all ate just plants, rather than animals which have eaten plants. This is not entirely possible, but if more people ate more plants and less animals, there would be more food to go round.

environment: the sum of the *abiotic* components of an ecosystem.

For example, for a pond ecosystem, the environment would include:

● the water
● the gases and nutrients dissolved in the water
● the soil at the sides and on the bottom of the pond

- the light from the sun
- the temperature of the water
- the pH of the water.

The term environment is also used loosely to mean our surroundings, including other organisms as well as the abiotic factors.

enzymes: proteins which speed up chemical reactions in living things: they are biological *catalysts*.

We often think of enzymes purely as chemicals which bring about *digestion*, and some enzymes do this – but they are only a tiny fraction of all the enzymes living things produce.

Most enzymes:

- operate inside cells rather than in the gut cavity as digestive enzymes do
- operate best at near a neutral pH, although some are specially adapted to work in more extreme pHs
- operate best at moderate temperatures (37°C for human enzymes) although some are adapted to work in cooler and warmer conditions
- are very specific – they will only catalyse one particular reaction.

Enzymes catalyse reactions by lowering the *activation energy* of the reaction. They can do this because a specially shaped *active site* brings the reactants closer together than they would normally be and this allows them to react. Enzymes are crucial to maintain life: without them the chemical reactions necessary to support life would proceed far too slowly.

enzymes, commercial applications: the use of enzymes in industry to catalyse a range of reactions at low temperatures and pressures.

Because enzymes are catalysts, they can make some reactions take place quickly at moderate temperatures. Without the enzymes, the reactions might need higher temperatures and pressures which would involve extra costs. *Immobilised enzymes* are often used in industry because they are more stable. The reaction conditions are carefully controlled as enzymes are affected by pH and temperature.

Many of the enzymes are produced from *microorganisms* in *bioreactors*. The table on page 99 shows some of the ways in which enzymes are used commercially.

enzymes, immobilised: *enzymes* which are not free-moving in a solution but fixed in some way.

Enzymes used in industrial processes are often immobilised – trapped either inside fibres or on the surface of tiny beads. The fibres/beads are then packed in a container and the substances which will react together are passed over them in a continuous stream. The product then flows out of the reaction vessel, and the enzymes remain in place to catalyse further reactions. There are several advantages in using immobilised enzymes.

- The enzymes do not contaminate the product of the reaction.
- The enzymes can be used over and over again.
- The enzymes are usually more stable than normal, and may withstand higher temperatures without being denatured.
- The running costs of the reactor are low because there is a continuous flow through it: periodic refilling is not necessary.

enzymes, commercial applications

Industry	Use	Enzyme	Source of enzyme
dairy industry	cheese manufacture	rennin	fungi
	manufacture of lactose-free milk	lactase	yeast
brewing industry	breaking down starch to sugar in the malt	amylase	bacteria
	breaking down yeast cells and reducing cloudiness of beer	protease	bacteria
	reducing cloudiness of wine	pectinase	bacteria
biological washing powder manufacture	removing protein-based stains, such as egg yolk, blood	protease	bacteria
	in dishwasher detergent for removing starch residues	amylase	bacteria
	removing grease/fatty stains	lipase	fungi
food industry	extracting fruit juices from fruits, olive oil from olives	pectinase	bacteria
	lowering protein content of flour for making biscuits, pre-digesting protein in baby foods	protease	bacteria
	producing glucose syrup as a sweetener from waste potato starch	amylase	bacteria
	producing fructose syrup, as a sweetener, from glucose	invertase	bacteria
medical uses	producing oxygen-rich dressings to reduce the chance of gangrene	catalase	fungi
	removing amino acids needed for tumour growth	asparginase	bacteria
	dissolving blood clots	trypsin	bacteria
textile industry	removing starch from fibres to make them smoother	amylase	bacteria and fungi

epidermis: a protective layer of cells around the outside of an organism.
- In plants and *invertebrates*, the epidermis is usually only one cell thick and is often covered by a *cuticle*.
- In *vertebrates* the epidermis is the outer layer of *skin* and is several cells thick. The outermost cells are dead and hardened and there is no cuticle.

ethanoic acid: the acid found in vinegar, used to be called acetic acid; chemical formula CH_3COOH.
Ethanoic acid is:
- a weak acid
- formed when bacteria oxidise ethanol (alcohol)
- used in some antiseptic jellies.

ethanol: the alcohol found in alcoholic drinks; chemical formula C_2H_5OH.
Ethanol is produced by the *fermentation* of glucose by yeast. This is a kind of *anaerobic respiration* and is summarised by the equation:

$$glucose \longrightarrow ethanol + carbon\ dioxide + 2ATP$$
$$C_6H_{12}O_6 \longrightarrow 2C_2H_5OH + 2CO_2 + 2ATP$$

Ethanol is a depressant *drug* and so slows down the working of the nervous system.
(See *alcohol abuse* for details of effects on our bodies.)

eutrophication: enriching a body of water (river, pond, lake) with nutrients.
Eutrophication is a naturally occurring process.
- A young lake or other body of water is often quite nutrient poor and cannot sustain much life.
- As time passes, more and more plants and animals live in the lake.
- The organisms die and are decomposed.
- Nutrients are released into the water.
- The level of nutrients in the water increases.
In this natural process, a balance is maintained between the decay and release of nutrients, growth of plants and the numbers of animals.
Eutrophication can be a problem when the time-scale of the nutrient enrichment is too short. This is very often the case when human activities are the cause of eutrophication.
When organic material enters a lake or pond, bacteria decompose it and release mineral nutrients into the water. *Fertilisers* sprayed on fields can leach into lakes and ponds and can also raise the level of nutrients in the water.

When the level of nutrients rises rapidly the following sequence of events occurs:

- *Algae* reproduce rapidly and either form a mat over the surface or unicellular algae form a 'pea soup' – an algal bloom.
- This cuts off the light from plants growing beneath the surface.
- These plants die and the oxygen released by the algae into the pond does not make up for the oxygen which would have been produced by the submerged plants.
- Many of the algae die as the nutrients get used up.
- *Bacteria* feed on the dead plants and algae and reproduce rapidly.
- They respire and use the oxygen in the water.
- Many animals die due to lack of oxygen.

The problem is not quite so acute when the nutrient level rises in a river because the water is moving and the nutrients are diluted.

---

evaporation: a change of state from liquid to gas (vapour) which occurs only at the surface of the liquid.

When particles evaporate, they take energy from their immediate surroundings which therefore become cooler. Evaporation of sweat draws heat from the *skin* which cools down, in turn, cooling the *blood*.

---

evolution: the process by which, over many generations, existing *species* give rise to new species.

Fossils provide evidence of evolution in a number of ways.

- A series of fossils of different ages can show gradual changes in form. The evolution of the modern horse from a much smaller animal is supported by a fossil series.
- Comparing modern forms with fossils can allow biologists to deduce possible paths of evolution and time-scales.

Other evidence for evolution includes:

- similarity in form of closely related species
- similarity in development of closely related species
- similarity in *DNA* of closely related species.

The mechanism of evolution is *natural selection*, identified by *Charles Darwin*.

---

excretion: removing waste products which have been made by chemical reactions in the cells of an organism.

Examples of excretion in humans include:

- breathing out carbon dioxide, produced in *aerobic respiration*
- removing urea, produced in the *liver* by deamination of surplus amino acids, in the urine.

You must be quite clear that egesting faeces from the anus is not excretion. The faeces are not waste products made by the body, but a mixture of dead cells, dietary fibre, dead bacteria and digestive fluids such as bile.

exercise: a physical activity which provides recreation, improves health or corrects an injury.

Exercise is broadly of two types.

- Dynamic (or aerobic) exercise – in this type of exercise large muscle groups perform regular, rhythmical movements and bring about a considerable increase in heart rate. Jogging, running, cycling and swimming are all examples of dynamic exercises.
- Static – in this type of exercise, individual muscle groups perform specific tasks for a short period of time. There is no real increase in heart rate. Weight lifting is an example of a static exercise.

Regular dynamic (aerobic) exercise has been shown to reduce the risk of a heart attack as well as making bone-loss less of a problem as people age. Static exercises do not reduce the risk of a heart attack, but can increase muscle strength. This is useful in treating muscles which have been damaged and in preventing muscle wasting with ageing. Some static exercises can improve flexibility.

exocrine gland: a *gland* which secretes a substance through a duct.
Examples of exocrine glands include:

- the *pancreas* secreting pancreatic juice into the duodenum through the pancreatic duct
- *sweat glands* secreting sweat onto the surface of the skin through sweat ducts
- *salivary glands* secreting saliva into the mouth through salivary ducts.

exoskeleton: a skeleton which is found outside the body.
Exoskeletons are made from non-living materials and so cannot grow. Two main groups of animals have exoskeletons.

- The *arthropods* have an exoskeleton which both protects and aids movement. Although it covers the whole of the body, it is thin and flexible at joints – where movement is needed. The exoskeleton must be shed periodically (moulting) to allow growth. As the arthropod emerges from its old exoskeleton, the new one is still soft and the animal is vulnerable to predators.
- Nearly all *molluscs* have a shell which protects but does not aid movement. The shell is big enough to allow growth.

exothermic reaction: a reaction which gives out energy to the surroundings as it proceeds.

The reactions involved in *respiration* are exothermic reactions. Some of the energy from the reactions escapes as heat but some is used to form molecules of *ATP*.

---

extinction: the loss of a *species* from the earth; a species is extinct only when the last individual has died.

Extinction is an important aspect of *evolution*. If the environment changes and organisms cannot adapt, they die out. Some biologists believe that for every species now existing, 2000 species have become extinct. In the short term, when a species dies out the earth loses some of its wildlife, but the long-term effect may be to gain new species.

Suppose a species which had been dominating an area suddenly became extinct. The following events may occur.

• When the dominant species dies out, the 'niche' it had been filling becomes 'vacant'.

• Other species may adapt, over time, so that some of their members fill the vacant niche.

• These new variants of existing species may, through *natural selection*, become new species.

If a whole dominant group becomes extinct, then there are even more chances for others to adapt and take their place. When the dinosaurs became extinct, 65 million years ago, it became possible for the primitive mammals and birds of the time to adapt and fill a whole range of niches left by the *dinosaurs*.

---

eye: a sense organ which detects light.

Many animal groups have eyes. The eyes of an octopus, for example, work in a very similar way to human eyes.

Humans have two eyes facing forwards; this gives us binocular vision and allows us to judge the distance of close objects very accurately, enabling us to carry out skilled movements.

Carnivores also have eyes facing forwards so that they can judge distance. When they get close to their prey, they must strike their prey first time or it will escape, so they must be able to judge their strike accurately.

Herbivores often have eyes on the sides of their heads. This gives them a wide field of view so that they can detect approaching predators.

The diagram on page 105 shows the structure of a human eye, and the table on page 104 shows the functions of the main parts of the human eye.

To see an object clearly, rays of light from the object must be focused onto the retina. To change the focus from a near to a more distant object the ciliary muscles alter the shape of the lens. This is called *accommodation*.

- To focus on near objects, the ciliary muscles contract, the suspensory ligaments slacken and the lens bulges to become more powerful.
- To focus on distant objects, the ciliary muscles relax, the suspensory ligaments are pulled tight and the lens is pulled thinner to become less powerful.

Part of eye	Description	Function
conjunctiva	a very thin transparent membrane covering the cornea and lining the eyelids	lubricates the cornea and eyelids
cornea	the transparent front part of the wall of the eye	allows light to enter and begins focusing (accommodation)
sclera	the tough white outer coat of the wall of the eye	protects the eye
choroid	the middle layer of the wall of the eye containing black pigment and blood vessels	supplies nutrients and oxygen to the retina and prevents reflection of light rays within the eye
retina	inner layer of wall of eye containing *rods* and *cones*	rods allow vision in dim light; cones allow detailed and colour vision in bright light
iris	the coloured disc at the front of the eye	contains muscles which control the size of the pupil
pupil	aperture or 'hole' at the centre of the iris	allows light to enter the eye
ciliary muscles	circular muscles around the rim of the choroid	control tension in suspensory ligaments and therefore the shape of the lens
suspensory ligaments	ligaments which attach the lens to the ciliary muscles	tension in ligaments determine shape of lens
lens	a crystalline structure held at the centre of the pupil	focuses rays of light onto the retina to form an image
optic nerve	the nerve at the back of the eye, made of many nerve cells	carries nerve impulses from the eye to the brain
blind spot	the region of the retina where there are no sense cells and so it cannot detect light	no function
fovea/ yellow spot	the region of the retina with the greatest concentration of cones	allows us to see objects in the greatest detail

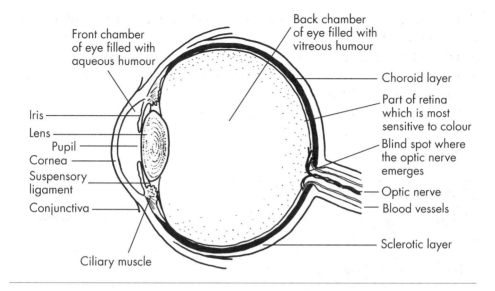

Front chamber
of eye filled with
aqueous humour

Back chamber
of eye filled with
vitreous humour

Iris

Lens

Pupil

Cornea

Suspensory
ligament

Conjunctiva

Ciliary muscle

Choroid layer

Part of retina
which is most
sensitive to colour

Blind spot where
the optic nerve
emerges

Optic nerve

Blood vessels

Sclerotic layer

F

F1 generation (1st filial generation): the offspring from a genetic breeding experiment of two *homozygous* parents.

For example, if a homozygous tall and homozygous dwarf pea plant were cross-bred and the seeds collected, the plants which grew from these seeds would be the F1 generation.

F2 generation (2nd filial generation): the offspring of the F1 generation in a genetic breeding experiment.

For example, if the offspring from the homozygous tall and dwarf cross described in the F1 entry above were allowed to interbreed and the seeds were collected, the plants which grew from these seeds would be the F2 generation.

faeces: solid waste material from the *digestive system* which is egested through the anus.

Faeces are composed of:
- indigestible components of food – largely *dietary fibre*
- dead *bacteria*
- dead cells from the lining of the intestines
- secretions from the digestive system (e.g. bile, mucus)
- water.

Faeces are formed as food which has not been absorbed in the small intestine enters the colon (large intestine). Water is reabsorbed along the length of the colon and the faeces become more and more solid. They are stored temporarily in the rectum before being egested through the anus.

Fallopian tubes: the tubes which extend from each side of the *uterus* to the *ovaries*.

The Fallopian tubes:
- carry the egg cells from the ovaries to the uterus
- are where *fertilisation* normally occurs.

farmer's lung: inflammation of the *alveoli* caused by inhaling spores of *fungi* which grow in hay and straw.

The walls of the alveoli become thickened and this has several effects, including:

- making breathing more difficult
- making gas exchange less efficient.

The inflammation usually occurs about six hours after exposure to the spores. Symptoms include:

- shortness of breath
- fever
- headache and muscle aches.

The symptoms may last for about 24 hours for a single attack.

Treatment uses anti-inflammatory drugs and complete recovery is possible. If the person is constantly exposed to the spores, then more permanent and serious lung damage can occur.

fat: a substance made from *fatty acids* and glycerol which is a solid at room temperature.

Fats and oils belong to a larger group called *lipids*.

Some fats are called *saturated fats* (hard fats like butter) and some are called unsaturated fats (soft fats like margarine). The difference is due to the fatty acids they contain.

Fats are necessary in our diet because:

- they are an essential component of all cell membranes
- we need to form a layer of fatty, insulating tissue under our skin to help prevent heat loss
- they contain fat-soluble vitamins such as vitamin A and vitamin D
- they are a secondary source of energy for respiration – during vigorous dynamic exercise we often respire fats; they give twice as much energy per gram as carbohydrates.

Too much saturated fat in our diet is dangerous because:

- it causes obesity which puts an extra strain on the heart
- it can be deposited in the lining of arteries causing atherosclerosis; this is especially dangerous in the coronary arteries where it is a major cause of heart attacks.

When we eat fats:

- they are emulsified by bile secreted from the gall bladder
- they are digested by lipase from the pancreas
- they are carried in the blood plasma as tiny particles attached to proteins.

fatigue: a state of exhaustion resulting from strenuous physical activity. When fatigued, *muscle* fibres are unable to contract, even when stimulated by nerve cells.

The most common reason for fatigue is lack of *ATP* in the muscle which may be due to:

- lack of oxygen in the muscle
- lack of glucose/glycogen in the muscle.

A build up of lactic acid in the muscle also contributes to fatigue.

Different types of muscle are more or less likely to suffer fatigue.

- Skeletal muscle fibres contract quickly and strongly and can become fatigued.
- Cardiac muscle fibres contract more slowly and rhythmically and do not suffer fatigue.

fatty acids: organic acids which combine with glycerol to form *lipids* (fats and oils).

There are three types of fatty acids: saturated, mono-unsaturated and poly-unsaturated fatty acids.

The diagrams show the differences between the types.

A saturated fatty acid

A monounsaturated fatty acid

A polyunsaturated fatty acid

- Lipids with a high proportion of saturated fatty acids are usually hard at room temperature. Most animal fats contain mainly saturated fatty acids.
- Fats in vegetables contain more mono-unsaturated and poly-unsaturated fatty acids.
- Vegetable oils and fish oils are high in poly-unsaturated fatty acids.

Saturated fatty acids raise blood *cholesterol* levels and increase the risk of coronary heart disease.

Polyunsaturated fatty acids actually lower blood cholesterol levels and so reduce the risk of coronary heart disease.

feather: a structure made from keratin possessed only by birds; feathers have several hundred branched filaments either side of a central shaft. Because of their construction feathers are:

Shaft

Branched filaments (barbs)

- excellent insulators – this helps birds to maintain a high, constant body temperature
- excellent aerofoils – the aerofoil shape helps to give lift when the bird is flying
- extremely light – this reduces the energy a bird must use to stay in the air.

Although all feathers have the same basic structure, feathers in different parts of a bird's body have different functions.

- The feathers on the body are for insulation only.
- The feathers towards the outside of the wings (primaries) give forward motion and some lift when flying.
- The feathers on the wings near the body provide lift only when flying.

feedback: a control mechanism in which a change in the amount of a product affects the rate of its production.

In *negative feedback* an increase in the product decreases the rate of production and so brings the level down again. A decrease in the product increases the rate of production and so the level rises. Many biological control systems are based on negative feedback.

In positive feedback, an increase in the product increases the rate of its production and a decrease decreases the rate of production.

fermentation: a type of *anaerobic respiration* which produces either ethanol (alcohol) or lactic acid from sugars and releases only a small amount of energy in the form of *ATP*.

glucose $\longrightarrow$ ethanol + carbon dioxide + little energy released

$C_6H_{12}O_6 \longrightarrow 2C_2H_5OH + 2CO_2 + 2ATP$

glucose $\longrightarrow$ lactic acid + little energy released

$C_6H_{12}O_6 \longrightarrow 2C_3H_6O_3 + 2ATP$

All plants, some fungi and some bacteria produce alcohol when they respire anaerobically, but fermentation by yeast is the best known as it is used to make beer and wine.

All animals, some fungi and some bacteria produce lactic acid when they respire anaerobically.

Some types of bacteria which produce lactic acid are used to make yoghurt and cheese.

(See *anaerobic respiration*, *brewing* and *winemaking* for details.)

---

fermenter: any reactor in which cells or enzymes are cultured in large numbers to make a useful product.

(See *bioreactor* for details.)

---

ferns: an ancient group of plants which have woody tissues, reproduce by spores, have stems which grow horizontally underground and young leaves which look like a 'fiddlehead'.

Bracken is a common fern in the United Kingdom and can be a troublesome weed in some agricultural areas. Bracken is troublesome because:

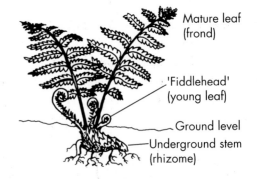

- it is poisonous in large amounts
- cattle cannot digest the woody tissue in bracken
- it is difficult to get rid of because of the underground stems
- it spreads quickly, taking over valuable grazing land.

The ancestors of modern ferns were much larger plants and grew in huge swamps millions of years ago. When they died, many fell into the water and, in the anaerobic conditions, did not decay fully but were compressed into coal. Imprints of the leaves of these ancient 'ferns' are common *fossils* in coal.

---

fertilisation: the fusion of male and female *gametes* (sex cells) to form a *zygote*.

- In flowering plants, the male gametes are contained in the pollen grains. The female gametes are the egg cells.
- In animals, the male gametes are the sperm and female gametes are the egg cells.

Many animals depend on external fertilisation. In this process:

- the egg cells and sperm are released into water: fertilisation (and development) takes place outside the animal's body
- water currents and predators make it unlikely that any one egg will be fertilised or survive to adulthood if it is fertilised
- to compensate, large numbers (sometimes millions) of egg cells are released.

Birds and mammals have evolved internal fertilisation. In this process:

- mating and copulation take place and fertilisation takes place inside the body
- because it is more likely that fertilisation will occur, only small numbers of eggs are released at a time.

Fertilisation is important in the life cycle of an animal or plant as:

- it starts the new generation
- with *meiosis* and *mitosis*, it keeps the number of chromosomes per cell constant from one generation to the next
- it mixes the genetic information from two individuals and so produces *variation*.

fertiliser: a substance used to make plants grow faster and better.
Fertilisers are used in agriculture to help farmers get a good yield from their crops. Many fertilisers contain the elements nitrogen (as nitrate), phosphorus (as phosphate) and potassium, and so are called NPK fertilisers. All three elements are important for growth of the plants and without them growth is poor.

Mineral element in fertiliser	Main use(s) in plant	Effect of deficiency	Reason for effect
nitrogen (as nitrate)	making proteins, DNA	stunted growth	not enough proteins made
	making *chlorophyll*	yellowing of leaves	not enough chlorophyll made
phosphorus (as phosphate)	making *ATP*	poor growth, especially of roots, due to poor uptake of other minerals	uptake of minerals from soil is by *active transport* which needs ATP
potassium	helps to activate many enzymes	poor growth of leaves and flowers	*photosynthesis* and *respiration* are inefficient

Overuse of fertilisers containing nitrates has caused *eutrophication* of waterways.

fertility: the ability to produce offspring: an organism which is unable to produce offspring is infertile.

In humans, there are two aspects to the ability to produce offspring: male fertility and female fertility.

Male fertility depends on:
- being able to produce enough *sperm* in the testes
- being able to ejaculate the sperm during intercourse.

Female fertility depends on:
- being able to ovulate (release an *ovum* or egg cell from the ovary)
- the egg being able to travel to the uterus
- any embryo resulting from *fertilisation* being able to implant in the uterus lining.

Female fertility is controlled by four hormones: *FSH* and *LH* from the pituitary gland and *oestrogen* and *progesterone* produced by the ovaries.

Women become fertile at puberty and remain fertile until the menopause, when they stop ovulating. This usually occurs at age 40–50.

---

fertility drug: a drug which increases fertility (the ability to produce offspring).

Most fertility drugs are either hormone based or use substances very similar to natural hormones.

Hormones released by the *pituitary gland* (FSH and LH) stimulate the formation of both sperm and eggs. Infertility drugs are of two main types:
- those which contain a substance that causes an increase in the release of the pituitary hormones – this causes an increase in production of sperm or eggs
- those which contain the pituitary hormones (or very similar substances) – these directly increase the production of sperm or eggs.

Sometimes, to produce maximum effect, both types are used together.

---

fetus: an *embryo* which has developed to the point where it is possible to recognise what *species* it is.

In humans, it is possible to recognise an embryo as human by the end of the second month of pregnancy.

---

fibrin: a fibrous protein which helps the blood to clot.

Fibrin is formed from fibrinogen in the blood plasma when we cut ourselves. (See *blood, clotting* for details.)

---

fibrinogen: the inactive form of the protein *fibrin* found in the blood plasma.

filter feeder: an organism which feeds by 'sieving' water through some structure which filters out small organisms.

The largest animal which has ever lived, the blue whale, feeds on some of the smallest organisms, the *plankton*, by filter feeding.

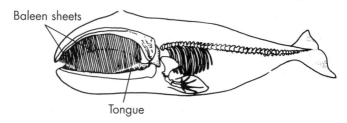

To obtain their food, blue whales:
- open their mouths and take in water
- force the water back out of their mouths through the sheets of baleen (whalebone) hanging from their upper jaw
- the organisms of the plankton are trapped on the baleen sheets and then washed into the stomach with more water.

Other filter feeders include sponges, mussels, daphnia, fan worms and many animals found in coral reefs.

filtration: a process which separates suspended solids from a liquid by using a membrane of some sort which will allow the liquid, but not the solid, to pass through.

The liquid which passes through is called the filtrate; the solid left behind is called the residue.

A mixture of sand and water can be separated by using a filter funnel and filter paper.

Filtration is the basis of:
- removing small molecules from the blood plasma in the *kidney*
- purification of water at a water treatment plant
- feeding in animals like the blue whale and fan worms.

fin: a structure on a fish used for propulsion, maintaining stability or for changing direction when swimming.

The median fins (dorsal and ventral fins) control:
- rolling – they help stop the fish from tilting over too much when swimming
- yawing – they reduce excessive side-to-side movements.

The paired fins (pectoral and pelvic fins):
- are hydrofoils – the angle at which they meet the water can be altered
- control the pitch of the fish when swimming – they control whether it moves up or down in the water

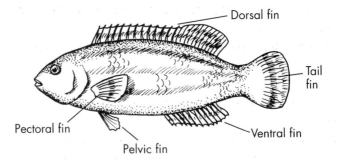

- help the fish to stop – they can be turned to give maximum resistance to the water.

The tail fin provides a large surface area in contact with the water for propulsion.

fish: vertebrate animals which live in water, breathe by gills, have scales, fins and reproduce by means of external *fertilisation*.

- Fish are the most primitive vertebrates – biologists think that all other vertebrate types have evolved directly or indirectly from fish.
- Most fish have a bony skeleton, but some, such as dogfish, sharks and rays, have a skeleton made from cartilage.
- Fish vary in size from the tiny clingfish (3 cm) to the massive whale shark (20 m).
- Fish are an excellent source of first class protein.
- The oils found in fish such as salmon and tuna are rich in poly-unsaturated *fatty acids*. The Inuit (Eskimos) had one of the lowest rates of heart disease in the world, largely because their diet contained a lot of oily fish.

fission: splitting into two or more parts.
- *Binary fission* is a kind of asexual reproduction where an organism splits into two parts.

- Multiple fission is a kind of asexual reproduction where an organism splits into many parts.

This sort of asexual reproduction is normally only carried out by unicellular organisms.

fitness, evolution: a description of how well adapted an organism is to its surroundings.

In his theory of *natural selection*, Charles Darwin suggested a process he called the 'survival of the fittest'. By this he meant that those most suited to their surroundings would survive to reproduce, whilst those less well adapted would die out.

fitness, physical: the ability of all the parts of the body to work together efficiently and to do the most work with the least amount of effort.

Physical fitness can have a number of benefits including:

- improved cardiovascular and respiratory fitness – the heart, lungs and circulation are all improved, reducing the risk of heart attacks and strokes
- improved strength – reducing the strain on muscles to carry out a task
- improved endurance – tasks can be undertaken for longer periods without *fatigue*
- improved flexibility – joints are more moveable and less likely to become arthritic
- changed body composition – reduced fat and increased muscle and bone density
- improved reaction times, coordination and balance.

Most of the above benefits come from dynamic *exercise*, although static exercise can be important in improving or maintaining strength and flexibility.

flaccid: a condition in which a plant cell has lost enough water to make the cytoplasm shrink away from the cell wall (see *plasmolysis*).

If a cylinder of potato tissue is placed in a strong salt solution:

- the cells lose water to the solution by *osmosis*
- the cytoplasm of the cells shrinks away from the cell wall
- there is now little outwards force on the cell walls from the cytoplasm – the cells are flaccid.

The cells in the potato cylinder no longer press against each other: it has little support and is very flexible.

Young plant stems with only a little woody tissue need to be kept watered so that their cells do not become flaccid. If they do become flaccid, the stems will wilt (droop).

flagellum (plural flagella): a long whip-like moveable structure found on some unicellular organisms and used in locomotion.

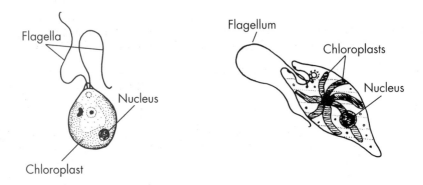

Flagella contain actin – one of the proteins found in muscle fibres.

Fleming, Alexander: a British microbiologist who discovered *penicillin*.
In 1928, Fleming was working in St Mary's Hospital in London. He noticed that a petri dish in which he had been culturing some bacteria was contaminated by a mould. When he looked closely, he could see that no bacteria were growing near to the mould, but they were growing everywhere else.
He drew two conclusions:
● the mould was secreting a substance into the agar in the petri dish
● the substance could inhibit the growth of bacteria.
Because the mould was called *Penicillium*, he called the substance penicillin.
Fleming never isolated penicillin in a pure form, although he did show that it was not harmful to mice.

Florey, Howard: a microbiologist who worked with *Ernst Chain*, following up Fleming's work on *penicillin*.
Florey and Chain isolated and purified penicillin and performed further experiments which confirmed Fleming's original conclusions. They also began to develop techniques to produce larger volumes of penicillin.

flower: a specialised shoot of a plant which contains the reproductive organs. Most flowers contain both male and female reproductive structures, although a few contain only male or female structures.
There are two main stages in reproduction in plants.
● *Pollination* – the transfer of pollen from the anther to the stigma (in either the same or a different plant). This can be done by either wind or insects. Flowers are usually adapted to either one or the other method of pollination.

- *Fertilisation* – the pollen grain nucleus fuses with the egg cell nucleus.

The zygote formed develops into an embryo which is enclosed in a *seed*.
The table describes the functions of the parts of a flower.

Structure	Description and function in insect-pollinated flower	Description and function in wind-pollinated flower
petals	large, showy, brightly coloured and scented to attract insects	very small to expose anthers and stigmas to wind
sepals	protect the flower when in bud	protect the flower when in bud
stamens and (anther filament)	enclosed within the petals so that a visiting insect must touch them and collect the pollen grains they produce	exposed so that the wind can blow away the pollen they produce
carpels (ovary, stigma and style)	enclosed within the petals so that a visiting insect must touch the stigma and leave pollen on it; the stigma is often sticky; after fertilisation of the egg cells, ovules develop into seeds	exposed to catch pollen blown by the wind; the stigma is often feathery to give an increased surface area for catching pollen; after fertilisation of the egg cells, ovules develop into seeds
nectaries	a reward: the 'what's in it for me?' factor for the insect; insects are attracted by the scent/colour and receive the reward of nectar and so visit other flowers of the same type.	

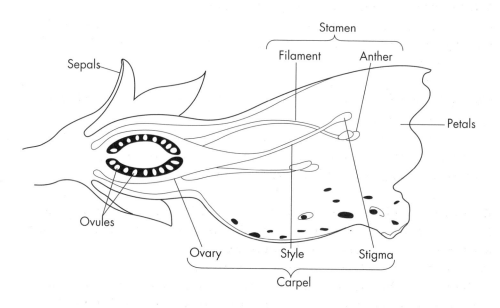

follicle: a group of cells in an *ovary* which contains an egg cell.
A woman has all the follicles she will ever have at the time she is born.
After *puberty*, one follicle matures each month and releases the egg cell at *ovulation*.
The remains of the follicle after ovulation is called the *corpus luteum* and it maintains the uterus lining for the first three months of pregnancy.

follicle stimulating hormone: see *FSH*.

fluid feeder: an organism which feeds only or mainly on fluids.
Most fluid feeders are insects which possess specialised mouthparts to allow them to suck liquids from a variety of sources.
Insects are not the only fluid feeders: the 300 species of humming birds which live mainly in South America have long slender beaks and can hover so that they can suck nectar from flowers.

Mouth parts of a bee

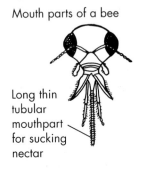

Long thin
tubular
mouthpart
for sucking
nectar

food: substances which are ingested either to supply energy or to be used in body structures or functions.
Producers can make their own food. The various foods eaten by *consumers* make up their diet.
(See *balanced diet* for details.)

food chain: a flow diagram which shows how food is passed through a series of organisms living in the same environment.
The following are examples of food chains.

A LAND BASED FOOD CHAIN:

   rose plant $\longrightarrow$ aphid $\longrightarrow$ ladybird $\longrightarrow$ bluetit

A FOOD CHAIN FROM A RIVER:

   photosynthetic $\longrightarrow$ small $\longrightarrow$ stickleback $\longrightarrow$ pike
   plankton   crustaceans   (small fish)   (large fish)

Notice that both food chains begin with organisms which can photosynthesise. This is true of all food chains. These are the only organisms which can produce their own food and are called *producers*. All other organisms must eat or consume organic materials (food) and are called *consumers*.

A general formula for a food chain is:

producer (photosynthetic organism) $\longrightarrow$ primary consumer (herbivore) $\longrightarrow$ secondary consumer (carnivore) $\longrightarrow$ tertiary consumer (top carnivore)

Few food chains contain more than four organisms; this is because energy is lost along the food chain. (See *energy flow diagram* for details.)

Food chains rarely exist on their own in nature: they are interlinked with others to form *food webs*.

food poisoning: a term used to describe any sudden illness caused by eating contaminated food or organisms not suitable for consumption.

Symptoms of food poisoning often include:

- sickness and diarrhoea
- stomach pains
- shock and collapse (in severe cases).

Food can be contaminated by a range of bacteria and also, sometimes, by viruses.

The table describes some important types of food poisoning.

Type of food poisoning	Caused by	How spread	Treatment/Prevention
salmonellosis	*Salmonella* (a bacterium)	infected chickens, eggs, raw milk, meat and pork (especially where intensive production is used – bacteria can be transmitted via faeces)	rest with enough fluids to rehydrate good hygiene in the food industry and at home; thorough cooking of food
listeriosis	*Listeria* (a bacterium)	soft cheese made from unpasteurised milk, ready prepared coleslaw and salads, cook-chill foods	antibiotics avoid unpasteurised milk products
non-specific	toxins from *Staphylococcus* (a bacterium)	infected skin of a handler in the food industry	rest with enough fluids improved hygiene in the food industry
botulism	toxins from *Clostridium* (a bacterium)	improperly canned foods	antibiotics reduce death risk to 25% check for evidence of gas production in canned food

Food poisoning can also be caused by eating certain types of fungi and shell-fish contaminated with viruses.

food preservation: any technique or process which reduces contamination of food and therefore reduces transmission of organisms causing *food poisoning*. The table describes some of the more common food preservation techniques.

Technique	Description	How it works	Drawbacks
pasteurisation	food is heated to 63°C for 20 minutes or to 72°C for 15 seconds	kills harmful bacteria but not those which give flavour	none
UHT (ultra-heat treatment)	food is heated to 140°C for 1–2 seconds	kills all bacteria	may alter flavour
canning	food is sealed in cans and heated to 100°C	kills all bacteria and prevents re-infection	destroys some vitamins
pickling	food is stored in an acid solution – usually vinegar containing ethanoic acid	the pH is too low for the enzymes in the bacteria to work effectively	alters the flavour of foods
dehydration	water is quickly removed	enzymes cannot operate without water	alters flavour of food
quick freezing	food is cooled quickly to –10°C to avoid large ice crystals forming in food	bacteria are not killed but stop reproducing	none
food irradiation	food is irradiated with ionising radiation	can kill all bacteria	destroys vitamins and may alter texture and flavour of food
salting (curing)	food (often bacon and ham) is covered in salt	salt draws water out of food by osmosis; bacteria cannot multiply and enzymes cannot work in the high salt concentrations	alters flavour of food

food tests: chemical tests performed to determine whether a certain nutrient is present or absent in a food sample.

The food tests you must know are shown in the table on the next page.

The food must be made liquid or made into a solution before the test is carried out.

Food test	Nutrient tested for	How performed	Result if present
Benedict's test	reducing sugar	heat sample with Benedict's solution for 5 minutes	brick red colouration forms
iodine test	starch	add iodine solution to sample in a spotting tile	blue-black colouration develops
emulsion test	lipids (fats and oils)	shake sample with alcohol, pour mixture into a test tube of water	cloudy/white emulsion develops
Biuret test	protein	mix sample with potassium hydroxide and dilute copper sulphate, (or mix with Biuret solution)	purple/mauve colouration develops
DCPIP test	vitamin C (ascorbic acid)	dissolve sample and mix with DCPIP	purple DCPIP is decolourised

food web: a diagram showing the feeding relationships between the organisms in an *ecosystem*.

A food web is usually made up of several inter-related *food chains*.

The diagram shows a simplified food web of a freshwater ecosystem.

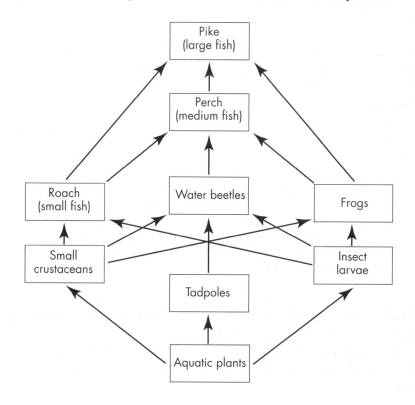

Because all the food chains in the web are inter-related, a change in the number of one organism may affect the number of another. Look at the food web shown on page 121.

What would happen if the number of tadpoles emerging from frogspawn was greatly reduced one year?

Possible effects include:

- fewer water beetles – as these depend in part on the tadpoles for food
- fewer small crustaceans and insect larvae – the water beetles may eat more of these to compensate for the lack of tadpoles
- more small crustaceans and insect larvae – there are fewer tadpoles so there are more aquatic plants to eat
- fewer frogs – there are fewer tadpoles and possibly fewer insect larvae (food for the frogs)
- fewer pike – fewer frogs means less food for the pike.

fossil: a record of life in the past.

These records can include, bones, teeth, petrified remains (remains turned to rock), impressions of various parts, trails, tracks.

Most fossils can be placed in one of the following groups.

- Unaltered hard parts of an organism – shells, teeth and bones of a variety of ancient organisms have been found relatively unchanged.
- Unaltered soft parts of an organism – these are much rarer, but whole mammoths have been found preserved in the permafrost and dehydrated insects have been found preserved in amber.
- Altered hard parts – such as bones, teeth and plant material where part of the structure has been replaced by rock of some sort.
- Altered soft parts – complete removal of the soft parts of an animal some-times leaves an imprint in the rock of what those parts had been like.

Fossils are preserved in rocks and older rocks contain older fossils. By studying a sequence of fossils from rocks of different ages, it is sometimes possible to see how an organism has evolved over time.

fossil fuel: a fuel, such as coal or oil, which is formed over a long period of time from the partially decayed remains of plants or animals.

Fossil fuels include:

- coal – formed from ancient fern-like plants
- oil – formed from the partly decayed remains of small animals which lived in the seas
- natural gas – formed at the same time as oil.

Fossil fuels took millions of years to form and they are non-renewable. Once the existing reserves have been used, there will be no more.

---

fossilisation: the process or processes involved in turning the remains of an organism into a *fossil*.

Some fossils are simply the remains of ancient organisms, unaltered. There is no special fossilisation process involved in producing these.

Fossils which are found as imprints or whole structures in rock are formed in the following way.

- The organism falls to the ground or sea floor.
- It becomes covered in sediment.
- The mud or sand is compressed by more sediment or the weight of water above it.
- It hardens and turns to stone.
- Parts of the remains are either lost and an imprint is left, or turned to rock which might be a little different from the surrounding rock so the structure of the fossil is visible.

As time goes by, more and more of the original material is lost as it gets compressed further and further. As a result, older rocks generally contain fewer fossils.

---

fovea: the part of the retina in the *eye* with the greatest concentration of *cones*.

The fovea is located directly opposite the centre of the lens. When we look directly at an object, the lens focuses the rays of light onto the fovea and we are able to perceive it in maximum detail.

If you look directly at a notice, you will be able to read what it says. If you look slightly to one side of it, then, although you will be aware of the letters, you will not be able to read them because you will not perceive them in enough detail. The rays of light from the notice will not be falling on your fovea.

Franklin, Rosalind: an English scientist who provided evidence which helped in the discovery of the structure of *DNA*.

Rosalind Franklin studied at Cambridge University before leaving to research into new uses of coal.

Whilst carrying out this research, she used X-rays to determine the arrangement of the atoms in coal. The technique is called X-ray diffraction. In 1951, she used this technique to produce X-ray photographs of the DNA molecule.

The photographs she produced helped James Watson and Francis Crick to work out the famous double helix structure of the DNA molecule in 1953. Rosalind Franklin died in 1958 and was unable to share with Watson and Crick the Nobel prize for the discovery of the structure of DNA as this award is never made posthumously.

fruit: a structure which contains *seeds*.

Biologically, a tomato is a fruit as it contains seeds. So is a pea pod and the spiky case which contains the horse chestnut seeds (conkers).

Fruits are formed from the ovary and its contents after fertilisation.

- An ovary will contain at least one ovule which, when fertilised will form a seed.
- The ovary wall changes and becomes the wall of the fruit.
- Fruits are adapted in some way to disperse the seeds they contain.

FSH (follicle stimulating hormone): the hormone released by the *pituitary gland* which, in females, stimulates the development of follicles in the ovaries. In males it stimulates the production of sperm in the testes.

In females:

- FSH is released when levels of *oestrogen* and *progesterone* in the blood-stream decrease at the end of a *menstrual cycle*
- the release of FSH by the pituitary causes a follicle to mature and to secrete oestrogen
- the increasing levels of oestrogen inhibit the release of FSH by the pituitary.

This is an example of negative feedback control.

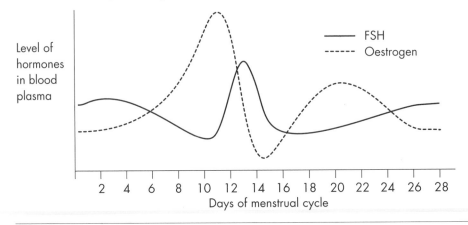

fungi: non-photosynthetic organisms with cell walls not made of cellulose. Fungi reproduce by producing spores.

Many feed using thread-like structures called *hyphae* which are organised into a mycelium. If you leave damp bread out for too long, you may see a white mass of threads develop on the bread. This is the mycelium of the common mould, *Mucor*. If you can see any small black spots among the white threads, these are the spore cases.

Fungi are important economically and ecologically because:

- some produce *antibiotics* (e.g. *penicillin* from the mould *Penicillium*, streptomycin from the fungus *Streptomyces*)
- some are important as *decomposers* in making available nutrients contained in dead organisms
- *yeast* is used to produce alcohol
- some are used to produce new foods such as mycoprotein.

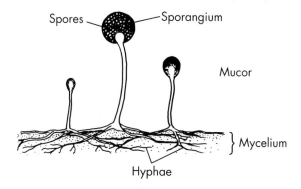

fusion (of gametes): the joining of male and female *gametes*.

gall bladder: a sac about 7–10 cm long, found on the undersurface of the liver.

The gall bladder:

- receives about 0.5 litres of *bile* per day from the liver
- stores the bile and concentrates it by a factor of 10
- when stimulated, it contracts and forces the bile into the duodenum.

(See *digestive system*.)

---

gamete: a sex cell.

In animals the male sex cells are the *sperm* and the female sex cells are the ova (*egg cells*).

In plants, the male sex cells are found in the *pollen grains* and the female sex cells are the ova.

We can talk about male and female in plants because, as in most animals, male sex cells are usually:

- smaller than female sex cells
- produced in greater numbers than the female sex cells
- motile – they move to the female sex cells which remain stationary.

Sex cells are formed by *meiosis* so they contain only half the normal number of chromosomes. When two sex cells fuse, the *zygote* they produce contains the full complement of chromosomes. The new individual which develops from this will have the same number of chromosomes in its cells as its parents.

---

gas: a state of matter in which the particles are able to move quickly and independently of each other.

Gases can change size and shape and will expand to fill whatever container they are placed in.

Because of the rapid motion of their particles, diffusion occurs quicker in gases than in liquids and solids.

Biologically important gases include:

- oxygen (for *aerobic respiration*)
- carbon dioxide (for *photosynthesis*)
- nitrogen (to be converted to ammonia by *nitrogen fixing bacteria*).

---

gas exchange: the exchange of gases between an organism or a cell and its environment.

In a simple unicell such as *Amoeba*, all gas exchange takes place by *diffusion* through the cell membrane.

Larger and more complex animals have evolved specialised gas exchange structures. This was necessary as the surface area of a large organism could never meet the demand for oxygen created by the volume of the animal.

Specialised gas exchange structures include:

- *alveoli* (in mammals)
- gill filaments (in fish)
- tracheoles (in insects. (See *trachea, insects*.)

All these structures have in common:

- a large surface area
- a thin surface
- a rich blood supply (except tracheoles)
- a moist surface.

gender: whether an individual is male or female.

In humans, gender is determined by the X and Y *chromosomes*.

Males have one X and one Y chromosomes in each cell (written XY).

Females have two X chromosomes in each cell (written XX).

These chromosomes make up the 23rd pair of chromosomes in human cells.

gene: a length of *DNA* on a chromosome which determines a specific feature, such as eye colour.

Genes often have two (sometimes more) forms called *alleles*. For example:

- the gene for eye colour has blue and brown alleles
- the gene for melanin production (skin pigmentation) has normal pigment and albino alleles
- the gene for earlobe development has free-hanging and attached-to-neck alleles.

Usually, one of the two alleles is dominant and the other is recessive.

A gene carries a code for a particular protein to be manufactured. (See *protein synthesis* for details.)

The protein made may be:

- an *enzyme* – which then controls a reaction in the cell
- a structural protein – e.g. part of a cell membrane or muscle fibre.

gene pool: all the *alleles* of all the *genes* in a *species*.
- The gene pool represents the total genetic variety of a species.
- Modern selective breeding may reduce the gene pool of the species involved as only certain types will be bred together.
- Other, less desirable alleles (to humans) may get more and more rare in the species and eventually be lost.
- This loss means that the species may not be able to adapt to changes as the alleles that would have helped it survive have been 'bred out' of the species.

gene therapy: a special kind of *genetic engineering* which attempts to replace genes which cause genetic diseases with normal genes.
One inherited disease which is currently being treated with gene therapy is *cystic fibrosis*.
- The normal genes are placed into fatty spheres (liposomes) or viruses, using genetic engineering technology.
- The liposomes/viruses are inhaled and pass into cells lining the lungs: the normal genes become incorporated into the DNA of those cells.
- The new genes start to work and the over-production of mucus is reduced.
This is not a one-off treatment. It must be reapplied from time to time and has the drawback that although, in time, the technique may cure the condition, it cannot prevent it being passed on.

genetics: the study of how similarities and differences are inherited.
The science of genetics is a relatively young one.
- In 1865, the Austrian monk *Gregor Mendel* discovers some of the basic laws which govern inheritance, but his work is ignored for 40 years.
- At the start of the 20th century, biologists are able to link Mendel's work to the structure of cells: they begin to map where genes are found on chromosomes.
- 1941 – the link between genes and enzymes is established.
- 1944 – *DNA* is identified as the hereditary material.
- 1953 – Watson and Crick lay the foundation for modern genetics by discovering the structure of DNA.
- 1966 – the basis of the genetic code is solved.
- 1988 – a man is convicted of murder on the basis of his DNA profile.
- 1997 – the first mammal is cloned: Dolly the sheep arouses controversy about the technique of *cloning*.
- 1999 – there is concern about genetically modified food.

genetic engineering: the technology which allows biologists to remove sections of *DNA* (*genes*) from one organism and transfer it to another.
Organisms which have had foreign genes transferred to them are called *transgenic* organisms.

The stages in transferring a gene from one organism to another are as follows:
- The location of the gene on a chromosome is found.
- The gene is cut out using restriction enzymes.
- The gene is transferred to a vector (a sort of molecular lorry which will carry the gene into cells of the new organism).
- The vector is introduced to the new organism.
- The gene is now part of the DNA of the new organism and will replicate when the rest of the DNA replicates.

The flow chart shows how the gene for human *insulin* can be transferred to bacterial cells.

Being able to transfer genes from one organism to another brings many exciting possibilities, such as:
- making human insulin in large quantities for *diabetes* treatment
- creating new crops with desired features more quickly than with traditional breeding techniques
- transferring the genes for nitrogen fixation from legumes to other crops, so that they are not as dependent on nitrates in the soil to make proteins.

genotype: the type of *alleles* an organism contains: its genetic make-up.
Usually:
- there are two alleles for each characteristic
- one of these alleles is dominant and the other is recessive
- the alleles are represented by single letters
- the dominant allele is represented by the first letter of the feature, written as a capital
- the recessive allele is represented by the same letter, but written as lower case
- any individual contains two alleles in the cells.

Consider the ability to taste PTC as an example. Individuals can either taste the chemical (it tastes very bitter if you can) or not.
Tasting is dominant and so the symbol for the tasting allele is T.
Non-tasting is recessive and the symbol for this allele is t.
Possible genotypes are therefore TT, Tt, tt.

geotropism: the response of plants to gravity: sometimes called gravitropism.
- Roots grow towards gravity – this is positive geotropism.

- Shoots (stems) grow away from gravity – this is negative geotropism.

At the moment, the mechanism which produces the geotropic response is poorly understood.

germination: the initial growth of a seed, spore, or pollen grain.
In seeds it includes the changes which take place when it starts to grow, up to and including the appearance of the root and shoot.
Many seeds are dormant over winter and then begin to germinate in the spring. They need:
- oxygen – for *aerobic respiration*: energy is needed to produce new cells
- water – the seed was dry and the cells must rehydrate so that *enzymes* can work and the chemical reactions of germination can take place
- a suitable temperature – this varies from plant to plant, but enzymes work better in warm temperatures than in cold ones.

The diagram shows some of the stages of germination and early growth of a broad bean seed

gills: the gas exchange organ of many aquatic animals, including fish.
A fish's gills are well adapted as gas exchange organs because they have many gill filaments which:
- have a large surface area
- have a good blood supply
- are thin walled.

Fish move a current of water over their gills so that there is always oxygenated water next to the gill filaments. Oxygen diffuses from the water into the blood and carbon dioxide diffuses in the opposite direction.

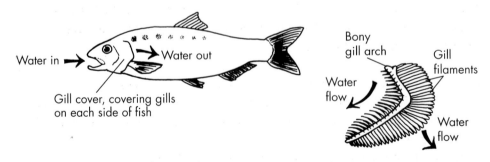

gland: a structure which produces and secretes a specific substance.
Some glands are endocrine and secrete substances directly into the bloodstream.
Other glands are exocrine and secrete substances through ducts onto a surface or into a space.
The table on the next page gives some examples of different types of glands.

Gland	Type of gland	Examples of substance(s) secreted	Secreted into/onto
pituitary gland	endocrine	growth hormone FSH (follicle stimulating hormone)	blood plasma
adrenal gland	endocrine	adrenaline	blood plasma
sweat gland	exocrine	sweat	surface of skin
gall bladder	exocrine	bile	lumen of duodenum
salivary glands	exocrine	saliva (containing the enzyme amylase)	buccal cavity (mouth)

global warming: an increase in the earth's temperature.

Global warming and cooling have happened many times in the history of the earth, but these changes have taken place over many thousands of years or even longer. There is concern now about the possibility of global warming taking place in just decades.

If significant global warming does occur, there will be many consequences which may include:

- the ice caps may melt and sea levels rise
- a change in rainfall and general climatic patterns
- *ecosystems* will be altered and some species will die out as their habitat changes
- agriculture will be affected by changes in rainfall and water levels; some pests may become more abundant in the warmer climate.

Many scientists think that global warming is brought about by the *greenhouse effect*. Others think that variations in the intensity of the sun's radiation could be part of the cause.

glucagon: a hormone secreted by islet cells in the *pancreas*.

Glucagon helps to maintain a constant level of glucose in the blood plasma. If the plasma glucose concentration falls too low the following sequence of events takes place.

- The islet cells secrete glucagon into the blood plasma.
- The glucagon travels to the liver.
- In the liver, glucagon causes glycogen to be broken down into glucose which is released into the blood plasma.
- The concentration of glucose in the plasma rises to normal.
- The secretion of glucagon stops.

glucose: a simple carbohydrate (a monosaccharide) with the formula $C_6H_{12}O_6$.

Glucose is a very important biological molecule because:

- it is the first product of *photosynthesis*
- it is the main source of energy in both *aerobic* and *anaerobic respiration*.

Glucose can be converted to other molecules, such as:

- *starch*, in plants – an insoluble storage product
- *cellulose*, in plants – a major component of plant cell walls
- *proteins*, in plants – glucose can be combined with mineral ions from the soil to form amino acids which can be converted into proteins
- *fats*, in both animals and plants
- *glycogen*, in animals – a storage product similar to starch, sometimes called animal starch.

glycerol: an alcohol which is found in all *lipid* molecules.

Glycerol is usually combined with three fatty acids to form the lipid molecule.

glycogen: a complex carbohydrate (a polysaccharide) made from hundreds of *glucose* molecules joined together.

Glycogen is sometimes called animal starch, because the molecule is similar to the starch molecule.

Glycogen is found mainly in muscles and the liver where it acts as a reserve of glucose. During exercise, the glycogen is broken down rapidly to replace the glucose which is being used up in *respiration*.

The correct level of glucose in the blood plasma is maintained by the inter-conversion of glucose and glycogen under the influence of the hormones *insulin* and *glucagon*.

$$\text{glucose} \underset{\text{glucagon}}{\overset{\text{insulin}}{\rightleftharpoons}} \text{glycogen}$$

greenhouse effect: the prevention of radiation leaving the earth due to a build up of certain gases in the atmosphere.

There has always been a greenhouse effect because of the gases in the earth's atmosphere. This greenhouse effect has made life on earth possible. Without it, the earth would be as cold as the moon and only very primitive life, if any at all, would have evolved.

The gases which cause the greenhouse effect are known collectively as the greenhouse gases and include:

- *carbon dioxide*

- methane
- nitrous oxide
- chlorofluorocarbons (*CFCs*).

The concentrations of all the gases have increased since the start of the industrial revolution (CFCs were only recently synthesised and their use is now banned). As a result, the greenhouse effect is greater now than it was previously and is correctly referred to as the enhanced greenhouse effect. Global warming is one of the consequences of the greenhouse effect.

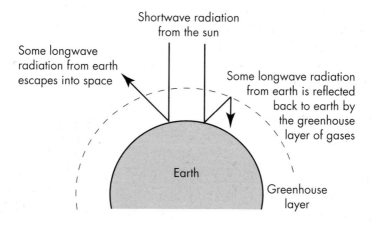

grey matter: the parts of the *central nervous system* (CNS) which are made mainly of the cell bodies of *neurones*.

In the brain, the grey matter is mainly found in the outer layers of the *cerebrum*.

In the *spinal cord*, the grey matter is mainly found in the inner layers.

growth: an increase in the amount of living substance of an organism. This usually means:

- an increase in the number of cells of a multicellular organism
- an increase in the amount of cytoplasm in a unicell.

Growth does not just mean getting larger (although this usually happens) as some organisms can get larger through taking in water by *osmosis* and then lose the water and shrink.

Growth in humans is controlled by a number of hormones including *growth hormone* from the *pituitary gland*.

growth hormone: a hormone secreted by the *pituitary gland*.

Growth hormone stimulates the production of protein in most tissues by:

- promoting the uptake of amino acids by the cells (to be built up into proteins)

- causing more fatty acids to be released into the blood plasma (these are an extra source of energy for protein synthesis).

If the secretion of growth hormone is not properly controlled during childhood, there are two possible results:

- gigantism resulting from over-secretion of the hormone
- dwarfism resulting from under-secretion of the hormone.

Dwarfism can be treated by administering controlled amounts of growth hormone.

Pituitary growth hormone is now manufactured on a large scale by genetically engineered microorganisms.

growth rate (individual): the growth produced over a set time period. In humans, the most rapid growth rates occur in the *fetus*. Growth rates then fall and remain constant until the growth spurt associated with *adolescence*. The graphs show the growth and growth rates of girls and boys from fertilisation to the age of 20.

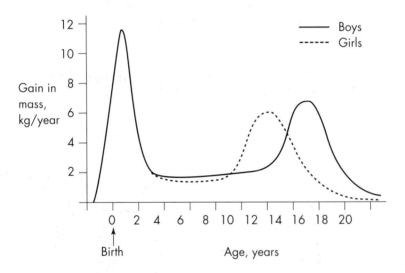

growth rate (population): the change in numbers per thousand individuals. The growth rate is calculated from the formula:

(births + immigration) – (deaths + emigration)

If the figure is negative, then the population is shrinking.

guanine: one of the bases that makes up the structure of *DNA*. Guanine on one strand of DNA is always paired with cytosine on the other strand. This is because of the base pairing rule.

guard cells: pairs of cells which surround the *stomata* in the lower and upper epidermis of leaves.

They are the only cells in the epidermis with *chloroplasts*.

When it is light, the following sequence of events occurs.

- The guard cells photosynthesise and make glucose
- The glucose causes an increase in concentration of the solution in the vacuole.
- Water is drawn from surrounding cells by *osmosis*.
- The guard cells swell.
- Because of the irregular thickening of guard cell walls, the swelling makes them change shape and open the pore.
- Because of this, more carbon dioxide can enter the leaf, which can then photosynthesise faster.

When it is dark, the opposite happens and the guard cells close the pores.

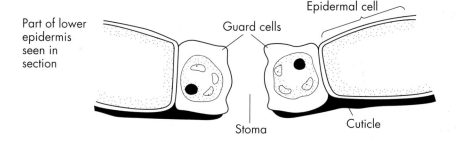

Part of lower epidermis seen in section

Guard cells

Epidermal cell

Stoma

Cuticle

Part of lower epidermis – surface view

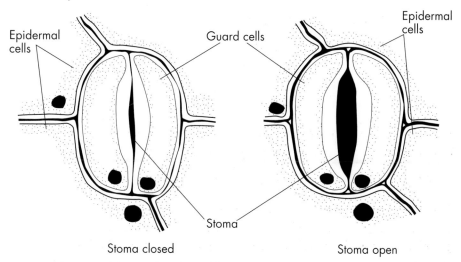

Epidermal cells

Guard cells

Epidermal cells

Stoma

Stoma closed

Stoma open

habitat: a part of an *ecosystem* which is the home of one particular species. Some organisms are very specific in their requirements and live in only one habitat; others, such as humans, are more adaptable and can live in a number of different habitats.

haemoglobin: a protein found in blood which can carry oxygen. In vertebrates, the haemoglobin is found inside the *red blood cells*.

As the blood passes through capillaries in the *gas exchange* organ (lungs, gills etc.):

- oxygen diffuses into the red blood cells
- it joins with the haemoglobin forming oxy-haemoglobin.

As blood passes respiring cells:

- the oxy-haemoglobin breaks down and releases the oxygen
- the oxygen diffuses from the blood into the cells.

Haemoglobin can also combine with *carbon monoxide* to form carboxy-haemoglobin. This is a very stable substance and prevents the haemoglobin from combining with oxygen in the lungs. As more and more carbon monoxide is breathed in, less and less oxygen is collected in the lungs and the individual may become unconscious or even die due to lack of oxygen.

haemophilia: an inherited condition in which *blood clotting* is defective. The condition is caused by a recessive allele on the X chromosome. Because of this, most of the sufferers are male. (See *sex-linked inheritance* for details.)

- The person cannot make one of the factors which cause blood to clot (usually factor VIII).
- Even the slightest injury may be life-threatening as much blood will be lost before clotting eventually takes place.
- Treatment is by administering the missing clotting factor either when bleeding starts or at frequent intervals as a preventive measure.

haemophiliac: a person who suffers from *haemophilia*.

Most haemophiliacs are male because the condition is caused by a recessive allele on the X chromosome. (See *sex-linked inheritance* for details.)

A number of haemophiliacs have, in the past, contracted AIDS. This was because the clotting factor they were given (from donated blood) had not been properly screened for the virus. Now screening is much more rigorous and donated blood is heat treated to destroy the virus.

A genetically engineered product has recently been produced and should solve the problem of transmitting the AIDS virus to haemophiliacs.

hallucinogen: a type of *drug* which causes us to perceive things which are not physically present.
- LSD, solvents, magic mushrooms and mescaline are hallucinogens.
- *Alcohol* can sometimes produce hallucinations when taken in large amounts.
- Alcohol withdrawal can also produce hallucinations.

Using hallucinogens is dangerous because:
- perception of time and movement may change
- perception of objects and colour may become distorted
- the user cannot stop the 'trip' once it has started
- the alteration of perception can cause accidents.

haploid: the number of *chromosomes* present in a sex cell (*gamete*).
The haploid number of chromosomes is:
- half the *diploid* number present in other cells
- made up from one chromosome from each pair in a normal cell
- the result of sex cells being formed by *meiosis*.

Harvey, William: the English doctor who, in 1628, discovered the circulation of the blood.

By observing the heart beating and through other simple experiments, Harvey was able to disprove beliefs that had been held for centuries. Before Harvey's book in 1628, people had believed:
- the heart was not a pump
- blood was able to pass freely between the left and right ventricles
- the food we eat is converted directly into blood.

By measuring the amount of blood coming from the heart, Harvey showed that a normal man's diet just couldn't supply that amount of blood. Harvey reasoned, from his observations, that the heart must pump 4.5 kg per minute – or 6500 kg per day. Some diet to form that amount of blood!

By demonstrating bleeding from an artery near the heart and bleeding from a vein much further from the heart, Harvey showed that the blood was circulating. He reasoned that the heart must pump it.

Harvey also showed the presence of valves in veins and was able to deduce their function.

hazard symbols: symbols on chemicals or apparatus which give warnings about potential dangers.

Some common hazard symbols are:

Oxidising
These substances provide oxygen which allows other materials to burn more fiercely.

Highly flammable
These substances easily catch fire.

Toxic
These substances can cause death. They may have their effects when swallowed or breathed in or absorbed through the skin

Corrosive
These substances attack and destroy living tissues, including eyes and skin.

Harmful
These substances are similar to toxic substances but less dangerous

Irritant
These substances are not corrosive but can cause reddening or blistering of the skin.

heart: the muscular organ which pumps blood through the *circulatory system*. In the cardiac cycle:
- blood returns to the atria in the pulmonary veins and the vena cava
- the atria contract and force blood through the atrio-ventricular valves into the ventricles
- the ventricles contract and force blood through semi-lunar valves into the aorta and pulmonary artery.

The valves prevent backflow of blood:
- the atrio-ventricular valves are closed by the contraction of the ventricles so blood cannot flow back into the atria
- the semi-lunar valves close when the ventricles stop contracting so that blood cannot flow back into the ventricles from the aorta and pulmonary artery.

Exam hint: to identify which is the left side and which is the right:
- the wall of the left ventricle is thicker than the wall of the right ventricle
- the aorta curves towards the left
- most diagrams show the heart from the front, so right is on the left and vice versa.

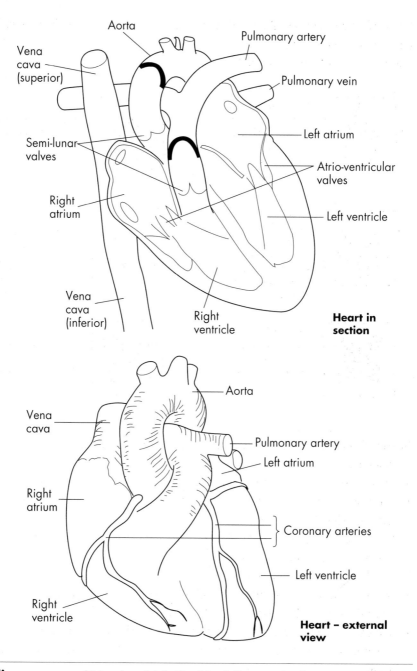

Aorta

Vena cava (superior)

Pulmonary artery

Pulmonary vein

Left atrium

Semi-lunar valves

Atrio-ventricular valves

Right atrium

Left ventricle

Vena cava (inferior)

Right ventricle

Heart in section

Aorta

Vena cava

Pulmonary artery

Left atrium

Right atrium

Coronary arteries

Left ventricle

Right ventricle

Heart – external view

heart disease: a condition in which the blood flow to the heart muscle is reduced, usually because of a blockage or narrowing of the coronary arteries. When the coronary arteries become narrower:

- less oxygen is carried to the heart muscle
- the heart muscle is therefore unable to contract as efficiently, especially during exercise

● the sufferer may feel the pains of angina or have a heart attack.

The coronary arteries often become narrower as a result of *atherosclerosis* (a build up of fatty deposits in the wall of the arteries). They may become blocked as a result of coronary thrombosis, in which a blood clot lodges in the artery.

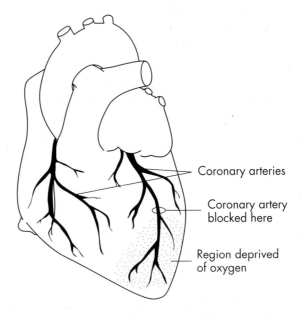

Coronary arteries

Coronary artery
blocked here

Region deprived
of oxygen

The diagram below shows some of the risk factors which make heart disease more likely.

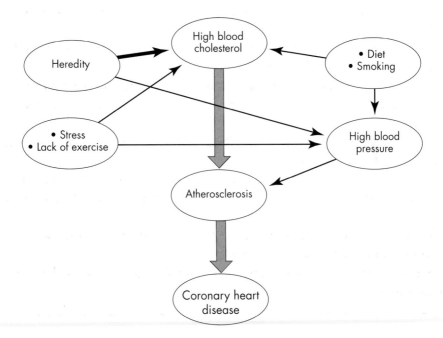

hepatitis: any inflammation of the *liver*, usually accompanied by death of liver cells.

Hepatitis can be caused by:

- viruses – there are five types of viral hepatitis, A,B,C,D and E
- overuse of some *drugs* (such as paracetamol)
- exposure to dry-cleaning fluids.

Hepatitis has the following symptoms:

- a 'flu-like illness, followed by
- jaundice – yellowing of the skin and *sclera*.

Hepatitis A is called infectious hepatitis and is spread in infected food and water.

Hepatitis B is called serum hepatitis and this type (and types C and E) can be spread through:

- contaminated blood products
- sexual activity
- needle-sharing by drug users.

There is no specific treatment for any type of viral hepatitis, but bed rest, a good diet and no alcohol often result in recovery.

herbicide: a weedkiller.

Herbicides are used by farmers to keep fields free from weeds to obtain the maximum yield from crop plants.

This has had important effects on wildlife.

- Some herbicides are persistent and may remain in the soil for up to 10 years.
- Creating large fields and keeping them weed-free has greatly reduced the number of wild flowers in these areas.
- The lack of wild flowers means that many insects have been reduced in numbers, and so any animals which feed on the insects must find new foods or die.

Herbicides are, generally, not passed along *food chains* in the same way that some insecticides have been.

There are many different herbicides and they can be grouped according to:

- the way they act – some kill by direct contact, some are absorbed from the soil
- whether they are selective or total herbicides – some kill only certain types of plants, others kill all plants
- their chemical nature – some resemble natural plant hormones, others are based on *urea*.

herbivore: an animal which feeds only on plants.
Herbivorous mammals have specially adapted *teeth* and *digestive systems*.
They often have:
- small, chisel-like canines on the lower jaw and none on the upper jaw
- ridged molars and pre-molars
- a side-to-side jaw action so that the ridges on the molars and premolars grind plant material.
- a long *digestive system* with some part enlarged and containing billions of bacteria to digest the cellulose in the plant cell walls.

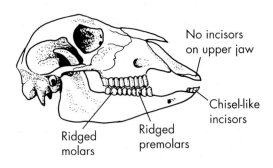

No incisors on upper jaw

Chisel-like incisors

Ridged molars

Ridged premolars

hermaphrodite: possessing both male and female sex organs.
(See *reproduction, plants* and *self-fertilisation*.)

heterotroph: an organism which shows *heterotrophic nutrition*.
Heterotrophs include *animals, fungi* and some *bacteria*. Compare with *autotroph*.

heterotrophic nutrition: nutrition in which the organism must feed from other organisms or from decaying matter.
Organisms which feed in this way are called heterotrophs or *consumers*.
They cannot synthesise their own food like *autotrophs*.

heterozygous: possessing both *dominant* and *recessive alleles* of a gene.
For example:
- in pea plants the gene for height has two alleles, tall and dwarf
- all pea plants contain two alleles for height in each cell (except the sex cells)
- a pea plant which is heterozygous for the height gene would have one tall allele and one dwarf allele in each cell.

Let T represent the allele for tallness and t the allele for dwarfness.
The *genotype* of a heterozygous pea plant would be Tt.
(See also *homozygous*.)

homeostasis: maintaining a constant internal environment.

The sum of all the chemical reactions occurring in our bodies is our *metabolism*. If conditions change too much in our bodies, our metabolism works less efficiently and systems may fail. Some examples of the benefits of homeostasis to our metabolism are:

- maintaining a constant body temperature allows enzyme-controlled reactions to work at peak efficiency
- an individual can be independent of varying temperatures of the external environment
- maintaining a constant blood pH keeps enzymes working at peak efficiency
- maintaining a constant blood concentration prevents cells losing or gaining water by *osmosis*: this would affect many reactions in cells.

Most homeostatic mechanisms involve *negative feedback*.

homozygous: possessing either two *dominant* or two *recessive alleles*.
For example:

- in pea plants the gene for height has two alleles, tall and dwarf
- all pea plants contain two alleles for height in each cell (except the sex cells)
- a pea plant which is homozygous for the height gene could have either two tall alleles or two dwarf alleles in each cell.

Let **T** represent the allele for tallness and **t** the allele for dwarfness.

The *genotype* of a homozygous tall pea plant would be **TT**.

The genotype of a homozygous dwarf pea plant would be **tt**.

See also *heterozygous*.

hormone (animal): a substance secreted from an *endocrine gland* which acts as a chemical messenger to produce a response only in certain target organs.

The effects of some of the main hormones are shown in the table overleaf.

hormone (plant): see *auxin*.

host: the organism on which a *parasite* depends for its food and which is usually harmed by the parasite.

Parasites can live on or in a host.

Those living on the outside of a host are called *ectoparasites*.

Those living on the inside of a host are called *endoparasites*.

hormones

Hormone	Secreted by	Target organ	Effect
ADH (anti-diuretic hormone)	pituitary gland	kidney	reduces amount of water lost in urine
FSH (follicle stimulating hormone)	pituitary gland	ovary	development of follicles and secretion of oestrogen
		testis	stimulates development of sperm
LH (luteinising hormone)	pituitary gland	ovary	stimulates ovulation and formation of corpus luteum
		testis	stimulates production of testosterone
thyroxine	thyroid gland	general	increases metabolic rate
insulin	islet cells in pancreas	liver	causes conversion of glucose to glycogen: lowers blood glucose levels
glucagon	islet cells in pancreas	liver	causes conversion of glycogen to glucose: raises blood glucose levels
adrenaline	adrenal gland	heart arterioles	increases heart rate dilates arterioles in muscles, constricts arterioles in skin, kidney
oestrogen	ovary (cells in follicle)	uterus	stimulates production of uterus lining
		pituitary gland	inhibits production of FSH
progesterone	ovary (follicle/corpus luteum)	uterus pituitary gland	maintains uterus lining inhibits production of FSH and LH
testosterone	testis	testis general	sperm production secondary sex characteristics

humus: the part of the *soil* made up of dead and decaying organisms. Humus is important because:
- as it decays it releases mineral ions into the soil
- it helps soils to retain water without becoming waterlogged

- it helps to prevent *soil erosion* by binding small soil particles together.

Compost (formed from decaying vegetable matter) is a kind of humus.

- If a soil has too much clay, it will become waterlogged because the tiny clay particles pack close together. By digging compost into the soil, the structure of the soil is made more free-draining.
- If a soil is too sandy, it will drain too freely. Digging compost into this type of soil helps to bind the sand particles together and improve water holding.

Huntington's disease (Huntington's chorea): an inherited condition in which the sufferer develops dementia (progressive loss of memory) and chorea (rapid, involuntary jerky movements).

Huntington's disease:

- is caused by a dominant *allele* on chromosome 4
- usually develops between the ages of 35–50
- proves fatal 15–30 years after the appearance of the symptoms.

Until recently, because of the late onset of the disease, a sufferer may already have had children and passed on the allele to them. Now tests (including *DNA* analysis) are available to determine whether a person carries the allele. In a sexual relationship between a person *heterozygous* for Huntington's disease and a non-sufferer, there is a 50% chance that a child will be affected. Let **H** be the dominant allele for Huntington's disease and **h** be the recessive allele for normal condition:

heterozygous sufferer – Hh
non-sufferer   – hh

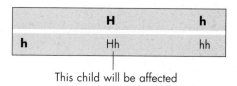

	H	h
h	Hh	hh

This child will be affected

hybrid: the offspring obtained by mating two different *species* or two different breeds or varieties of the same species.

Hybrids between different species are nearly always infertile – they cannot themselves produce any offspring. The mule is a good example of an infertile hybrid between two species (female horse and male donkey).

It is often possible to produce fertile hybrids between different breeds of the same species. A breed is a population of animals of a certain species that has been selectively bred to have certain features.

In plants, we call these varieties. There are many different breeds of dogs and many different varieties of roses.

Hybrids between different breeds/varieties are often more healthy and disease resistant than the parents. This is called hybrid vigour.

hybridisation: breeding different species or breeds or varieties of a species to produce a *hybrid*.

hydrochloric acid: a strong acid produced when hydrogen chloride gas dissolves in water; both hydrogen chloride and hydrochloric acid have the chemical formula HCl.
Hydrochloric acid:
- dissociates into H^+ ions and Cl^- ions in water
- is produced in our stomach where it kills many of the bacteria which are ingested with food.

hydroponics: growing plants on a large scale in nutrient solution, or in a sterile medium such as sand with nutrients passing through it.
Growing crops by hydroponics is expensive because:
- artificial lighting and heating must be provided
- the nutrient solution must be constantly monitored and adjusted to ensure the correct balance of nutrients
- the roots must be constantly aerated.
The benefits can include:
- crops can be grown in areas normally unsuitable (e.g. in very dry areas) or at times of the year not normally possible
- crops can be grown in the area where they are needed, reducing transport costs
- crops can be grown in disease-free environments (this also means that pesticides need not be used on the crop).
Crops currently being grown hydroponically include tomatoes, lettuce and herbs in winter.

hydrostatic skeleton: a 'skeleton' in which the support is provided by the pressure of a liquid inside the animal's body.
Invertebrates with hydrostatic skeletons include:
- animals like jellyfish and *Hydra*
- earthworms.

hygiene: taking measures which help to preserve health.
Hygiene is often taken to mean cleanliness, and this is certainly part of personal hygiene, but hygiene involves more than just keeping ourselves clean.
Public hygiene includes:
- all the measures taken to ensure we have pure water supplies
- maintaining high standards of sanitation

- ensuring that housing is well maintained.

Industrial and occupational hygiene include all the measures taken to ensure that the workplace is safe and unlikely to cause any occupational disease.

hyphae (singular hypha): thread-like structures which make up the main part of many *fungi*.

The hyphae form a mass of threads called a *mycelium*. A mycelium is easily seen if you leave damp bread out for a few days. Soon a white mass of threads like cotton wool appears – this is the mycelium of the mould Mucor.

- Hyphae have cell walls which are not made from cellulose like plant cell walls.
- They have cytoplasm which contains many nuclei.
- They secrete digestive enzymes from their tips.
- The hyphae absorb the soluble materials produced by the external digestion of food materials.

hypothermia: a fall in body temperature to below 35⁰C.

Hypothermia may cause:

- drowsiness
- drop in heart rate and breathing rate leading to further hypothermia
- unconsciousness
- possibly death.

Most deaths from hypothermia occur in elderly people because:

- they are more likely to live in poorly heated homes
- as the body ages it loses sensitivity to the cold
- as the body ages it becomes less able to reverse a fall in body temperature, especially if the person has a disorder.

Babies are also at risk of hypothermia, because they can lose heat quickly and cannot easily regenerate the lost heat.

Surgical hypothermia is the deliberate reduction of body temperature during surgery to prolong the period of time organs can be deprived of oxygen. This allows more time for the surgery.

identical twins: twins which have developed from the same *zygote* (fertilised egg).

Because they develop from the same zygote, identical twins:

- are sometimes called monozygotic twins
- have identical *genotypes*
- share the same placenta when developing in the uterus
- will look almost exactly alike
- will always be the same sex.

If the separation of the two cells is incomplete, then the twins will develop still joined together at some part(s) of their body. Such identical twins are called conjoined or Siamese twins. Sometimes, conjoined twins can be separated successfully by surgery.

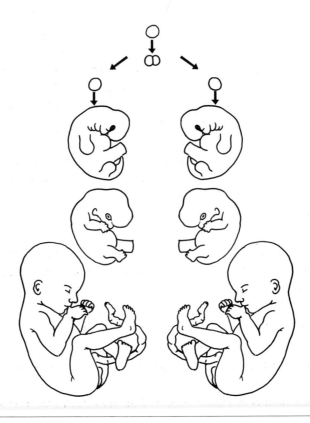

immobilised enzymes: see *enzymes, immobilised.*

immune (immunity): not (being) susceptible to *infection.*
(See *immune response, immune system* and *immunisation.*)

immune response: a response by the *immune system* to cells or substances in the body which carry *antigens* recognised as non-self (not part of the body's own set of antigens).
The immune system responds to:
- invading microorganisms
- the toxins produced by microorganisms
- tissues or organs which have been transplanted from another individual
- cancer cells
- in some individuals, dust, pollen and other 'foreign' particles.

The immune response can include some or all of:
- *phagocytes* engulfing invading microorganisms
- B-*lymphocytes* producing antibodies to kill the microorganisms
- B-lymphocytes producing antitoxins to destroy toxins produced by bacteria
- T-lymphocytes destroying cells infected with viruses
- B and T-lymphocytes producing *memory cells* to give long lasting immunity.

immune system: a collection of cells and chemicals which work together to destroy non-self *antigens* (usually on invading microorganisms).
The main cells of the system are *phagocytes* (these engulf microorganisms at the site of an infection) and *lymphocytes.*
B-lymphocytes:
- recognise non-self antigens on the surface of invading microorganisms
- produce *antibodies* and *antitoxins* to destroy microorganisms or the toxins they produce
- some become memory cells.

T-lymphocytes:
- recognise the antigens on the surface of invading microorganisms
- produce chemicals to kill cells which are already infected with viruses
- some become memory cells.

immunisation: the process of producing immunity to prevent someone catching an infectious disease.
There are two main types of immunisation, active and passive.
In active immunisation:
- the person is injected with a *vaccine* of dead or modified microorganisms

- *lymphocytes* in the immune system produce antibodies against the microorganism in the vaccine and *memory cells*
- the memory cells remain in the blood
- if the person is then infected with the actual disease-causing organism, the memory cells bring about a much quicker response so that the microorganisms are destroyed before they have a chance to make the person ill.

In passive immunisation:

- the person is injected with antibodies taken from another person (or sometimes an animal) who has already had the disease
- the antibodies provide immediate protection and destroy the microorganisms
- there are no memory cells produced, so passive immunity is short lasting.

Babies obtain antibodies across the *placenta* and from their mother's milk: this is natural passive immunity.

immunosuppressive drug: a *drug* which reduces the ability of the *immune system* to produce an *immune response*.

Immunosuppressive drugs are often used:

- after transplant surgery – to reduce the risk of *rejection* of the newly transplanted tissue or organ
- to treat disorders where the immune system is attacking some of the body's own tissues (some kinds of *arthritis* are caused in this way).

They work by decreasing the formation of *lymphocytes*, essential to the normal immune response.

implantation: attaching an *embryo* to the lining of the *uterus*.

At the stage of implantation, the human embryo:

- is about six days old
- is a hollow ball of cells with a small mass of cells inside the ball

The embryo implants by secreting *enzymes* which digest away an area of the lining and allow the embryo to settle in. The embryo then starts to develop structures which will eventually become the *placenta*.

Some people believe that implantation, rather than fertilisation, is the moment at which a new life has begun.

impulse: see *nerve impulse*.

in vitro fertilisation: a method of treating infertility in which an ovum (egg cell) is surgically removed and fertilised outside the body. In vitro means 'in glass'.

The procedure followed is shown below.

- Between days 1–8 of her *menstrual cycle*, the woman is given *fertility drugs* to stimulate the ripening of several ova.
- Between days 9–13 the ripening of the ova is monitored using an ultrasound scanner.
- Days 14–15, the ova are removed surgically, mixed with the man's semen and incubated.
- Days 16–17, the dish is checked to see if fertilisation has occurred.
- If fertilisation has occurred, several *embryos* are placed in the *uterus* to implant naturally.
- The woman's condition is monitored for a few days to check that implantation has occurred.

Embryos which implant usually go on to develop normally, although there is a slightly higher risk of an early miscarriage than with normal pregnancies. Multiple pregnancies are quite common with in vitro fertilisation as several embryos may implant successfully.

incineration (of household rubbish): burning household rubbish.
Household rubbish is usually either disposed of by incineration or by *landfill tipping*.
Incineration has several advantages, including:
- land is not used up
- it does not attract pests
- it does not contaminate ground water supplies
- the heat generated can be used in local heating schemes.
Incineration also has some drawbacks, including:
- the plant is costly to build
- it may generate toxic fumes.

indicator: a substance used to show how acidic or alkaline a solution is.
Different indicators change colour at different pHs, for example:
- litmus turns red in solutions below pH 7 and blue above that
- methyl orange turns red in solutions below pH 3, orange above that and yellow above pH 4.5
- phenolphthalein is colourless in solutions below pH 8.3, pink above that value and red above pH 10.4.
Universal indicator is a mixture of indicators which gives a range of colours over almost the whole range of the *pH scale*.

indicator organisms (indicator species): species which indicate by their presence a certain environmental condition or set of conditions.

Examples of indicator species include:
- lichens – different lichens can tolerate different levels of pollution by sulphur dioxide
- blood worms – can survive in water which is heavily polluted by organic material
- some orchids – can only grow in soils which are rich in calcium.

infection: establishing a colony of disease-causing organisms in the body.
A few bacteria or viruses entering the body does not constitute an infection.
They must enter in sufficient numbers to be able to multiply and establish themselves in the body.
The disease-causing microorganisms can enter the body:
- in air-borne droplets
- in contaminated food
- in contaminated water
- through skin contact
- through sexual contact
- through insect bites
- across the placenta
- through blood contact.

An infection usually provokes an *immune response* from the *immune system*.

influenza ('flu): a viral *infection* of the breathing system spread in airborne droplets breathed out by an infected person.
Symptoms of 'flu include:
- chills and fever
- headache
- muscular aches and tiredness
- loss of appetite.

Periodically, a very active form of the virus appears and a 'flu epidemic results. In 1918 Spanish 'flu killed millions across the world. Other serious forms include the Asian 'flu (1957) and Hong Kong 'flu (1968).

infrared radiation: radiation with a wavelength just longer than red light and so invisible to humans.
Infrared rays are sometimes used in the treatment of muscle tears because:
- the infrared rays heat the skin and the tissues below the skin
- the warmth stimulates increased blood flow to the area
- the increased supply of oxygen and nutrients is thought to promote healing.

inheritance: passing on characteristics from one generation to the next through the *genes*.

The study of inheritance is called *genetics*. The basic rules of genetics, which control how characteristics are passed on, were discovered at the end of the 19th century by *Gregor Mendel*.

Some of these basic rules are:

- the characteristics are controlled by inherited structures called *genes*
- many genes can exist in two forms (*alleles*) called dominant and recessive
- all the cells of an individual (except the *gametes* or sex cells) contain two alleles for each characteristic
- if an individual contains both dominant and recessive alleles, the dominant allele will decide the appearance of the individual: the recessive allele is effectively 'switched off'
- the sex cells (gametes) contain only one allele for each characteristic
- all male sex cells have an equal chance of fertilising the female sex cells: it is a random process.

inorganic substances: substances which do not contain carbon combined with hydrogen.

Inorganic substances include:

- all substances which do not contain carbon
- substances like carbon dioxide (CO_2), carbon monoxide (CO), carbonates, such as calcium carbonate ($CaCO_3$) and carbon itself (C) as these contain carbon, but not combined with hydrogen.

insect: a type of *arthropod* with three body sections, compound eyes, one pair of *antennae* and three pairs of legs.

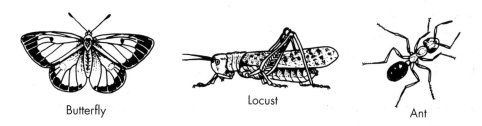

Butterfly

Locust

Ant

Like all arthropods, insects have an *exoskeleton* and jointed legs. Butterflies, flies, bees and mosquitoes are all insects.

There are over 750 000 known species of insects and many biologists believe that there are actually well over one million species. This makes insects the largest and most successful animal group in terms of diversity, numbers of species and actual number of individuals.

Insects have always had an impact on human life, sometimes beneficial and sometimes harmful.

Beneficial insects include:
- bees, wasps, beetles and other insects which are pollinators of crop plants
- bees which provide us with honey and beeswax
- silkworms (insects, not worms) which provide silk.

Harmful insects include:
- flies, lice and fleas which can transmit diseases
- termites which may destroy whole buildings
- insect pests which destroy huge amounts of crops every year.

insecticide: a substance which kills *insects*.

Insects cause billions of pounds worth of damage to crops every year. Because of this, farmers have used insecticides for many years. Insecticides have reduced crop damage considerably and the use of *DDT* to get rid of mosquitoes has eradicated *malaria* in some parts of the world.

There have, however, been problems such as the following with the use of insecticides:
- Insecticides are usually non-specific – they kill beneficial insects, and in some cases birds, as well as the insect pests.
- Some are non-*biodegradable* and can persist in the soil for many years.
- Organochlorine insecticides, such as DDT, are stored in fatty tissue and accumulate along *food chains*, producing harmful and sometimes lethal concentrations in top carnivores.
- Insect pests can become resistant to the insecticide, making it useless.

insemination: introducing semen, containing sperm, into a female's body.

Insemination occurs naturally during sexual intercourse.

Semen can be introduced without intercourse. (See *artificial insemination*.)

insulin: a *hormone* released from *islet cells* in the *pancreas* which reduces the level of glucose in the blood plasma.

If the plasma glucose concentration becomes too high:
- the islet cells detect this and secrete insulin into the blood plasma
- the insulin travels to the liver
- liver cells take up more glucose and convert it to glycogen
- the concentration of glucose in the plasma drops to normal
- the secretion of insulin stops.

(See *diabetes*.)

intercostal muscles: muscles which are found between the ribs and help in *breathing*.

There are two sets of intercostal muscles, internal and external.

- The external intercostal muscles contract and raise the ribs when we breathe in. This helps to create a low pressure in the *thorax* which causes air to enter.
- The internal intercostal muscles contract and lower the ribs when we breathe out. This raises the pressure in the thorax and forces air out.

intestine: the part of the gut between the stomach and the anus.

There are two main regions to the intestine, the small intestine and the large intestine.

The table compares the structure and function of the two regions.

Region	Structure	Function
small intestine	tube, 6 m long, 2.5 cm diameter	most digestion occurs in the lumen of the small intestine
	inner wall has • *villi*	increase surface area for *absorption*
	• secretory cells	secrete digestive enzymes
	outer layers of wall contain muscle	*peristalsis* squeezes food along gut
large intestine	tube, 1.7 m long, 6 cm diameter	secretion of mucus
	smooth inner wall has secretory cells	water is reabsorbed along the large intestine to form semi-solid faeces

The intestines of different animals are *adapted* to their diet.

invertebrate: an animal without a backbone.

Invertebrates make up about 95% of animal species. Invertebrates include:

- *arthropods*
- *annelids*
- *molluscs.*

involuntary muscle: muscle which is not under conscious control.

There are two types of involuntary muscle:

- *cardiac muscle* – found only in the wall of the *heart*
- *smooth muscle* – found in the walls of many hollow organs, like the *stomach*, *intestine*, *blood vessels* and *uterus*.

Cardiac muscle produces rhythmical contractions of the chambers of the heart to pump blood.

Smooth muscle generally produces wave-like contractions which can:

- mix substances – the stomach mixes food with gastric juice secreted by the stomach lining

- move materials – the intestine moves food by *peristalsis*
- move a baby to the exterior when it is born – the contractions of the smooth muscle in the uterus wall push the baby though the vagina.

iodine: a purple-black crystalline solid.

Iodine dissolved in potassium iodide solution (often just called iodine solution) is brown in colour. This solution turns blue/black when it reacts with *starch*, which is the basis of the 'iodine test'.

Iodine is also:

- essential in the diet to make the hormone *thyroxine*
- a *disinfectant*.

ion: a charged particle.

Atoms are neutral – the number of negatively charged electrons is balanced by an equal number of positively charged protons. If an electron is lost or gained, there is an imbalance and the particle formed will have one extra positive or negative charge. It is now an ion.

- If an atom loses electron(s), the ion formed will be positively charged. For example, sodium (Na^+) and calcium (Ca^{2+}).
- If an atom gains electron(s), the ion formed will be negatively charged. For example, chlorine (Cl^-) and oxygen (O^{2-}).
- Groups of atoms can also form ions. For example, ammonium (NH_4^+) and nitrate (NO_3^-).

ionising radiation: any radiation which causes the formation of *ions* as it passes through a substance.

X-rays and gamma rays are examples of ionising radiation.

Ionising radiation is high energy radiation and is potentially very dangerous. It can cause:

- changes in the structure of *DNA (mutation)*
- *cancers* to develop.

X-rays can also be used to treat some cancers, because of their high energy. The X-rays must be carefully targetted so that they kill the cancer cells without causing too much damage to other cells.

iris: the structure which controls the amount of light entering the *eye*.

Too much light entering the eye may damage cells on the retina.

Too little light entering the eye makes it difficult to see anything.

In bright light:

- the circular muscles contract
- the radial muscle relaxes

- the iris enlarges and the pupil becomes smaller
- less of the available light enters the eye.

In dim light:
- the circular muscles relax
- the radial muscles contract
- the iris becomes smaller and the pupil enlarges
- more of the available light enters the eye.

Bright light

Iris

Small pupil

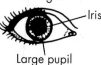

Dim light

Iris

Large pupil

iron: a hard, magnetic metal.

Iron is important in many ways to living things because:
- it is part of the *haemoglobin* molecule
- it is needed to make *chlorophyll* (although not part of the molecule itself)
- it is needed in the process of *aerobic respiration*.

With insufficient iron in our diet we cannot make enough haemoglobin. This condition is called *anaemia* and the person often appears pale and tires easily.

islet cells (islets of Langerhans): clusters of cells in the *pancreas*.
- They are called islets because they are clusters of different cells among the normal pancreas cells (like islands dotted in the sea).
- They can produce and secrete the hormones *insulin* and *glucagon* which help to maintain a contant plasma glucose concentration.
- They secrete directly into the *blood plasma* and so are *endocrine glands*.

J

Jenner, Edward: an English doctor who gave the first effective *vaccination*. At the time Jenner lived (1749–1823), smallpox was a major killer in England. Jenner was a country doctor and noticed that people who caught the mild disease cowpox hardly ever caught smallpox.

In 1796, he carried out a famous 'experiment'. In this he:

- infected a small boy with cowpox
- allowed him to recover for two months
- infected the boy with smallpox.

The boy did not contract smallpox because Jenner's 'vaccination' had made him *immune*, although Jenner knew nothing of how this had happened.

Following Jenner's work, vaccination against smallpox became common in England and deaths from the disease decreased. In 1979 after a massive worldwide vaccination programme, smallpox was officially declared to have been eradicated.

The word 'vaccination' (first used by Jenner) comes from the Latin word 'vacca' – meaning cow.

---

joints: structures at which two or more *bones* are held together.
There are two main kinds of joints:

- fixed, or immovable joints, like the joints between the different bones in the skull
- movable or *synovial joints* such as the hinge joint at the elbow, and the ball and socket joint of the upper arm to the shoulder.

---

joule (J): a measure of heat energy.
4.2 joules will make one gram of water hotter by 1°C.
In many biological contexts, the joule is too small a unit to use and so we use the kilojoule (kJ), which is 1000 joules, or even the megajoule (MJ), which is 1 000 000 joules.
The energy value of foods is often given in kilojoules per 100 g of food.

---

kidneys: paired organs found in the *abdomen* which filter *urea* from the *blood plasma* and regulate the water content of the blood.

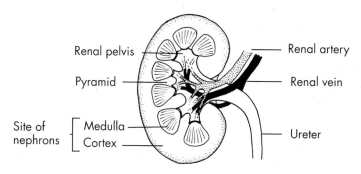

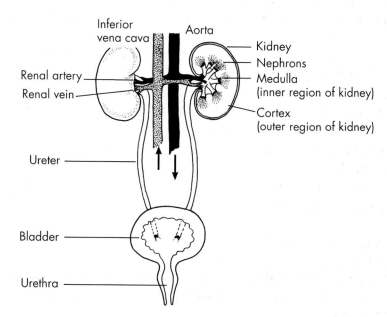

In the kidney are structures called *nephrons*. Each nephron has its own blood supply and is a complete filtration unit in its own right. To remove urea from the blood plasma, the nephron:
- first filters from the blood any molecule small enough to be filtered
- then returns useful molecules to the bloodstream.

kidney transplant: an operation in which the function of a diseased *kidney* is taken over by a kidney from a donor.

The normal procedure is as follows.

- The left kidney is removed from the donor through an incision just below the ribcage.
- The patient is prepared and an incision is made low in the abdomen, over the pelvis.
- The donor kidney is placed in the pelvis.
- The renal artery and vein of the new kidney are joined to an artery and vein in the leg.
- The ureter is stitched into the bladder.
- The kidney begins to work immediately.

Kidney transplants have a high success rate because:

- a national donor scheme means that close tissue matching is possible, which helps to avoid rejection
- the surgery is relatively straightforward
- the patient takes *immunosuppressive* drugs for the rest of his/her life to avoid rejection.

The health of the donor is not affected as the remaining kidney grows to take over full function.

kidney, artificial: the common name for the machine used in treatment of kidney failure by *dialysis*.

kinetic energy: the energy of a body which is due to its motion.

As particles get more kinetic energy they move about more and we call this energy heat. Temperature is a measure of the kinetic energy in the particles of a substance.

Koch, Robert: a German bacteriologist who made several important advances in methods of culturing bacteria.

- Koch was the first to culture bacteria on plates of jelly, rather like the *agar* plates used today.
- He was able to grow pure cultures of bacteria by taking samples from different colonies of bacteria and growing them separately.
- He devised a technique called the 'hanging drop mount' in which he was able to look at bacteria growing in a drop of liquid on an upside-down slide.
- He discovered the life cycle of the bacterium causing anthrax in cattle and, later, isolated the bacterium responsible for tuberculosis.

Many of Koch's techniques are still used today, with very little change.

kwashiorkor: a disease caused by a lack of protein and energy in the diet. Because of the low energy intake, the little protein which is eaten is used mainly as an energy source and not for body building.

At first glance a child with kwashiorkor does not look underfed. This is due to water retention in the tissues (oedema) which makes the child seem plump. The water retention is due to a lack of protein in the blood plasma. Children suffering from kwashiorkor should be fed little and often as the disease has serious effects on the *intestine* and *pancreas*.

lactation: the production and secretion of milk to feed a newborn mammal. In humans, milk is produced in the *breasts,* in tiny sacs called alveoli (not to be confused with alveoli in lungs).

During pregnancy, the higher than usual levels of the hormones *oestrogen* and *progesterone*:

- stimulate development of the alveoli
- prevent the production of milk.

After childbirth, a rapid fall in the level of these hormones stimulates the *pituitary gland* to release other hormones which:

- stimulate the alveoli to secrete milk
- stimulate the alveoli to force the milk into ducts in the breast leading to the nipple.

lacteal: a *lymph* vessel in a *villus* in the small intestine.
Lacteals are found in the centre of each villus and absorb *fats* from the small intestine.
The lymph fluid they contain eventually drains into the blood system in veins near the shoulder, and so fats enter the blood plasma.

lactic acid: the substance formed by animals, some fungi and some bacteria during the *anaerobic respiration* of glucose.
In animals, the build up of lactic acid during exercise in muscles:

- can contribute to *fatigue* of muscle fibres
- causes cramp/stitch
- produces an *oxygen debt.*

After the period of exercise, lactic acid is either converted back to glucose or is oxidised. These processes takes place in the liver and the muscles, and require oxygen.

Bacteria which make lactic acid are used in the manufacture of cheese and yoghurt from milk. The lactic acid sours the milk (makes it acidic) and makes it start to solidify.

Lamarck, Jean Baptiste: a French naturalist who proposed a theory of evolution before *Charles Darwin*.

Lamarck suggested, correctly, that characteristics could be inherited, but extended this to characteristics acquired during a lifetime.

By Lamarck's theory, a person who acquired a talent would be able to pass that talent on to his/her children. Lamarck's famous example is his explanation of how the giraffe got its long neck.

Giraffes originally had short necks. According to Lamarck, they got their long necks because:

- they frequently stretched their necks to reach the leaves on trees and so their necks became longer
- their offspring inherited the extra long necks that the parents had developed
- these giraffes too stretched their necks and they became even longer
- this further increase was inherited by the next generation
- this was repeated over many generations until the giraffes had the very long necks they have today.

Lamarck's theory had little support and was completely rejected in favour of Darwin's theory of *natural selection*.

---

landfill tipping: a method of disposing of household refuse by tipping it and covering it with topsoil.

Traditional landfill sites were a health hazard because:

- rubbish was tipped over an exposed area over a long period
- the area was covered with soil only when the entire site was full of rubbish
- it attracted vermin
- it could affect water supplies if leakage occurred.

Modern landfill sites are often 'cellular' and overcome some of these disadvantages because:

- the rubbish is contained in smaller cells which are sealed as soon as they are full
- the whole site is covered, so there is a double seal.

Modern sites can help with:

- land reclamation
- local energy schemes – methane collected from the sites can be burned to give heat.

---

large intestine: the part of the gut between the *small intestine* and the *anus*.

In the small intestine, *digestion* and *absorption* of food occurs. The unabsorbed materials pass into the large intestine where:

- vitamins and mineral salts are absorbed into the bloodstream

- water released in digestive secretions is reabsorbed
- fibre and other materials, such as dead intestinal cells and dead bacteria remain in the large intestine
- the mixture becomes more and more solid as it passes along the large intestine, forming faeces
- the faeces are stored temporarily in the rectum, before being egested from the anus.

larynx: the organ in the throat responsible for speech, commonly called the voice box.

The larynx is found at the top of the windpipe. It contains folds of tissue called the vocal cords. As air is being breathed out, it passes over the vocal cords and can cause them to vibrate and produce sounds.

The larynx also prevents food from passing into airways when we swallow because:

- the larynx moves up under the floor of the mouth
- a flap of tissue (the epiglottis) closes over it.

leaching: washing soluble materials out of soil.

Heavy rainfall can leach fertilisers out of soil because they are extremely soluble. Sometimes the fertilisers can be carried into nearby lakes, ponds and rivers and can cause environmental problems such as *eutrophication*.

Rain can also leach naturally occurring mineral ions from the soil.

The extent to which leaching takes place depends on:

- the solubility of the ions
- the amount of rainfall
- the type of soil (soils with a high proportion of clay particles leach less than others).

leaf: the plant organ specially adapted for *photosynthesis*.

To photosynthesise efficiently the leaf must:

- absorb light effectively
- allow carbon dioxide to enter
- be supplied with water
- be able to export any surplus glucose manufactured
- allow surplus oxygen to leave.

Stomata allow carbon dioxide to enter the leaf. However, they also allow water vapour to be lost. To minimise this loss, leaves usually have most stomata in the lower epidermis. This reduces the loss of water vapour as it reduces evaporation due to the effect of heat from the sun.

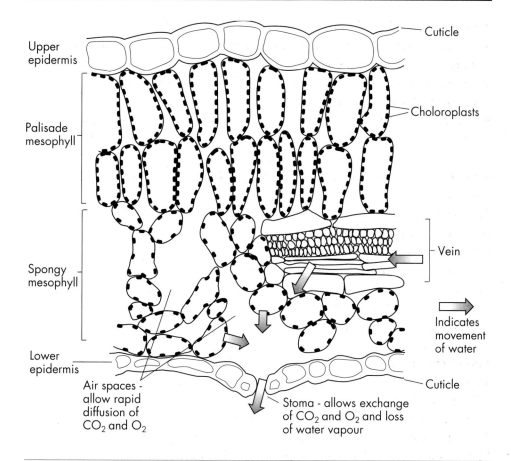

Upper epidermis

Cuticle

Palisade mesophyll

Choloroplasts

Spongy mesophyll

Vein

Lower epidermis

Indicates movement of water

Air spaces - allow rapid diffusion of CO_2 and O_2

Stoma - allows exchange of CO_2 and O_2 and loss of water vapour

Cuticle

leguminous plant (legume): a plant which produces seeds in pods. Peas, beans, soybeans and lentils are all legumes and are important crop plants as:

- they have nodules on their roots which contain *nitrogen fixing bacteria*
- these bacteria can use nitrogen in the air and turn it into ammonia
- the bacteria give the plants ammonia in return for glucose from *photosynthesis*
- the plants use the ammonia to make amino acids and then proteins.

Because of the association with the nitrogen fixing bacteria, legumes:

- can grow in soils containing few nitrates (as the ammonia from the bacteria supplies the nitrogen normally obtained from nitrates)
- make seeds with a high protein content and so they are important sources of protein, especially to vegetarians.

Clover is a legume which is sometimes grown to feed livestock, but also to enrich the nitrate-poor soils. To do this:

- clover is sown in a field
- the plants grow and develop root nodules

- the nitrogen fixing bacteria begin to pass ammonia to the clover, which uses it to make protein
- at the end of the growing season, the clover crop is ploughed into the soil
- soil bacteria decay the clover and release extra nitrates into the soil.

lens: the transparent structure in the eye which focuses rays of light onto the *retina*.

In humans the lens is able to change shape so that rays of light from near or more distant objects can be focused on the retina.

(See *accommodation* and *eye* for details.)

leucocytes: white blood cells.

There are three main types of white blood cells you should know about:

- *phagocytes* – these engulf and then digest invading microorganisms
- B-lymphocytes – these produce antibodies and memory cells to combat microorganisms directly, and antitoxins to neutralise toxins produced by bacteria
- T-lymphocytes – these destroy cells infected with viruses and produce memory cells.

(See also *immune response* and *immune system*.)

LH (luteinising hormone): the *hormone* released by the *pituitary gland* which stimulates *ovulation*.

In females, the pituitary gland secretes LH throughout the *menstrual cycle*, but there is a surge about day 12 caused by increasing levels of oestrogen. The extra LH causes:

- a *follicle* to rupture and release an egg into the Fallopian tubes
- the remains of the follicle to form the *corpus luteum* which secretes *progesterone*.

In males, LH from the pituitary gland causes some cells in the *testes* to release *testosterone*.

ligament: a structure which holds *bones* together at a *joint*.

Ligaments must be able to hold the bones firmly at a joint and limit movement to only what the structure of the joint permits.

To do this they must be:

- strong
- inelastic.

Ligaments are made largely from the protein collagen.

light: a kind of electromagnetic radiation visible to humans.
Different wavelengths of light correspond to different colours.
Red light has the longest wavelength of visible light and blue light the shortest wavelength.
We are able to distinguish between different colours because of different *cones* in the *retina* being sensitive to different wavelengths.

limewater (Ca(OH)$_2$ aq): a solution of calcium hydroxide which turns cloudy when carbon dioxide is bubbled through it.
Limewater is often used to show that respiring organisms are giving off carbon dioxide.

limiting factor: the factor which is controlling the *rate of reaction*.
If a reaction is affected by several factors, then the limiting factor will be the one which is in short supply.
Photosynthesis is affected by light intensity, carbon dioxide concentration, and temperature. On a bright day in the middle of winter, temperature is most likely to be the limiting factor.
In the late evening in midsummer, light will most likely be limiting the rate of photosynthesis.

lipase: an *enzyme* which digests *lipids* (*fats* and *oils*).
In humans, fats and oils are:
- emulsified by bile salts released in the bile from the gall bladder (this gives a much larger surface area for lipase to act on)
- digested by a lipase secreted by the *pancreas*
- digested into *fatty acids* and *glycerol*.
The fatty acids and glycerol are absorbed into *lacteals* in the *villi*.

lipids: a group of chemicals which includes *fats* and *oils*.
All lipids are very similar, chemically. They are made from *fatty acids* joined to a *glycerol* molecule.
Fats are solid at room temperature whilst oils are liquid.
Lipids are an essential component of our diet. We need them to:
- build cell membranes
- form an insulating layer beneath our skin
- supply energy during vigorous exercise
- supply lipid-soluble vitamins like vitamins A and D.

Some lipids in the diet can increase the level of *cholesterol* in the blood plasma. Others do not do this and may even reduce the levels of cholesterol. Healthy lipids are found in:

- fish liver oils
- nuts and pulses
- vegetable oils.

Lister, Joseph: a British surgeon who pioneered antiseptic techniques during operations.

Lister was working in Glasgow in 1865 when:

- he read Louis Pasteur's work on 'the germ theory of disease'
- he thought that germs in the air could infect wounds during surgery
- he devised methods of eliminating contamination
- he started to use carbolic acid (phenol) as an *antiseptic.*

Deaths from infected wounds fell sharply in the patients under his care and, soon, his antiseptic procedures were followed by surgeons in hospitals everywhere.

liver: the largest internal organ in the human body.

The liver is found just underneath the *diaphragm* on the right-hand side of the body, but extending over to the left.

The liver is a very important organ with many functions including:

- producing *bile*
- taking up excess *glucose* from the blood plasma and storing it as *glycogen* (and breaking down the glycogen to glucose when plasma glucose levels are low)
- producing blood plasma proteins
- converting excess amino acids into *urea*
- destroying toxins in the body
- storing iron and some vitamins
- helping to maintain a constant body temperature: the liver is a very active organ and so produces a lot of heat.

lock and key hypothesis: a hypothesis which attempts to explain how *enzymes* work.

Enzymes are biological *catalysts*: they speed up biological reactions by lowering the *activation energy* needed to make the reaction take place.

One model which tries to explain how this is possible is the lock and key hypothesis. In this model:

- the *active site* of the enzyme and the reacting molecules have shapes which complement each other

- the reacting molecules fit into the active site of the enzyme
- this brings the molecules into very close contact with each other
- only a very small amount of extra energy is needed to make the reacting molecules finally 'collide' and react.

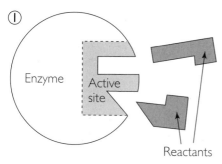

①

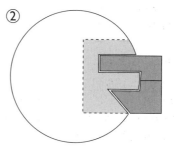

②

Shapes of active site and reactants are complimentary - like a lock and key

Reactants brought very close together on the active site

③

Product formed then detaches to leave the active site free

---

lungs: paired organs in the *thorax* of mammals and other vertebrates which enables them to breathe air.

The diagram on page 170 shows the structure of human lungs.

Each lung contains:

- a system of branching tubes called *bronchioles*
- millions of *alveoli* at the end of the finest bronchioles
- a large number of *capillaries* around each alveolus
- a moist, double membrane over its surface to allow it to slide over the ribs during breathing.

The large numbers of alveoli and capillaries:

- give a large gas exchange surface
- make the lungs very efficient at obtaining oxygen and eliminating carbon dioxide.

The linings of the bronchioles contain:

- cells which secrete mucus to trap dust and *bacteria*

● cells with cilia to 'waft' the mucus/bacteria towards the *larynx*.
These two features help to reduce lung *infections*, but the lungs have no
defence against tobacco smoke and toxic fumes inhaled in some workplaces.

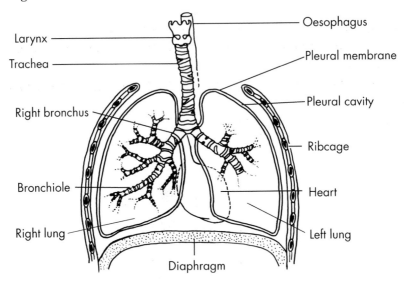

lymph: a clear watery liquid found in vessels called *lymphatics*.
Lymph has two main functions:
● it helps to maintain the fluid balance of the blood
● it has an *immune* function.

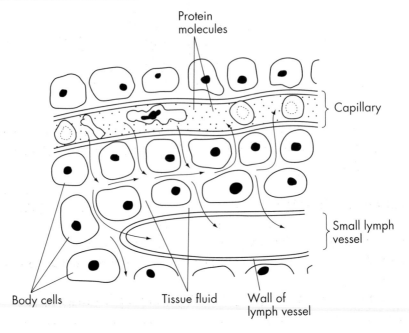

Lymph is formed from blood as it flows through *capillaries*. Lymph is formed because:

- blood enters the capillaries under high pressure (due to the force from the heart)
- capillary walls are only one cell thick and are 'leaky'
- some water and small molecules in the blood plasma are forced out of the capillary as *tissue fluid*
- the tissue fluid passes around nearby cells delivering nutrients and collecting waste materials
- some of the tissue fluid passes back into the blood
- the rest of the tissue fluid drains into lymphatics.

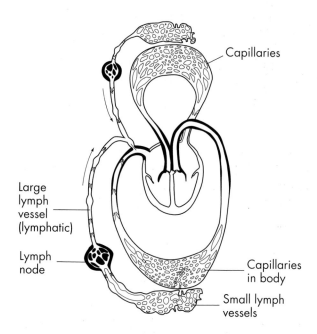

Lymph travels through the body in lymphatics and is eventually returned to the blood. As it travels through the lymphatics it passes through structures called *lymph nodes*.

lymph node (gland): a bundle of tissue along the course of a *lymphatic*. Lymph nodes have an immune function; they:

- add lymphocytes to the lymph and so, eventually, to the blood
- filter bacteria and harmful particles (e.g. tiny particles of soot) from the lymph
- contain phagocytes which engulf and destroy the filtered particles.

lymphocytes: white blood cells which are responsible for the *immune response*.

There are two main types of lymphocytes:

- B-lymphocytes – these produce *antibodies* and *memory cells* to combat microorganisms directly, and *antitoxins* to neutralise toxins produced by *bacteria*.
- T-lymphocytes – these destroy cells infected with *viruses* and produce memory cells.

magnesium: a mineral ion needed by plants and animals.

In animals, magnesium is needed to:
- build strong bones and teeth
- activate many enzymes
- conduct nerve impulses.

In plants, magnesium is needed to:
- build molecules of chlorophyll
- activate many enzymes.

---

malaria: a serious, often fatal disease of the blood.

Malaria is one of the world's biggest killer diseases. It is caused by a proto-zoan called *Plasmodium* which is spread by the bite of the female *Anopheles* mosquito.

When an infected female mosquito feeds from a human, the following occurs.
- She pierces the skin and injects saliva (to prevent the blood from clotting as she feeds).
- *Plasmodium* enters with the saliva.
- *Plasmodium* enters liver cells, changes form and multiplies.
- The new form is released from the liver cells and enters red blood cells.
- It multiplies in the red blood cells, causing them to burst and release more of the parasites into the blood.
- These then infect other red blood cells and the cycle continues.
- Some of the parasites form sex cells inside red blood cells.
- These can then be transferred to another female mosquito when she feeds.
- Fertilisation takes place in the mosquito and the cycle of infection can begin again.

The most characteristic symptom of malaria is the fever it produces: this can make body temperatures rise to 40.5°C. The fever is caused by the red blood cells bursting and develops in three stages:
- a cold stage with uncontrollable shivering
- a hot stage in which body temperature rises as high as 40.5°C
- a sweating stage in which profuse sweating reduces the temperature again.

A number of anti-malarial drugs (such as chloroquine) are used to treat malaria, but resistance to the drug is an increasing problem. Scientists are still researching into producing an effective *vaccine*, which could, if used on a worldwide scale, eradicate the disease.

maltose: a disaccharide sugar made from two *glucose* molecules joined together.
Maltose is not a naturally occurring sugar: it is only formed when starch is digested.
(See *carbohydrates*.)

mammal: a type of *vertebrate* which has hair and mammary glands.

Mammals also have:
- external ears
- a double circulation and a four chambered heart
- a constant, high body temperature.

Mammals reproduce by internal fertilisation and early development usually takes place inside a *uterus*. While in the uterus, they receive nutrients and oxygen across a *placenta*. After birth, the young are fed milk from the mammary glands (see *breasts*).
Monotreme mammals (like the duck-billed platypus) lay eggs and marsupials (like the kangaroo) complete early development in pouches.

mammary glands: see *breasts*.

mass flow: the bulk transport of substances from one place to another in living things.
The term is self-explanatory – substances are flowing 'en masse', or together.
Mass flow systems are essential in larger organisms when it would take too long for a substance to move by *diffusion* from one place to another.
Examples of mass flow systems include:
- the human *breathing system* – this moves air in and out of the lungs far quicker than it could diffuse
- the human *circulatory system* – the blood transports materials around the body faster than would be possible by diffusion

- the *phloem* in plants – this moves sugars around the plant faster than they could diffuse.

measles: a viral disease which usually affects children rather than adults. Measles is caused by the *Morbilli* virus and is spread in airborne droplets breathed out by an infected person.

Symptoms of measles include:
- initially, a fever, runny nose, sore eyes and cough
- after 2 days, red spots with white centres (Koplik's spots) appear on the lining of the mouth
- after 3–4 days a rash appears, on the head first then spreading downwards
- after one week all symptoms start to disappear.

There is an effective *vaccine* against measles which usually has few side effects. The use of this vaccine has greatly reduced the number of cases of measles in England.

meiosis: cell division in which the *chromosome* number is halved.

Sex cells (*gametes*) are formed by meiosis. Because of this:
- they have half the normal number of chromosomes
- they have one chromosome from each pair of chromosomes
- when two sex cells fuse (in *fertilisation*) the *zygote* formed has the normal number again

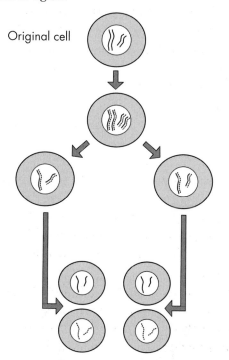

Original cell

Four chromosomes in nucleus; two pairs of chromosomes

Each chromosome duplicates itself; now there are eight chromosomes in the nucleus

Cell divides into two; each new cell with four chromosomes

Cells divide again to form four sex cells, each with only two chromosomes, one of each type present in the original cells

- all the cells of the next generation will have the normal number of chromosomes.

When a human cell divides by meiosis to form sex cells:

- all 46 chromosomes duplicate themselves – there are now 92 chromosomes in the cell
- the cell divides into two cells, then divides again into four cells
- each cell formed now has 23 chromosomes – one from each original pair
- the cells formed do not have exactly the same *alleles* – there is variation in the sex cells.

melanin: the brown pigment which gives skin, hair and the irises of the eyes their colour.
Melanin protects us from the harmful ultraviolet rays present in sunlight.
People with darker skins have more melanin and so are better protected.
Over-exposure to ultraviolet radiation can cause serious burning and, eventually, skin cancer.
Melanin is produced by cells in the skin called melanocytes.
The amount of melanin produced depends on:

- a person's genes – there are about six genes which affect how much melanin is produced
- sunlight – when we sunbathe or are exposed to the sun, the melanocytes produce more melanin.

People who do not produce any melanin are called *albinos*.

melanoma: a raised reddish brown lump which appears on the skin.
There are two types – juvenile melanoma and malignant melanoma.
Juvenile melanoma appears on the face or legs in early childhood and is almost always harmless.
Malignant melanoma is the most serious type of skin cancer. It is:

- a *tumour* which usually develops from an existing mole and then enlarges, may become lumpy and bleed
- most common in middle-aged people with fair skin (little *melanin*) who have been exposed to too much sunlight for many years
- extremely malignant and spreads quickly to other parts of the body.

membrane (1): a thin layer of cells which covers or lines a structure.
Examples include:

- the membranes around the brain and spinal cord (meninges)
- the membrane lining the abdomen (peritoneum).

membrane (2): a layer of lipid and protein molecules surrounding:

- a cell (see *cell membrane*)
- a structure within a cell.

memory cells: cells formed by *lymphocytes* which remain in the blood after an infection.

B- and T-lymphocytes can both form memory cells as part of the *immune response*. These memory cells:

- are formed in response to a specific *antigen* (usually on the surface of an invading microorganism)
- can remain in the blood for many years
- 'recognise' the same antigen if it re-enters the body
- organise a much quicker immune response so that the invader is destroyed before it has time to multiply and cause illness.

Mendel, Gregor: an Austrian monk who discovered the basic laws of *genetics*. Mendel lived in a monastery in Brno in the Czech Republic and became interested in inheritance. He began breeding experiments to find out how characteristics were inherited. His first experiments were with mice, but he was advised to use plants instead and so he began his now famous breeding experiments with pea plants.

As a result of his experiments, Mendel suggested the ideas that form the basis of genetics.

- He suggested something was passed on in the sex cells which determined characteristics in the next generation. Mendel called these 'heritable units'. We call them *genes*.
- He found out that some genes had *dominant* and *recessive* versions (*alleles*).
- He knew that pea plants showing a dominant characteristic could be *homozygous* or *heterozygous* for the gene for that characteristic.
- He showed that crosses between certain genetic types always produced exact ratios of types in the offspring.
- He was able to predict these ratios and then confirm them by experiment.

Mendel published his work in 1865, but it was largely ignored until 1900 when his work was rediscovered and confirmed by other geneticists.

menstrual cycle: the cycle of changes in sexually mature women which begins with the shedding of the lining of the *uterus* approximately once a month.

A menstrual cycle, which is counted from the first day of *menstruation*, lasts between 24 and 35 days. The average cycle lasts 28 days.

The changes which occur in the uterus lining during the cycle are controlled by levels of the *ovarian* hormones *oestrogen* and *progesterone* secreted by the *ovaries*. The levels of these hormones are influenced by *FSH* (follicle stimulating hormone) and *LH* (luteinising hormone) from the *pituitary gland*. The table summarises the main changes occurring during the menstrual cycle.

Changes in:	Days 1–4	Days 5–13	Day 14	Days 15–22	Days 23–28
uterus lining	menstruation: lining breaks down and is lost through vagina	new uterus lining starts to build and thicken	continues thickening, starts to become vascular (blood-filled)	continues to become more vascular	lining starts to show signs of breakdown due to low levels of progesterone
ovary	follicle starts to develop and secrete oestrogen	follicle continues to develop and secrete oestrogen	ovulation (egg cell released from follicle)	remains of follicle becomes corpus luteum, which secretes progesterone	corpus luteum shrinks and stops secreting progesterone
FSH	pituitary gland secretes FSH due to low level of oestrogen in blood	pituitary gland secretes less FSH due to inhibition by oestrogen	secretion of FSH rises quickly again and peaks	secretion inhibited by oestrogen and progesterone	secretion remains at a low level
LH	level of LH in blood is low	pituitary gland secretes more LH	secretion of LH peaks	level falls due to inhibition by oestrogen and progesterone	level remains low
oestrogen	level in blood is low	level increases and peaks on day 12–13	level falling	level low and falling	level rises slightly then falls again
progesterone	level low	level low	level low	level rising as corpus luteum starts to secrete progesterone	level falling as corpus luteum is regressing (shrinking)

menstruation: the loss of the uterus lining and blood during the first few days of the *menstrual cycle*.

Menstruation begins at *puberty* and continues until the menopause when a woman stops ovulating.

It does not occur when a woman is pregnant.

Menstruation can last for up to 8 days, but the average is about 5.

The amount of blood lost also varies from woman to woman, but averages about 60 cm^3.

The regular loss of the uterus lining in menstruation and its replacement following menstruation increases the likelihood of *implantation*. It ensures that the lining of the uterus is always in the correct condition every month at the time when an embryo might be ready to implant.

messenger RNA (m-RNA): the *RNA* which carries the code for a protein from the *DNA* in the nucleus to the *ribosomes* in the cytoplasm.

Like all RNA molecules:

- it is smaller than DNA
- it is single stranded
- the base thymine is not used: it is replaced by uracil.

(See *protein synthesis* for further details.)

metabolic rate: the rate at which an organism uses energy.

Energy is needed to drive all the complex chemical reactions which together make up an organism's *metabolism*.

Metabolic rate can be estimated by measuring the amount of oxygen used up over a period of time.

The amount of surface influences metabolic rate, since heat is lost through the skin. Because of this, metabolic rate is expressed in kilojoules per square metre of body surface per hour.

metabolism: all the chemical changes going on in the cells of an organism. (See *metabolic rate*.)

metacarpal: a bone in the hand.

The metacarpal bones are cylindrical and lie between the carpals (in the wrist) and the *phalanges* (in the fingers).

The heads of the metacarpals are the knuckles.

metatarsal: a bone in the foot.

The metatarsal bones are cylindrical and lie between the tarsals (in the ankle) and the phalanges (in the toes).

They are held in an arch shape by surrounding *ligaments*.

metamorphosis: a change in body form which corresponds with a new stage in the individual's life cycle.

There are two types — incomplete metamorphosis and complete metamorphosis.

INCOMPLETE METAMORPHOSIS

In incomplete metamorphosis, gradual changes transform the larva into the adult. This is shown by insects like the locust in which the larva has the same basic form as the adult but lacks wings. These gradually develop through several stages.

COMPLETE METAMORPHOSIS

In complete metamorphosis, the larva is completely different to the adult and a complete restructuring of the body occurs. This is typical of flies, butterflies and moths. The larva develops from an egg, feeds voraciously and grows quickly. To change into the adult, however, it must form a pupa. During this stage, the body completely restructures and the adult form emerges.

micropropagation: producing large numbers of genetically identical plants from a single parent plant by *tissue culture*.

You can walk into garden centres and see rows and rows of potted plants which look almost identical. These plants have been produced by micropropagation. In this technique:

- A 'stock plant' with desirable features is chosen and the tips of stems or side shoots are removed from it – these are called explants
- these explants are cut to size (about 0.5–1 mm) and disinfected
- the explants are then placed on an agar which contains nutrients and plant hormones to encourage shoot formation
- as new shoots form on the explants, more explants are taken from them and the whole process repeated several times
- the explants with shoots are transferred to a different agar medium to induce root formation
- when they have grown roots, they are removed to greenhouses, transplanted to soil and gradually acclimatised to normal growing conditions.

Micropropagation has several advantages.

- The plants produced are genetically identical because they have all been formed from one stock plant by *mitosis* and growth. No new genes have been introduced.
- The plants can be produced at any time of the year because the process is carried out in controlled conditions.
- The new plants produced are disease-free.

It is, however, expensive to set up and is very labour-intensive, which keeps costs high.

microorganisms: organisms whose structure can only be seen through a microscope.

Most microorganisms are unicellular and include *bacteria*, *protozoa*, some *fungi* and some *algae*.

Viruses are sometimes referred to as microorganisms but, strictly, are not organisms at all (micro or otherwise).

When we think of microorganisms, we usually think first of those which cause disease. Yet most microorganisms are not pathogenic and many are helpful. Without microorganisms, there would be no decay and recycling of nutrients, cows could not digest grass in their stomachs and we would not have the delights of beer and wine!

microvilli (singular microvillus): microscopic projections on the surface of some cells.

Microvilli are found on the surface of cells specialised for absorbing materials. The cells on the surface of the *villi* in the small intestine have microvilli.

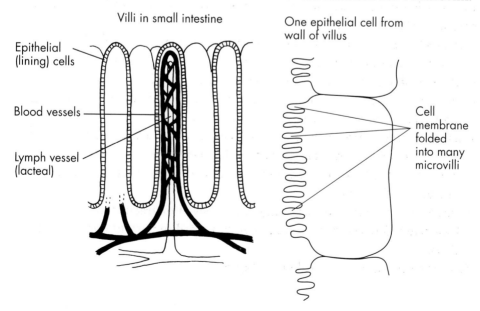

Villi in small intestine

Epithelial (lining) cells

Blood vessels

Lymph vessel (lacteal)

One epithelial cell from wall of villus

Cell membrane folded into many microvilli

The microvilli increase the surface area of each cell and make *absorption* more efficient.

microscope: an instrument for producing enlarged images of small objects. Biologists use two types – light microscopes and electron microscopes.

LIGHT MICROSCOPES:

- use a beam of light shone through an object which is mounted on a slide
- the light which passes through the object is used to produce an image of the object
- the image you see has been magnified twice: first by the objective lens (the lens nearest the object), then this magnified image is further magnified by the eyepiece (the lens you look through)
- the overall magnification is the product of the magnification of each lens.

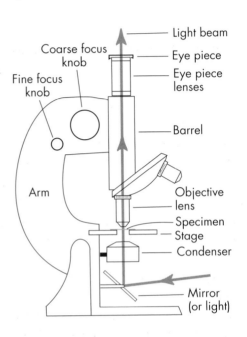

ELECTRON MICROSCOPES:

- use a beam of electrons instead of a beam of light
- are capable of much higher magnifications
- can show much finer detail than light microscopes
- have allowed us to understand the structure of cells and the *organelles* they contain.

mildews: a group of *fungi* which are *parasites* of plants.
Plants parasitised by mildews include roses, cereals, grasses, apples and hops.
When a spore from a mildew fungus lands on an appropriate host plant:
- it develops hyphae
- the hyphae secrete an enzyme which digests the cuticle
- the hyphae produce special branches (haustoria) which grow through the cuticle
- these branches have two functions: they anchor the hyphae to the plant and absorb food from the plant

- using the food from the plant, an extensive *mycelium* develops over the surface of the plant
- spore cases are formed and spores released
- the spores can infect other plants: this occurs mainly in the summer.

Infected plants often die prematurely and mildews are responsible for considerable crop damage.

---

minerals: biologists use this term to describe inorganic nutrients such as *calcium, magnesium, iron* and *nitrogen* required by cells.

Animals obtain minerals from the foods they eat. Milk, cheese, green vegetables and bread are usually good sources of calcium for humans. Iron is found in red meat (especially liver), green vegetables and bread.

Plants obtain minerals from the soil.

Minerals are absorbed by plants and animals as *mineral ions*.

---

mineral ions: *ions* of *minerals* in solution.

When organic materials decay the mineral elements in them are converted into ions by the action of a range of bacteria and fungi.

- The *nitrogen* in proteins is converted to nitrate ions (NO_3^-).
- Magnesium from bones and chlorophyll molecules is released as magnesium ions (Mg^{2+}).

These ions dissolve in the water in the soil.

Plants are able to absorb these mineral ions and re-use them to make new *organic substances*.

- Nitrates are used to make amino acids (then proteins), chlorophyll and DNA.
- Magnesium ions are used to make chlorophyll.

---

mineral salts: compounds which contain *minerals* needed by cells.

Fertilisers contain mineral salts. When these compounds enter the soil, they dissolve in the water in the soil and form *mineral ions*.

Potassium nitrate (KNO_3) contains both potassium and nitrogen (in the nitrate). When it dissolves, it will form potassium (K^+) and nitrate (NO_3^-) ions. Ammonium nitrate (NH_4NO_3) contains nitrogen in the ammonium and the nitrate. When it dissolves, it will form ammonium (NH_4^+) and nitrate (NO_3^-) ions.

Plants can then absorb the ions and use them to make *organic substances*. (See *mineral ions* for details.)

---

mitochondrion (plural mitochondria): a cell *organelle* where many of the reactions of *aerobic respiration* take place.

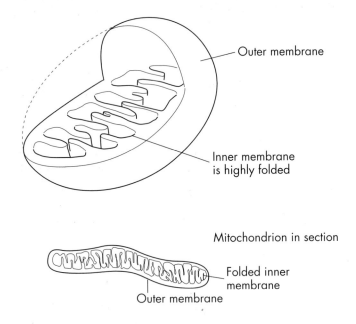

Mitochondrion in section

- Mitochondria are usually long, sausage-shaped structures.
- They have two membranes surrounding them.
- The inner membrane has many folds.
- They are numerous in active cells such as muscles, nerve cells and cells which are for *absorption*. All these cells need a lot of energy for their functions. Many mitochondria can supply this energy.

mitosis: a type of *cell division* in which the cells formed have the same number and type of *chromosomes* as the cell which divided to form them. (See the diagram on page 135.)

All cells except sex cells (*gametes*) are formed by mitosis. Because of this:
- they all have the same number and type of chromosomes
- they all have the same *alleles*.

When a human cell divides by mitosis:
- the chromosomes duplicate themselves (there are now 92 chromosomes instead of 46)
- the cell divides into two, each with 46 chromosomes
- each new cell receives either the original or the copy of each of the original 46 chromosomes
- two new, genetically identical cells are formed.

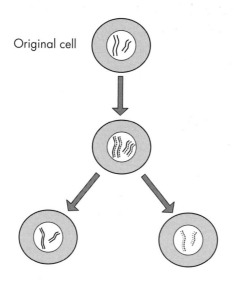

Original cell — Four chromosomes in nucleus; two pairs of chromosomes

Each chromosome duplicates itself; now there are eight chromosomes in the nucleus

Cell divides to form two daughter cells; each daughter cell has exactly the same chromosomes as the original cell

molecule: the smallest particle of a substance which can exist in a free state. A molecule is made from two or more atoms bonded together, forming a larger particle.

Some elements exist as molecules.

- Oxygen exists as O_2 – two oxygen atoms bonded to form a molecule.
- Chlorine exists as Cl_2 – two chlorine atoms bonded to form a molecule.

Some compounds exist as molecules. Most biological compounds are molecular, although some are ionic.

- Glucose exists as $C_6H_{12}O_6$ – each particle of glucose contains six carbon atoms, twelve hydrogen atoms and six oxygen atoms bonded together to form a molecule.
- Ethanol (alcohol) exists as C_2H_5OH – each particle of ethanol contains two carbon atoms, six hydrogen atoms and one oxygen atom bonded together to form a molecule.

molluscs: *invertebrates* with a soft, non-segmented body, 'foot' and a shell. Molluscs are second only to *insects* in diversity and number of *species*. 50 000 living species and 35 000 fossil species are known.

The diagrams on the following page show some of the many forms of molluscs.

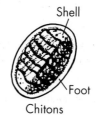

Shell

Foot

Chitons

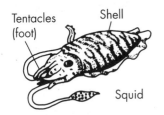
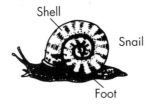
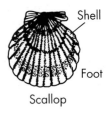

monoclonal antibodies: *antibodies* produced by one specific type of cell against one *antigen*.

In our bodies, antibodies are produced by B-*lymphocytes* as part of our *immune response* to *infection*. Individual antibodies can be used to test for and isolate the protein or antigen which stimulated their production.

One major problem to manufacturing specific antibodies outside the body is that the B-lymphocytes which make the antibodies do not grow well in *tissue culture*. To overcome this biologists have developed a special process.

- They inject a small mammal with the antigen which they wish to be able to screen for.
- The mammal produces B-lymphocytes which make antibodies against this antigen.
- These B-lymphocytes are obtained from the mammal (other types of B-lymphocytes are screened out).
- These are then fused with other cells which do grow well in tissue culture (the fused cells are called hybridomas).
- The hybridomas multiply and produce just one type of antibody – a mono-clonal antibody – in bulk.

Because of the special nature of the hybridomas, they can multiply for long periods of time before a new culture needs to be established.

Monoclonal antibodies bind to just one protein or antigen and can therefore be very useful in diagnosing whether that antigen/protein is present in a sample.

Monoclonal antibodies are used in:
- detecting some cancers – the cancer cell antigens are used to produce monoclonal antibodies which can then be used to see if other samples contain the same antigen
- detecting some viruses – this works in the same way as detecting cancer cells
- pregnancy testing – the monoclonal antibodies in pregnancy testing kits will only bind with a hormone produced by a human embryo, so a positive result means pregnancy
- delivering toxins to kill only one type of cell – the toxin is attached to the

monoclonal antibody which will only bind to certain infected cells, so only these receive the toxin.

motor neurone: a nerve cell (*neurone*) which carries *nerve impulses* away from the *central nervous system*. The impulses carried by motor nerve cells bring about a response in an *effector*. This response is usually either the contraction of a *muscle* or secretion of a substance by a *gland*

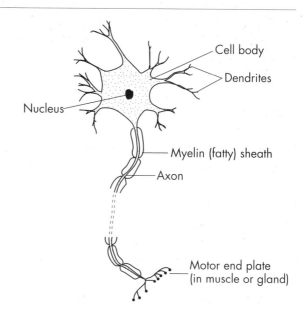

moulds: *fungi* which have a *mycelium* and grow on dead material.
Moulds often look like a piece of velvet or a mass of cotton wool. This appearance is due to the mycelium made from thousands of *hyphae*. Moulds often grow on dead material and start off the process of recycling by decaying the material.
Moulds feed by extra-cellular digestion. To do this they:
● secrete *digestive enzymes* from the tips of their hyphae onto the material
● the enzymes digest large, insoluble molecules, such as starch, into small soluble ones, like glucose
● the soluble molecules diffuse into the hyphae and are used for *growth* or *respiration* in the mould.
Organisms which feed on dead material in this way are called *saprobionts* (saprophytes).
Moulds are very common and easily grown. The white mould which grows on damp bread is called *Mucor*. The blue/green mould growing on citrus fruits is a kind of *Penicillium* (some species of this mould produce *penicillin*).

mucus: a sticky mixture of water, protein and a carbohydrate.
Mucus is secreted in several places in humans. These are summarised in the table.

Mucus secreted by	Name of secretion containing mucus	Function of mucus in secretion
salivary glands	saliva	lubricates food as it passes down oesophagus
stomach glands	gastric juice	protects stomach lining from attack by hydrochloric acid
small intestine glands	intestinal juice	lubricates passage of food along intestine
pancreas	pancreatic juice	lubricates passage of food along intestine
cells in bronchioles in lungs		traps dust and bacteria entering lungs to be 'wafted' out by cilia

muscle (1): *tissue* which is specialised for contraction.

There are three types of muscle tissue in our bodies:

- *skeletal muscle* – the type of muscle which moves bones when it contracts
- *smooth muscle* – the type of muscle found in the walls of the intestine, uterus, blood vessels and also in the iris
- *cardiac muscle* – found only in the heart.

Skeletal muscle is also called voluntary muscle as it is under conscious control. Cardiac and smooth muscle are not under conscious control and are types of involuntary muscle.

The table compares the three types of muscle tissue.

Property of muscle	Skeletal muscle	Smooth muscle	Cardiac muscle
location	in skeletal system, at *joints*	in walls of intestine, uterus and blood vessels	in wall of heart only
type of control	voluntary	involuntary	involuntary
speed of *contraction*	fastest	slowest	intermediate
style of contraction	strong, rapid twitch	prolonged contraction	wave-like contractions
suffering *fatigue*	can become fatigued	does not fatigue	does not fatigue

muscle (2): an organ mainly made of muscle tissue which contracts to produce movement.

The biceps and triceps are muscles attached to the skeleton which bend and straighten the arm at the elbow. They are organs because they contain several tissues each contributing to the overall function of the muscle contraction to produce movement.

The table shows the tissues which are found in the biceps:

Tissue in biceps	Contribution of tissue to overall function of muscle (contraction)
muscle	generates the force for the *contractions* of the whole muscle
blood	brings oxygen and glucose for *respiration* to supply the necessary energy
nerve	*nerve impulse* stimulates the muscle to contract

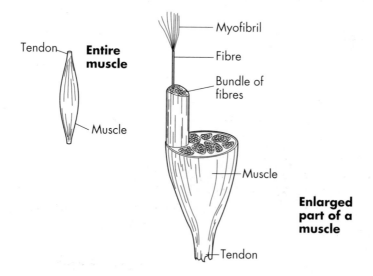

mutagen: anything which can produce a *mutation*.
Mutations are potentially harmful since the *DNA* of a cell is altered.
Mutations can be caused by over-exposure to any high-energy radiation (X-rays, gamma rays, ultraviolet rays) and some chemicals, such as mustard gas, many of the chemicals in cigarette smoke and some of the chemicals used in the rubber industry.

mutant (1): a *gene* which has undergone *mutation*.
The altered gene will be a new *allele* of the gene. It will have some effect on the same *characteristic*, but the effect of the mutant will be different to that of the original form.

mutant (2): an organism which carries a mutant *gene*, usually with an observable effect.

mutation: a change in the *DNA* of a cell.

A change in the DNA will alter a gene. It will produce a new form, or *allele*, of that gene.

Mutations are happening all the time: all of us contain some mutant alleles. Most of these mutations are harmless, but a few may be harmful and kill the cell in which the mutation occurs. Some mutations may cause a cell to become cancerous (see *cancer*).

Most mutations occur in ordinary body cells and can only affect the individual in which they occur. If the mutation were to occur in a sex cell (*gamete*), or one of the cells which form the sex cells, then the mutation could be inherited.

mycelium: the mass of threads which makes up the main body of a *fungus*. The mycelium is the main feeding part of the fungus. It is made of threads called *hyphae* which secrete *enzymes* from their tips to digest food material outside the body of the fungus.

mycoprotein: a high protein food product made from a *fungus*.

The fungus used in the process is called *Fusarium*. It is grown in a *fermenter* using waste materials from flour making.

Under the ideal conditions provided in the fermenter, the fungus produces extra *hyphae* rapidly. Because the mycoprotein is made from filaments (the hyphae), it has a texture similar to meat. It can be flavoured to taste like beef or chicken and used as a substitute for either of these meats.

Compared to beef and chicken, mycoprotein contains:
- less protein (but still about 60% of the protein content of these meats)
- a lot less *fat* than beef and chicken
- a reasonable amount of *fibre* (there is none in beef and chicken).

myotomes: blocks of muscle found either side of the backbone of a fish. The myotomes on opposite sides of the backbone function as antagonistic muscles. They move the tail in opposite directions.

The side-to-side movement of the tail displaces water and provides propulsion.

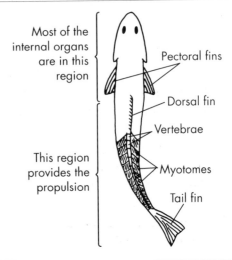

Most of the internal organs are in this region

Pectoral fins

Dorsal fin

Vertebrae

This region provides the propulsion

Myotomes

Tail fin

natural selection: the process by which new *species* evolve (see *evolution*). The Theory of Natural Selection was put forward in 1858 by Charles Darwin. He had gathered evidence from his observations when working as ship's naturalist on HMS Beagle. Much of his important work was done on the Galapagos islands. He also received information confirming his ideas from another naturalist, Alfred Wallace.

Darwin's theory was based on two main observations:
- all living things tend to over-reproduce
- all living thing vary.

From this he made three important deductions:
- there will be a 'struggle for existence' (because they over-reproduce, resources will be limited)
- some will be better adapted to their environment than others (because they vary)
- those best adapted will survive and reproduce in greater numbers than those less well adapted.

The last point, Darwin called the 'survival of the fittest'.

We can modify Darwin's last point with our knowledge of *genetics*.

Those best adapted will survive to reproduce in greater numbers than those less well adapted. They will pass on their advantageous *alleles* to the next generation. Over time, these alleles will increase in frequency in the species.

Resistance to *penicillin* in bacteria gives an example of natural selection in action.
- Originally, none of the bacteria were resistant and penicillin was not used.
- Doctors began to use penicillin, which killed the bacteria.
- A chance *mutation* gave some bacteria resistance to the antibiotic.
- These bacteria were better adapted to an environment in which penicillin was used.
- They survived in greater numbers and passed on the 'resistance allele'.
- This was repeated with each generation of bacteria.
- The proportion of bacteria with the resistance allele increased until most had the allele.

The original penicillin is now useless against these bacteria and new antibiotics must be used.

negative feedback: a homeostatic mechanism in which a change in some condition from its normal 'set' value triggers a response which restores the set value. (See *homeostasis*.)

Examples of negative feedback systems include the regulation of body temperature and the regulation of blood plasma glucose concentration.

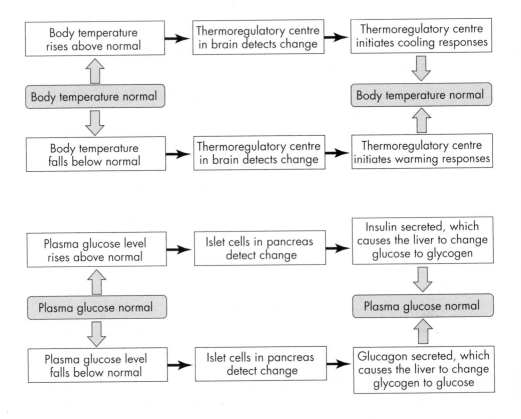

nephrons: the microscopic tubular structures in the *kidney* which remove *urea* from the *blood plasma*.

- Blood enters the capillaries in the Bowman's capsule under high pressure.
- *Ultrafiltration* forces out of the blood any molecules small enough to pass through the membrane which separates the capillaries and the space inside the Bowman's capsule. This filtrate includes the waste urea as well as water, glucose, amino acids and mineral ions. Only the plasma protein molecules are not small enough to be forced out.
- The filtrate flows along the rest of the nephron.
- In the first and second convolutions, glucose, mineral ions and other useful substances are reabsorbed into the blood plasma by *active transport*. Water is also reabsorbed.

- In the collecting duct, the amount of water which passes out of the kidney with the urine is varied. If the hormone *ADH* is released, more water is reabsorbed into the blood and less is lost. If ADH is not produced, all the water entering the collecting ducts is lost in the urine.

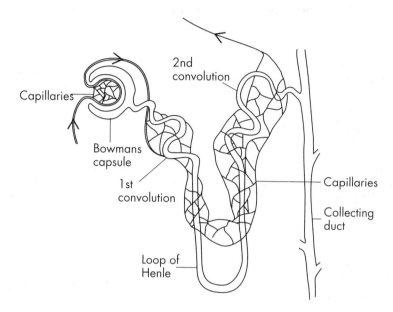

As the filtrate passes along the nephron, the concentration of the urea increases. This is because water is being reabsorbed from the filtrate.

nerve: a bundle of *neurones* (nerve cells) surrounded by other tissue and which connects to the *brain* or *spinal cord*.
Most nerves contain both *sensory neurones* and *motor neurones* and so can carry *nerve impulses* into and out of the *central nervous system*. The individual neurones which make up a nerve are surrounded by a layer of fibrous tissue.
They usually carry impulses to and from a certain organ or area of the body. The *optic nerve* carries impulses from the eye to the brain. The facial nerve carries impulses to and from the face.

nerve cell: see *neurone*.

nerve impulse: an electrical change in the membrane of a *neurone* which sweeps along the axon of the cell.
It is important to realise that a nerve impulse is not like an electric current. Nothing physically moves along a neurone like electrons flow through a wire. So how can anything pass along if nothing moves? A useful analogy is a

Mexican wave passing around a stadium. Nobody actually moves around the stadium, people just make the wave in turn and the wave gets passed along. When one end of a neurone is stimulated:

- the membrane of the axon changes electrically
- this makes the next portion of membrane change (and the original part restores itself to normal)
- then the next portion changes ... and the next ... and the next, all the way along the axon.

Nothing has moved along the axon: portions of the membrane have changed in turn and it is this electrical change being passed along which is the nerve impulse.

When the impulse reaches the end of the axon, it cannot cross the *synapse* (small gap between two nerve cells). It causes the axon to secrete a *neurotransmitter* which diffuses to the next neurone and starts an impulse in that axon.

nervous system: a system of interconnecting *neurones* (nerve cells) which coordinates the activities of an animal.

Nearly all multicellular animals have a nervous system.

In *vertebrates*, it is made up of two main parts:

- the *central nervous system* (the *brain* and *spinal cord*)
- the peripheral nervous system (the neurones in *nerves* which carry *nerve impulses* to and from the central nervous system).

neurone: a cell found in the *nervous system* specialised for transmitting *nerve impulses*.

All neurones have a number of adaptations which suit them to their function.

- They have at least one *axon*, or fibre, which transmits the impulse. Axons are usually long so that the impulse can be carried considerable distances.
- The axons are surrounded by a fatty sheath which allows the nerve impulse to be transmitted quickly.
- They have many dendrites at the ends of the axon which communicate with other neurones by forming *synapses* with their dendrites.

There are two main types of neurones:

- *sensory neurones* which carry impulses into the spinal cord or brain
- *motor neurones* which carry impulses out of the spinal cord or brain.

neurotransmitter: a substance which passes from one *neurone* to another across a *synapse*.

When a *nerve impulse* reaches the end part of the *axon*:

- the end of the axon secretes a neurotransmitter
- the neurotransmitter diffuses across the synapse to the axon of the next neurone
- the axon absorbs the neurotransmitter
- the neurotransmitter initiates a new nerve impulse.

Different neurotransmitters are found in different parts of the *nervous system.*

neutralisation: the reaction between an acid and a base (or alkali) to produce a salt (neutral substance) and water.

nitrate: an ion (NO_3^-) containing nitrogen and oxygen.
Nitrates are formed in the *soil* when *nitrifying bacteria* oxidise ammonia. Plants can absorb nitrates and use them to synthesise *amino acids* and, from them, proteins.

nitric acid: a strong acid with the formula HNO_3, formed when nitrogen dioxide (NO_2) dissolves in water.
It is an extremely important acid and is used in the manufacture of fertilisers which contain nitrates.
Nitric acid is one of the components of *acid rain*. Oxides of nitrogen (gases) from car exhausts dissolve in water in the air to form the acid, which falls with rain.

nitrifying bacteria: bacteria in the soil which convert ammonium to *nitrate*. Nitrifying bacteria are not generous benefactors – they do not produce the nitrates just so that plants can absorb them. The bacteria obtain energy from oxidising the ammonium, just as we obtain energy from oxidising glucose during respiration. The energy is used to drive their *metabolism*.

nitrogen: an element essential to all organisms; it is found in all *amino acids, proteins* and *DNA*.
(See *nitrogen cycle*.)

nitrogen fixing bacteria: bacteria which can absorb nitrogen gas and convert it into ammonia.
There are two main types of nitrogen fixing bacteria:
- those that live free in the soil
- those that live in nodules on the roots of *leguminous plants* like peas, beans and clover.

Both types use energy from *respiration* to convert nitrogen gas into ammonia. Those which live in the root nodules receive glucose for respiration from the plant root cells. They release some of the ammonia they make to the plant cells which use it to synthesise amino acids (and, from them, proteins). So both the bacteria and the plant benefit from their association – an example of *symbiosis*.

nitrogen cycle: the processes which recycle the element nitrogen through living things and their environment.

First, you must be quite clear about exactly what is cycling around! 'Nitrogen' can mean the gas nitrogen or the element nitrogen in whatever state. In the nitrogen cycle we are talking about the element nitrogen. Second, you must be clear about what sort of compounds in living things contain nitrogen. This is quite easy: all you have to do is remember that the symbol for nitrogen is N.

These compounds contain **N**itrogen: protei**N**s, ami**N**o acids, D**N**A.

These do not contain **N**itrogen: carbohydrates, fats, oils.

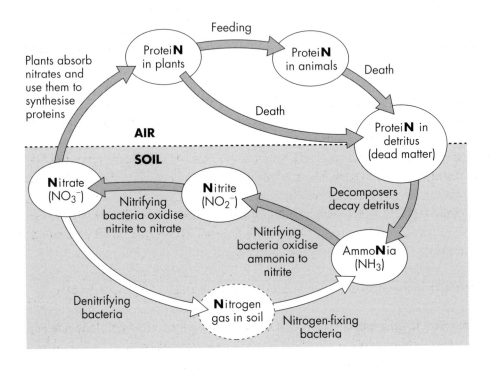

To find your way around the cycle:

- Plants absorb **N**itrates from the soil.
- Plants use the **N**itrates to manufacture ami**N**o acids and then, from them, protei**N**s.

- The plants are eaten by animals which digest the plant material. They make their own protei**N**s.
- Some excretory products contain **N**itrogen and these enter the soil. Plants and animals die and their remains enter the soil.
- Bacteria in the soil decompose the excretory products and dead remains and convert the nitrogen-containing compounds into ammo**N**ia.
- *Nitrogen fixing bacteria* convert **N**itrogen gas into ammo**N**ia.
- *Nitrifying bacteria* in the soil convert the ammo**N**ia into **N**itrates.
- *Denitrifying bacteria* convert some of the **N**itrates in the soil to **N**itrogen gas.

---

nitrogen oxides: gases which contain nitrogen and oxygen chemically combined.

There are several of these gases with different ratios of nitrogen to oxygen. As a result, they are given the general formula NO_x.

Nitrogen oxides are released from car exhausts and rise into the *atmosphere*. They combine with water to form a mixture of acids including *nitric acid*. The nitric acid dissolves in rainwater forming *acid rain*.

---

nose: the first part of the *breathing system* and the sense organ which gives us our sense of smell.

Special sense cells inside the nose are activated when chemicals, usually gases, bind to them. The sense cells then trigger a *nerve impulse* to the brain which interprets the sensation as the smell of, for example, peppermint (or whatever the particular 'smell' is).

Humans have a sense of smell which is less sensitive than many other animals, but most individuals can distinguish between several hundred smells. Some can distinguish several thousand smells.

The nose is also the opening to the breathing system. It is lined with cells which secrete *mucus* and other cells with *cilia*. These filter dust and bacteria from the air entering the breathing system.

---

nucleoid: the term sometimes used to describe the genetic material in *bacteria*.

Bacteria do not have a true nucleus enclosed by a membrane. They usually have one, circular piece of *DNA*. This is sometimes called the nucleoid.

---

nucleus: the structure in cells which contains the genetic material.
The nucleus:
- is surrounded by a *membrane* – the nuclear membrane
- contains *DNA* (the genetic material) in the *chromosomes*

- determines the activities of the cell, because DNA controls *protein synthesis*.

The nucleus of any human cell (except *gametes* or sex cells) contains 46 chromosomes. All the cells therefore contain all the genes. So why are your toes not brown (or blue) like your eyes? Although all the genes are in all the cells, some genes are only 'allowed to work' in certain cells.

---

nutrients: substances needed either as an energy source or for making chemicals needed by the individual.

Plants obtain their nutrients in two ways:

- they manufacture their own *carbohydrates* in *photosynthesis*
- they absorb *mineral ions* from the *soil*.

All other chemicals the plant needs are made using these two main groups of nutrients as a starting point.

Animals obtain their nutrients from the food they eat.

Nutrients needed in large amounts by an organism are called macronutrients. Those needed in small amounts are called micronutrients.

---

nutrition (1): obtaining and using food.

There are two main types of nutrition.

- *Autotrophic nutrition* – organisms which use this type are able to synthesise food molecules from simpler chemicals. *Photosynthesis* is the best known type of autotrophic nutrition. All green plants are autotrophs.
- *Heterotrophic nutrition* – organisms using this type of nutrition must ingest food, digest and absorb it before they can use it. All animals are heterotrophs.

---

nutrition (2): the science of food, the nutrients it contains and their use in relation to the health of the organism.

obesity: a person is obese if his or her body mass is 20% above the maximum desirable mass for his or her height.

Obesity is a serious condition because it increases a person's risk of developing:

- high *blood pressure*, *strokes*, coronary *heart disease* and adult *diabetes*
- *cancer* of the colon, rectum and prostate gland (in men)
- cancer of the cervix, breast and uterus (in women).

Obesity may make worse any joints affected by *arthritis*: the extra weight on these joints can cause extra damage.

The causes of obesity are not obvious. It is not just simply a person overeating which makes them obese. Some people inherit a *metabolism* which does not use energy quickly – they have a low *metabolic rate*. Such a person may eat the same amount as a slim person and still put on weight.

---

oesophagus (gullet): the tube leading from the mouth to the *stomach*.
Food is rolled into a bolus (ball) in the mouth and swallowed. The tongue flicks the bolus into the throat and it is then forced down the oesophagus by *peristalsis*.

Mucus in the *saliva* lubricates the bolus as it is forced down the oesophagus. The lining is thicker than in other regions of the digestive system, to protect it from abrasion as the food moves through it.

No enzymes are secreted by the oesophagus.

---

oestrogen: one of the female sex hormones.
Oestrogen is produced and secreted by *follicle* cells in the *ovaries*. It is sometimes called the 'feminising hormone' as, at puberty, it causes:

- the development of *breasts*
- broadening of the *pelvis*
- redistribution of body fat
- *menstrual cycle*s to begin.

It is produced in response to increasing amounts of *FSH* secreted from the *pituitary gland*. During the first part of each menstrual cycle, oestrogen causes the lining of the *uterus* to thicken in preparation for *implantation* of an *embryo*.

The levels of oestrogen secretion fall as a woman goes through the menopause (stops ovulation).

oil: a substance made from *fatty acids* and *glycerol* which is liquid at room temperature.

Oils and fats together make a larger group called *lipids*.

omnivore: an animal whose diet includes both animal and plant material. *Carnivores* have pointed teeth which are adapted to crushing bones and tearing meat. *Herbivores* have teeth which can grind plant materials. *Omnivores* often have relatively unspecialised teeth which can process both.

In a *food web*, omnivores can be both:
- a primary consumer, because they eat plants
- a secondary consumer, because they eat animals.

optic nerve: the *nerve* which carries *nerve impulses* from the *eye* to the *brain*.

organ: a structure made from several *tissues* which performs a major function.

Organ	Main function	Tissues	Functions of tissues
heart	pumps blood around body	• cardiac muscle	• contracts to provide the force to pump the blood
		• blood	• supplies oxygen and glucose for respiration to give the energy for contraction
		• nerves	• alter the rate of contraction so that the correct amount of blood is circulating
leaf	photosynthesis	• palisade tissue	• photosynthesises
		• lower epidermis	• stomata in lower epidermis allow uptake of carbon dioxide
		• spongy mesophyll	• air spaces allow rapid diffusion of carbon dioxide to palisade layer
		• veins	• bring water to the leaf
bone	support and movement	• bone tissue	• provides the strength
		• blood	• provides oxygen and nutrients for the bone cells
		• cartilage	• provides a slippery surface at the end of the bone to prevent damage from two bones rubbing together

The tissues which make up an organ each perform different functions, but all are necessary to the main or overall function of the organ.

organ system: a number of *organs* linked together to form a system which often carries out one of the main life processes.
Because of their simpler structure, plants do not have true organ systems. The table describes some of the organs systems in *mammals*.

Organ system	Function of system	Organs it contains	Contribution of each organ
circulatory system	carries blood around body to deliver oxygen and nutrients to organs and to remove waste materials	• heart • blood vessels	• provides the force to move the blood • carry the blood around the body
nervous system	allows body to respond to changes in environment	• brain • spinal cord • nerves	• interprets sensory impulses, generates motor impulses • links brain to lower nerves • carry impulses into and out of brain and spinal cord
digestive system	converts food molecules into a form which can be absorbed	• mouth • oesophagus • stomach • small intestine • large intestine	• food is chewed; starch digestion begins • carries food to stomach • digestion of proteins begins • most digestion occurs here; absorption of products of digestion • reabsorption of water; faeces formed

organelle: a small structure within a *cell* with a specific function.
Some organelles are found in all cells: others are only found in certain types (see the table on the following page).

organic substances: substances which contain carbon nearly always combined with hydrogen.
Nearly all biological molecules are organic: they contain carbon, hydrogen and usually oxygen as well. Some organic substances contain other elements such as *magnesium* and *iron*.
• *Carbohydrates* contain carbon, hydrogen and oxygen.
• *Lipids* contain carbon, hydrogen and oxygen.

- *Proteins* contain carbon, hydrogen, oxygen and nitrogen.
- *DNA* contains carbon, hydrogen, oxygen, nitrogen and phosphorus.

organelle

Organelle	Function	Plant cell	Animal cell	Bacterial cell
nucleus	controls activities of cell by controlling *protein synthesis*	present	present	no true nucleus, but DNA is present
mitochondrion	release of energy in *aerobic respiration*	present	present	absent
chloroplast	synthesis of glucose in *photosynthesis*	present	absent	absent
ribosomes	protein synthesis	present	present	present
vacuoles	storage of water, waste and other materials	present	usually absent: sometimes small vacuoles present	absent

osmosis: movement of water from a weak solution to a stronger one across a *partially permeable membrane.*

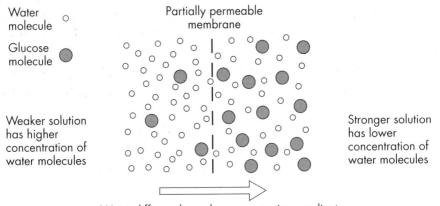

Water diffuses down the concentration gradient

You can think of osmosis as a special case of *diffusion*. It is the diffusion of water between two solutions when a membrane separates them. The diagram illustrates this situation.

The weak solution has a higher concentration of water molecules than the stronger one and so water can diffuse down its *concentration gradient* from the weak solution to the stronger one.

Cell membranes are partially permeable and so if the solution outside a cell is a different strength to the solutions inside the cell, water will move across the membrane into or out of the cell.

ova (singular ovum): female *sex cells* (*gametes*) in an *ovary*. They are also called *egg cells*.

ovary (animal): one of a pair of organs which produce *egg cells* (ova) and female sex hormones.
(See *uterus* for a diagram showing the position of human ovaries.)
At birth, a woman's ovaries contain all the *follicles* (which contain the ova) she will ever have. From *puberty*, one follicle a month develops in an ovary. As the follicle develops, it bursts and releases an ovum into the *Fallopian tubes*. This is called *ovulation*. The remains of the follicle is called the *corpus luteum*.
The female sex hormones produced in the ovary are *oestrogen* and *progesterone*.

- Oestrogen is produced by cells of the developing follicle and causes the uterus lining to thicken each month in preparation for *implantation* of an embryo.
- Progesterone is produced by the corpus luteum and maintains the uterus lining and causes blood spaces to develop in preparation for pregnancy. If an embryo does not implant, progesterone is no longer produced and the uterine lining breaks down and is lost in *menstruation*.

ovary (plant): the part of the *carpel* which contains the ovules. (See *flower*.)
Each ovule in an ovary contains an *egg cell* which can be fertilised by the nucleus of a *pollen grain*.
The *stigma* receives the pollen from another plant and a tube grows from the pollen grain through the *style* to the ovule in the ovary. The pollen nucleus can pass down the tube and fertilise the egg cell.

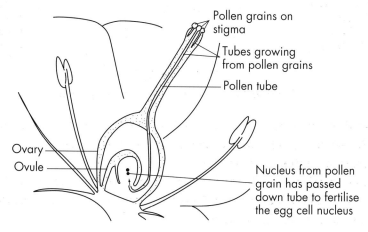

Pollen grains on stigma

Tubes growing from pollen grains

Pollen tube

Ovary

Ovule

Nucleus from pollen grain has passed down tube to fertilise the egg cell nucleus

After fertilisation:
- each ovule will become a *seed*
- the ovary will become a *fruit*.

oviduct (Fallopian tube): in *mammals*, one of the tubes which carries *egg cells* (ova) from the *ovary* to the *uterus*.
Following *ovulation*, special fringes at the end of the oviduct collect the egg cell (ovum) and sweep it into the oviduct proper. Some of the cells lining the oviduct have *cilia* which beat and sweep the ovum along towards the uterus.
Fertilisation usually takes place when the ova are in the oviducts.
(See *reproductive system, human*.)

ovulation: the release of an *egg cell* (ovum) from a *follicle* in an *ovary*.
In humans, ovulation is triggered by a sudden rise in the amount of luteinising hormone (LH) from the *pituitary gland*. It normally occurs on day 14 of a *menstrual cycle*, but the timing can vary considerably between individuals. The precise timing of ovulation can also vary from month to month in the same woman.

oxidation: a chemical reaction in which the substance that is oxidised loses electrons.
Although this is the correct definition, for practical purposes you can think of oxidation in biological situations as involving a reaction with oxygen.
In *aerobic respiration*, glucose is oxidised to carbon dioxide and water.
Lactic acid formed during exercise is oxidised to carbohydrate in the liver.

oxygen: a colourless and odourless gas, with the formula O_2.
Oxygen is needed by almost all living things for *respiration*: without oxygen this process could not continue and life as we know it would not exist.
It is produced in *photosynthesis*. All the oxygen in our *atmosphere* was put there by plants, algae and some photosynthetic bacteria. It now makes up 21% of the atmosphere.
Many biological molecules contain oxygen: carbohydrates, fats, proteins and DNA all contain some oxygen.

oxygen debt: the amount of oxygen required to oxidise the *lactic acid* produced by *anaerobic respiration* during vigorous *exercise*.
During vigorous exercise, the *heart* and *lungs* cannot supply enough oxygen to the *muscles* to allow them to release all the energy they need aerobically. The muscles therefore respire anaerobically and lactic acid is produced as a result.

After the exercise, the lactic acid is converted to carbohydrate in the *liver*. The amount of oxygen needed to do this is the oxygen debt.

oxyhaemoglobin: the form in which *oxygen* is transported around the body of *vertebrates*. (See *haemoglobin*.)

ozone: a blue gas present in the upper *atmosphere*.
Ozone is a form of oxygen in which three oxygen atoms form a molecule, O_3 (rather than two in normal oxygen).
Ozone is sometimes formed at low levels by the action of sunlight on pollutants containing oxygen (e.g. nitrogen oxides) formed by heavy traffic. It can be seen as photochemical smog in large cities.
Ozone can be used for *oxidation* and *sterilisation*.

ozone layer: a layer of *ozone* in the upper *atmosphere*.
The ozone is found mainly at heights of 15–50 kilometres above the earth's surface. It has been formed by the action of sunlight on oxygen. The importance of this layer is that it shields life on earth from ultraviolet radiation which can induce *cancer*-causing *mutations*.
Scientists have found that *CFCs* in aerosols can destroy ozone – converting it back to ordinary oxygen. The CFCs can do extensive damage: one molecule of a CFC can destroy many thousands of molecules of ozone. If the ozone layer were to be significantly reduced, much more ultraviolet radiation would be able to reach the earth.
The ozone layer appears to becoming thinner in certain areas. Scientists talk of a hole in the layer over the Antarctic. Because of the concern about the effects of CFCs, their use has been banned in many countries.

palisade mesophyll: a layer of cylindrical cells below the upper epidermis of a *leaf*.

The palisade layer is the major region of *photosynthesis* in a leaf. This is because:

- the palisade cells contain more *chloroplasts* than other cells in the leaf
- they are near to the upper surface and so receive more light than other cells (except the upper epidermis).

Carbon dioxide is able to move rapidly to the palisade cells by *diffusion* from the *stomata* on the lower epidermis through air spaces in the spongy mesophyll. Water is carried in the *xylem* in the veins of the leaf, and moves from the veins by *osmosis* into the surrounding palisade cells.

---

pancreas: a *gland* present in *vertebrates* usually found near the first part of the *small intestine* (duodenum). (See *digestive system*.)

The pancreas secretes pancreatic juice into the small intestine. This 'juice' contains:

- *digestive enzymes* (amylase, protease and lipase)
- *mucus* (to lubricate the movement of food through the intestines)
- sodium hydrogencarbonate (to raise the pH to the optimum for enzyme activity).

Groups of special cells (called *islet cells*) also produce the hormones *insulin* and *glucagon*, which regulate the concentration of glucose in the blood plasma.

---

parasite: an organism which lives in or on another organism and feeds from that organism.

- The organism on which the parasite feeds is called the host.
- A parasite which lives inside its host is called an *endoparasite*.
- A parasite which lives on the surface of its host is called an *ectoparasite*.

Because a parasite feeds from its host, the host is harmed and may even be killed, although this is not normally the case. A well adapted parasite does not normally kill its host – this would result in the death of the parasite also.

Examples of parasites are shown in the table.

Parasite	Ectoparasite or endoparasite	Attachments to host	How it feeds from host
tapeworm	endoparasite (in guts of mammals)	head has hooks and suckers which attach to intestine wall	digested food in intestine is absorbed through body wall
flea	ectoparasite (on skin of mammals)	no permanent attachment, can jump from host to host	bites skin and sucks blood
liver fluke	endoparasite (in liver of mammals)	suckers attach to inner wall of bile duct	food is absorbed through body surface
dodder	ectoparasite (on stem of plants)	outgrowths of dodder stem (haustoria) grow into host stem	haustoria absorb food from phloem cells

parasitism: the type of association shown by a *parasite* and its *host*.

In parasitism, the parasite obtains a benefit from the association: usually it obtains food. The host is harmed by the association.

partially permeable membrane: a membrane which will allow certain molecules to pass through it, but not others.

Usually, it is the size of the molecule which determines whether or not it can pass through the membrane. Small molecules like water can pass freely through *cell membranes*, whereas larger ones may need to be 'carried' through the membrane.

(See *osmosis*.)

pascal (Pa): the unit of pressure: 1 pascal is equivalent to a force of 1 newton per square metre.

Pascals are relatively small units of pressure and we commonly work in kilopascals (kPa). One kilopascal = 1000 pascals.

Air pressure is 101 kPa.

The pressure of blood entering the *aorta* in humans varies between 10 kPa and 16 kPa.

passive immunity: *immunity* which is not due to an individual's own *immune response*.

Passive immunity involves obtaining *antibodies* from an external source. It can be either naturally induced or artificially induced.

Antibodies being passed to a fetus across the placenta and to a baby when breast feeding are examples of naturally induced passive immunity. Because the body's own *immune system* has not been involved in producing the antibodies, no *memory cells* are produced and the immunity is short-lived (lasts for only a few months).

Artificial passive immunity is induced when a person with hepatitis A is injected with antibodies against the hepatitis virus.

Pasteur, Louis: a French microbiologist who made great advances in the field of prevention and treatment of infectious diseases.

Louis Pasteur started his career as a chemist, but became interested in the idea that 'germs' caused disease.

In 1854, he proved that microorganisms in the air caused wine to go sour (they turned the alcohol to ethanoic acid) and:

- if he kept out the microorganisms in the air, the wine took longer to sour
- if he heated the wine first to kill any microorganisms in the wine and then excluded other microorganisms, the wine would stay fresh indefinitely.

This process of heating to kill microorganisms and then excluding others has been modified, but it is still named after the man who developed it. We call it *pasteurisation*.

Pasteur also knew of *Jenner's* work and the work of others developing *vaccines* and became involved in this work. He developed vaccines against:

- chicken cholera
- anthrax in cattle
- rabies.

In 1888, seven years before Pasteur died, the Pasteur Institute was founded to research the treatment of rabies.

pasteurisation: a heat treatment process used to kill harmful or *pathogenic bacteria* in milk and other products.

There are two methods of pasteurising milk: both involve heating the milk to destroy pathogenic bacteria, but the time and temperatures used are different.

- Method 1 – the milk is heated to a temperature between 62.8°C and 65°C for 30 minutes.
- Method 2 – the milk is heated to 71.7°C for 15 seconds.

Pasteurisation does not necessarily kill all bacteria in the milk, but it does kill all pathogenic bacteria. It is preferred to *sterilisation* because the higher temperatures used in this process alter the flavour of the milk.

Other products can also be pasteurised, including beer, yoghurt and ham.

pathogen: an organism which causes a *disease*.

All pathogens are *parasites*, but not all parasites are pathogens. A flea bite may cause irritation, but the bite itself does not cause a disease, so the flea, although a parasite, is not a pathogen.

All *viruses* are pathogens (even though they are not strictly organisms themselves): they all cause a disease in some living organism.
There are many *pathogenic bacteria*, but even more that are not.
Other pathogens include:
- some *protozoans* – e.g. the trypanosome which causes *malaria*
- some types of *yeast* which infect the urinary system.

Pavlov: see *conditioning*.

pectoral girdle: the ring of bones which circle the body at the shoulders. The pectoral girdle is made up of the two collar bones (clavicles) and the two shoulder blades (scapulas). It is joined to the spine by muscles. A ball and socket joint attaches the arm to the girdle.

pelvic girdle (pelvis): the bones which circle the body at the base of the spine.
The pelvic girdle is made up of the two hip bones, which are joined to the sacrum and coccyx at the back. It forms a complete bony ring around the body and protects the bladder and part of the large intestine (and reproductive organs in women) from physical damage. It also supports the upper body.
It is not joined to the spine by muscles, like the *pectoral girdle*, but is fused rigidly to it. The ball and socket joint which attaches the leg to the pelvic girdle is deeper than the one at the pectoral girdle. These two features allow thrust from the legs to be transmitted to the whole body efficiently.
The male and female pelvic girdles differ. The flatter and broader pelvic girdle of females allows childbirth more easily than a longer pelvic girdle would. The longer and generally bigger pelvic girdle of males supports a more heavily built upper body.

penicillin: an *antibiotic* produced by some species of the mould *Penicillium*. Penicillin was discovered in 1928 by *Alexander Fleming*. It was the first antibiotic to be discovered and when first used, it produced spectacular cures.
We now know that penicillin works by preventing bacterial cells from making new cell walls. This means that they cannot reproduce as they cannot make the cell walls for the new bacteria which would be produced.
Although penicillin was very effective when it was first used, strains of bacteria have now developed *resistance* to penicillin. They arose by chance *mutations* and had an advantage over other bacteria and so survived better. This is an example of *natural selection*. Scientists are now continually

developing new types of antibiotics as more and more resistant strains of bacteria evolve.

penis: the male sex organ through which *semen* passes into the *vagina* during intercourse.

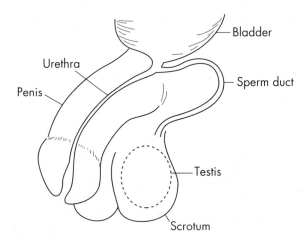

The penis consists mainly of three columns of spongy tissue full of tiny blood vessels. When the male is sexually aroused, blood flow through this tissue increases greatly and causes an erection.

The *urethra* runs through the centre of the penis and passes semen into the vagina during intercourse. It also carries urine from the bladder.

pentadactyl limb: a limb with five digits, (fingers, toes or equivalent). *Amphibians*, *reptiles*, *birds* and *mammals* all have pentadactyl limbs. This similarity between the limbs is used as evidence that all four types of *vertebrates* share a common evolutionary history.

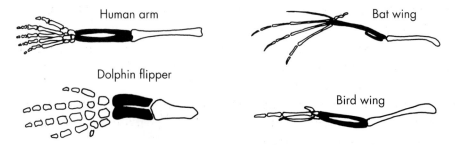

It seems unlikely that the same kind of limb would have evolved many times over. It is much more likely that it evolved once and then became modified by *natural selection* to suit many different purposes.

pepsin: a *protease* enzyme secreted by cells lining the *stomach* of *mammals*. Pepsin is the first enzyme in our *digestive system* to act on protein molecules. The proteins are only partially digested by the pepsin into shorter chains of *amino acids*.

Pepsin is different from other digestive enzymes in humans in one important way. It is adapted to work most efficiently in the acidic conditions in the stomach. All other human digestive enzymes work best in near neutral conditions.

percolating filter (biological filter): a method of sewage treatment involving percolating the untreated sewage through a filter bed.

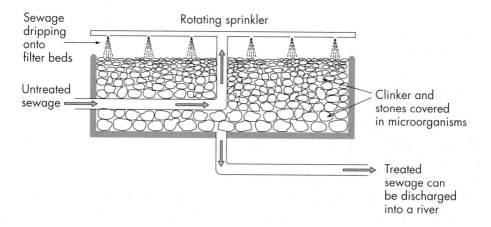

When raw sewage arrives at the treatment plant it is:
- screened to remove large objects
- allowed to stand in large tanks (settlement tanks) to allow solid material to settle out
- pumped through a pipe which rotates over the filter bed and trickles the liquid sewage onto the filter
- purified by bacteria, fungi and protozoa (growing on the stones of the filter) which remove any organic matter as a source of food
- discharged into a waterway.

The bacteria and other organisms in the filter are able to use the organic material for *aerobic respiration* because the large gaps between the stones ensure a plentiful supply of oxygen.

The sludge from the settlement tanks is transferred to special 'digesters' where other bacteria convert complex organic molecules into simpler ones. The sludge is then dried and sold as *fertiliser*.

perennial: a plant which lives for many years.

There are two types of perennials: herbaceous perennials and woody perennials.

Herbaceous perennials are plants which survive the winter as underground storage organs like bulbs or corms. These organs store food materials over winter and produce new roots, shoots and flowers in the spring. Daffodils and crocuses are examples of herbaceous perennials.

Woody perennials are plants like trees and shrubs. The stems of these plants do not die back in winter. The permanent stems form a starting point for each year's new growth. Some lose their leaves in winter (deciduous plants); others keep them through the winter (evergreens). They produce new flowers and seeds each year.

---

period: another name for *menstruation*.

(See also *menstrual cycle*.)

---

peristalsis: rhythmic waves of muscular contractions of the wall of a tube which move its contents along the tube.

You really only need to know about peristalsis as it occurs in the *digestive system*, but there are other examples:

● sperm are moved along the sperm ducts by peristalsis

● urine is moved along the ureters by peristalsis.

In the human digestive system, the walls of the various organs contain *smooth muscle* fibres which bring about peristalsis. The roles of peristalsis in the parts of the digestive system are:

● in the *oesophagus* – to force food to the stomach

● in the *stomach* – to mix the stomach contents then force food into the small intestine

● in the *small intestine* – to move the liquid food along the intestine

● in the *large intestine* – to move the faeces along the intestine.

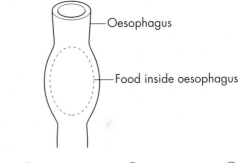

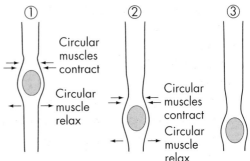

pesticide: a chemical which is used to kill pests (organisms which reduce the yield of crop plants).

There are many different kinds of pesticide, but the three most important types are:

- fungicides – these kill *fungi*
- *herbicides* – these are weedkillers and kill unwanted plants
- *insecticides* – these kill insects.

Pesticides have reduced the effect of many pests, but they have also brought their own problems.

Some insecticides have caused considerable environmental damage because they are accumulated along *food chains*. *DDT* used on a range of insects was passed along food chains and seriously reduced the fertility of peregrine falcons.

Some herbicides are persistent and traces of them remain in the crops on which they were sprayed.

Pesticides are often over-used and new, resistant forms of the pest emerge as a result of chance *mutations*. These resistant forms survive better and pass on their resistant *alleles*. As time passes, the proportion of resistant forms increases. This is an example of *natural selection* in operation.

Ideally, a pesticide should:

- control the pest effectively
- be *biodegradable*, so that toxic products are not left in the soil or on crops
- be specific, so that only the pest is killed
- not accumulate along food chains
- be safe to store and transport
- be easy and safe to apply.

petal: a structure in a *flower* which is usually brightly coloured to attract *insects*.

Flowers which are insect pollinated need to attract insects (so that they will come and collect the *pollen*) and reward the insects (so that they will visit other flowers of the same type and transfer the pollen). The petals of insect pollinated flowers:

- are large
- are brightly coloured
- are scented
- have a nectary – the nectar produced is the reward for the insect.

Wind pollinated flowers do not need to attract insects and so their petals (if present) are usually small, inconspicuous and not scented. They do not have nectaries.

pH scale: a scale which measures the degree of acidity or alkalinity of a solution.

The pH scale ranges from 1–14.

- Solutions with a pH of less than 7 are acidic.
- Solutions with a pH of more than 7 are alkaline.
- Solutions with a pH of 7 are neutral.

phagocyte: a cell which ingests and digests material.

Many single celled organisms are phagocytes: *Amoeba* feeds on smaller organisms by ingesting them and then releasing digestive *enzymes* to digest them.

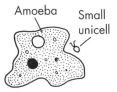

Amoeba Small
         unicell

Pseudopudia
surround unicell

Arrows show
direction of flow
of cytoplasm

Unicell enclosed
in a food vacuole

Unicell is now
digested by
enzymes secreted
by amoeba

Some of the *white blood cells* in our bodies are phagocytes. They form part of our *immune system* and are found both in the blood and wandering free through tissues. These phagocytes are able to recognise objects which should not be in our bodies, such as bacteria, viruses and dust particles. They then ingest them and digest them.

phagocytosis: the way in which *phagocytes* feed.

phalanges: the small bones which make up the fingers and toes.

The thumb and big toe have two phalanges. All other fingers and toes have three phalanges.

pharynx: the throat.

The pharynx is the passage which connects the back of the mouth and the back of the nose to the *larynx* and *oesophagus*.

The functions of the pharynx are:

- to pass air from the nose to the *trachea*
- to pass food from the mouth to the oesophagus
- to help in the formation of different vowel sounds by changing shape.

phenotype: the feature or *characteristic* which results from the *genotype*. For example, in the inheritance of *albinism* in humans, the *allele* for normal pigmentation (**N**) is dominant to the allele for albinism (**n**).

Possible genotypes	Phenotypes
NN	normal pigmentation
Nn	normal pigmentation
nn	albino

phloem: the *tissue* which transports dissolved *organic substances* and some *mineral ions* through a plant.

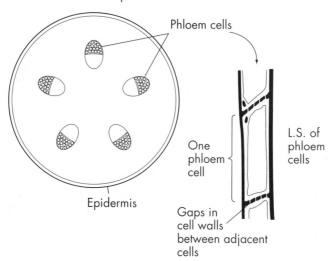

Transverse section of plant stem

- Phloem cells are tubular.
- They are found with the *xylem* tissue in the centre of a root, towards the outside of a stem and in the veins of a leaf.
- They transport sugars between leaves (where they are made) and other parts of the plant (where they are used or stored).

photosynthesis: a light-dependent process which makes glucose from carbon dioxide and water.

Photosynthesis can be summarised by the equation:

$$6CO_2 + 6H_2O \xrightarrow[\text{(suitable temperature)}]{\text{light energy absorbed by chlorophyll}} C_6H_{12}O_6 + 6O_2$$

(carbon dioxide) (water) (glucose) (oxygen)

Many factors are needed for photosynthesis to take place. If any one of them is absent, then the process will cease. If one is in short supply, then it will be a *limiting factor* and will determine the rate of photosynthesis.

Photosynthesis can only take place in organisms which can trap light energy and then use it to drive chemical reactions. The organisms which can do this are *plants*, *algae* and some *bacteria*.

Photosynthesis is probably the most important biological process on our planet as:

- it is almost the only process which builds a complex *organic substance* from simple *inorganic* substances
- the glucose formed in photosynthesis is the starting point for the synthesis of all other biological molecules – it can be converted to starch and stored, combined with nitrogen to form amino acids and then proteins, and it can be converted to lipids.
- the organisms which can photosynthesise start nearly all *food chains*
- all the oxygen in the earth's *atmosphere* has been released by photosynthesis.

photosynthesis, experiments: Photosynthesis produces *glucose* and *oxygen*. The glucose is used for *respiration* and any surplus is usually converted to *starch* and stored. The oxygen is also used for respiration and any surplus passes out of the leaf.

If we can show that a plant is producing starch or oxygen, then it must be photosynthesising.

Experiments you should know are:

- to show that *carbon dioxide* is needed for photosynthesis
- to show that light is needed for photosynthesis
- to show that light intensity affects the rate of photosynthesis.

For the first two experiments, you need a destarched plant. You destarch a plant by keeping it in a dark place for a few days so that it uses all its stores of starch.

TO SHOW THAT CARBON DIOXIDE IS NEEDED

1 Take two destarched plants.
2 Place one under a bell jar with a beaker of potassium hydroxide solution (to absorb any carbon dioxide).
3 Place the other under a bell jar with a beaker of sodium hydrogencarbonate solution (to give off carbon dioxide).
4 Leave both for 2–3 days in a warm place with constant light.
5 Test a leaf from each for the presence of starch.

TO SHOW THAT LIGHT IS NEEDED

1 Take two destarched plants.
2 Place one under a bell jar with a beaker of sodium hydrogencarbonate solution in a dark place.
3 Place the other under a bell jar with a beaker of sodium hydrogencarbonate solution in a light place.
4 Leave both for 2–3 days in a warm place.
5 Test a leaf from each for the presence of starch.

TO SHOW THAT LIGHT INTENSITY AFFECTS THE RATE OF PHOTOSYNTHESIS

1 Place some water in a boiling tube and add a little sodium hydrogencarbonate (to supply carbon dioxide).
2 Put some *Elodea* (pond weed) in the boiling tube.
3 Shield the boiling tube from the natural light.
4 Shine a light onto the *Elodea*.
5 Count the number of bubbles of oxygen it produces in one minute.
6 Repeat twice more and average.
7 Vary the light intensity by: (a) varying the distance of the light from the Elodea or (b) varying the electrical energy supplied to the bulb.

---

phototropism: a *growth* response made by plants in response to light. Phototropism occurs only in plant shoots; roots do not respond to light. The way in which light promotes growth in shoots occurs in three main stages.

- Cells in the tips of shoots are sensitive to light: when illuminated they produce a plant hormone called *auxin*.
- The auxin diffuses downwards from the tip and cells absorb the auxin as it passes them.
- The auxin causes the cells to grow.

If the illumination is the same on all sides of the shoot, it grows straight up. If the illumination is uneven, the shoot bends towards the light because:

- when illuminated from one side, the auxin moves away from the light
- the dark side has a higher concentration of auxin as a result
- the cells on the dark side therefore grow more than those on the light side.

---

phylum (plural phyla): a major grouping in a classification system. There are five main kingdoms in modern classification systems: *bacteria, protoctista, fungi, plants* and *animals*.

Within each kingdom there are several phyla. A phylum is a group with a major body plan. Some examples are shown in the table on the following page.

Kingdom	Phylum	Body plan of phylum
animal	• vertebrates • arthropods • annelids	• all have a backbone • all have jointed limbs and an exoskeleton • all have a segmented body with no limbs
plants	• angiosperms • conifers • ferns	• all have stem, roots, leaves, flowers, seeds inside a fruit • all have stem, roots, needle-like leaves, seeds formed in a cone • all have woody stems, underground horizontal stems, young leaves coiled in bud, no seeds – reproduce by spores

physiology: the study of the processes which go on inside living things.

phytoplankton: microscopic floating organisms, mainly *algae* and some kinds of *bacteria*.

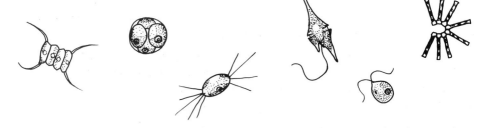

Phytoplankton are found in both freshwater and in the seas. They can *photosynthesise* and are therefore the basis of most aquatic *food chains* and *food webs*.

Although they are microscopically small, the sheer number of these organisms makes them the most productive organisms on the planet. They produce far more oxygen and new biomass each year than all the plants on land combined.

pituitary gland: an *endocrine gland* lying just beneath the centre of the *brain*.

The pituitary gland releases a number of hormones into the bloodstream. These influence a wide range of processes. Some pituitary hormones influence processes directly, such as *growth hormone* which influences growth. Others have an indirect effect because they influence the production of other hormones, such as thyroid stimulating hormone, which stimulates the *thyroid gland* to produce *thyroxine*.

The table shows the main pituitary hormones and their effects.

Hormone	Target organ	Effect
FSH (follicle stimulating hormone)	● ovary ● testis	● stimulates development of follicles and secretion of oestrogen ● stimulates development of sperm
LH (luteinising hormone)	● ovary ● testis	● stimulates ovulation and formation of corpus luteum ● stimulates some cells to produce testosterone
ADH (anti-diuretic hormone)	kidney – collecting ducts	stimulates reabsorption of water from urine and so conserves water
growth hormone	general	stimulates growth by increasing protein and fat metabolism
thyroid stimulating hormone	thyroid gland	stimulates production of thyroxine
adrenal stimulating hormone	adrenal gland	stimulates production of some adrenal hormones

placenta: the *organ* found in *mammals* only which exchanges materials between the *blood* of a fetus and the blood of the mother.

The placenta is formed partly from *tissues* of the *embryo* and partly from maternal tissue. It has several important functions which include:

● anchoring the developing embryo in the uterus
● exchanging materials between mother and embryo
● secreting hormones to maintain the *pregnancy*.

Before birth, the placenta acts as a lung, kidney and intestine for the developing embryo because:

● oxygen diffuses across the placenta from the mother's blood to the blood of the embryo and carbon dioxide diffuses in the opposite direction
● the products of digestion (such as amino acids, glucose, fatty acids and glycerol) and other soluble food materials diffuse across the placenta from the mother's blood
● urea and other waste materials diffuse from the embryo's blood across the placenta into the mother's blood to be excreted.

plankton: floating, mainly microscopic organisms in the upper layers of freshwater and the oceans.

There are two types of plankton:

● *phytoplankton*, which can photosynthesise and include microscopic algae and some bacteria
● *zooplankton*, which are non-photosynthetic and include tiny shrimp-like

crustasceans, jellyfish, unicellular organisms and the larvae of some animals.

plants: multicellular organisms which can *photosynthesise*; their cells have *cell walls* made of cellulose.

The plant kingdom includes:

- mosses – plants with non-woody stems which reproduce by spores; they are often found in damp environments
- *ferns* – plants with woody, horizontal, underground stems which reproduce by spores; their leaves develop from stems by 'uncurling'
- conifers – plants with woody stems, needle-like leaves and seeds produced in cones
- *angiosperms* – plants with woody stems, true flowers and seeds contained in a fruit.

plaque, atheromatous: a deposit of *fat* which forms in the inner lining of *arteries*.

Atheromatous plaques are the first visible stage in *atherosclerosis*. As more and more plaques form in the arteries:

- the lumen (or central space) becomes narrower and narrower
- blood flow is restricted
- a blood clot may form and block the artery completely.

If this happens in a *coronary artery*, then part of the heart muscle is deprived of blood and oxygen. A heart attack may result.

plaque, dental: a rough, sticky coating which forms on *teeth*.

Plaque is a mixture of:

- food debris
- *saliva*
- bacteria.

Plaque builds on teeth because the mucus in saliva holds it in place. Bacteria multiply within the plaque, using sugars in the food debris and producing acids in the process. The acids cause decay of the tooth enamel.

If plaque is not removed by regular brushing, it will build up and can lead to gum disease and cause loosening of the teeth.

plasma: the liquid part of *blood*.

(See *blood plasma*.)

plasma protein: any *protein* normally found in the *blood plasma*.

The main plasma proteins in humans are:

- *fibrinogen* – a protein which helps in blood clotting
- *antibodies* – proteins which help in our *immune response* to invading microorganisms
- albumin – maintains the osmotic potential of the plasma (see *osmosis*).

100 cm³ of plasma contains about 6–8 g of proteins.

plasmid: small circular pieces of *DNA* found in *bacteria*.
Plasmids are separate from the main DNA molecule in bacteria, but still reproduce themselves when the bacterium reproduces. They have become a convenient way of inserting foreign genes into bacteria in *genetic engineering*.

plasmolysis: occurs in plant *cells* when the *cytoplasm* shrinks away from the *cell wall*.

Turgid cell:Vacuole is large and full of liquid. Cytoplasm is pressed firmly against cell wall which is stretched slightly

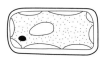

First stage of plasmolysis: Cell has lost water by osmosis: cytoplasm and vacuole have shrunk

Almost fully plasmolysed: Cytoplasm and vacuole have shrunk further: cytoplasm only has a few contacts with cell wall

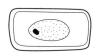

Fully plasmolysed: Vacuole is non existent and cytoplasm has completely shrunk away from cell wall

Plasmolysis occurs when plant cells are surrounded by a solution which is stronger than the solutions in the cell. As a result:

- water moves out of the cell, through the *partially permeable membrane*, by *osmosis*
- the cytoplasm starts to shrink as it loses water.

platelets: small fragments of *blood cells* which are important in *blood clotting*.

When we damage a *blood vessel* the platelets are activated. In this condition they release calcium ions and a number of other substances which trigger the clotting reactions.

pleural membranes: the *membranes* which lie outside the *lungs*.

There are two pleural membranes:
- the inner membrane lines the outside of the lungs
- the outer membrane lines the inside of the body wall of the *thorax*.

Between the two is a liquid called the pleural fluid which lubricates the movement of the lungs over the ribs as we breathe.

Sometimes the pleural membranes become infected and inflamed: this condition is called *pleurisy*.

pleurisy: any inflammation of the *pleural membranes*.

Pleurisy is sometimes due to a specific viral infection of the pleural membranes, but more commonly is a result of pneumonia or tuberculosis. Lung cancer can also cause pleurisy.

Pleurisy causes sharp chest pains when breathing and *analgesics* (painkillers) are often given to patients along with drugs to treat the cause of the infection.

plumule: the part of a *seed* which will develop into the *stem*.

When the seed germinates, the plumule will use food reserves from the *cotyledons* to grow and develop into a young stem. The stem will develop leaves which will *photosynthesise* and manufacture food materials needed for further growth.

(See *germination*.)

pollen grains: structures which contain the male sex cells (*gametes*) of plants.
- Pollen grains are formed in the *anthers* of the *stamens*.
- They are formed by *meiosis*.
- They contain only half the normal number of *chromosomes* and *genes*.
- The nucleus of a pollen grain fuses with the nucleus of an egg cell in the ovule (in the ovary) to form a *zygote* which develops into an *embryo* inside a *seed*.

Pollen grains are transferred from one flower to another by wind or insects. This transfer is called *pollination*.

pollen tube: the tube which grows from a *pollen grain* when it has landed on a *stigma* of the same *species* (see *ovary – plant*).

- The pollen tube grows through the *style* by secreting *enzymes* which digest a pathway for the tube.
- It grows to the opening in the *ovule* and the pollen grain *nucleus* passes down the tube.
- The pollen grain nucleus passes out of the tube and into the ovule where it fertilises the egg cell nucleus and forms a *zygote*.

pollination: transferring *pollen grains* from *anther* to *stigma*.

Pollination that takes place between anther and stigma in the same flower, or between flowers on the same plant, is called self-pollination. If the pollen is transferred to a stigma in a flower on a different plant, it is cross-pollination.

Pollination can be brought about by wind or *insects*. Flowers which are wind pollinated are very

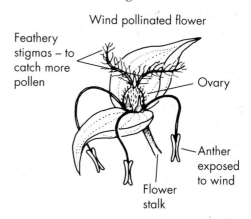

Wind pollinated flower

Feathery stigmas – to catch more pollen

Ovary

Anther exposed to wind

Flower stalk

Feature	Insect pollinated flower		Wind pollinated flower	
petals	• large • brightly coloured • scented	all these features attract insects to the flower	• small or absent • drab colours • no scent	there is no need to attract insects
nectaries	present	this is a reward for the insect	absent	
pollen grains	have hooks or are sticky	pollen grains must stick to insect	are light and often have 'wings'	pollen grains must be carried long distances by the wind
stamens	enclosed within flowers	insects must brush against anthers and collect pollen grains as they enter flower for nectar	hang outside flower	pollen grains must be blown easily from anthers
stigmas	often sticky, enclosed within flowers	insects must brush against stigmas and leave pollen grains as they enter flowers for nectar	hang outside flowers, often 'feathery'	feathery stigma has large surface area to collect pollen grains

different from those which are insect pollinated. The table on page 223 compares the two types of flowers.

---

pollution: releasing substances into the environment in amounts which cannot be easily removed by natural, biological processes and which cause harmful effects.

---

pollution, air: releasing substances into the air which cause harmful effects.

The table shows the main pollutants of the air and their effects.

Pollutant	Main sources	Effects
carbon dioxide	● burning fossil fuels ● deforestation	● builds up in the atmosphere and causes the *greenhouse effect* which leads to *global warming* ● reduces rate at which CO_2 is used in photosynthesis
sulphur dioxide	burning fossil fuels	dissolves in rain to form acid rain which causes: ● acidification of waterways ● death of trees ● damage to buildings
nitrogen oxides	burning petrol	dissolves in rain to form acid rain – as above
methane	● decomposition of waste in landfill sites ● fermentation in the rumen of ruminant herbivores	builds up in atmosphere and causes the greenhouse effect which leads to global warming
CFCs	● aerosols in some countries ● leaking coolant from old, damaged fridges	damage the *ozone layer* and allow more UV radiation to reach the earth; cause greenhouse effect and global warming

---

pollution, freshwater: releasing large amounts of harmful substances into ponds, rivers and lakes.

The table on page 225 shows some of the main freshwater pollutants and their effects.

---

pollution, marine: releasing substances in damaging amounts into the oceans.

The seas are sometimes treated as though they can absorb and dilute ever increasing amounts of harmful chemicals such as heavy metals (like mercury), *pesticides* and plastics.

The sheer size of the oceans does allow dilution and mixing of many pollutants and bacteria in seawater decompose many organic materials and other toxins. However, mixing and dilution of chemicals is not guaranteed.

- They become concentrated in some areas, especially near to large seaside towns which dump their wastes directly into the sea.
- They may be re-concentrated in living organisms as they pass along *food chains* (e.g. *insecticides* like *DDT*).
- Some pollutants (especially those from oil) float in the top few millimetres of water.

The most obvious pollution of seawater occurs when oil is spilled from a tanker. The millions of gallons of oil which can escape has many effects, e.g:

- clogging feathers of sea birds so they cannot fly: the birds try to clean themselves, swallow poisonous compounds in the oil and die
- blocking out light from the water so the phytoplankton cannot photosynthesise.

pollution, freshwater

Pollutant	Main sources	Effects
organic materials	● sewage ● farmyard manure	● bacteria and fungi reproduce rapidly and use up much of the oxygen in respiration; other organisms die ● may cause *eutrophication* as bacteria release nitrates and phosphates from the organic matter: these nutrients encourage the growth of algae
nitrates	fertilisers being leached into waterways	cause eutrophication
detergents	some enter rivers with sewage	release phosphates from sewage which causes eutrophication

pollution, land: adding large amounts of harmful substances to the land. The land can be polluted through deliberate measures and also by carelessness. Potential sources of pollution include the following.

- Landfill sites – exposed sites may contain substances toxic to wildlife and, once covered, chemical reactions may produce other pollutants. The sites may also leak and release toxins into the environment.
- Not clearing away glass, plastic and other non-*biodegradable* materials following picnics and other activities.
- Mining destroys the structure of the land and adds pollutants from the machinery and processes involved.

pollution, thermal: pollution of the environment by heat.

There is a fairly narrow range of temperatures in which life can exist. Each species has a 'cold death point' and a temperature above which enzyme systems fail and death results.

Human activities which alter the temperature of the environment either locally or globally are called thermal pollution.

Some examples of thermal pollution are shown in the table.

Example	Source of waste heat	Effect(s)	Possible remedies
warming of stretches of river water	water used to cool machinery in power stations	levels of oxygen in the water may be reduced so fish and other animals cannot survive	ensure that the warm water returned to the river is as highly oxygenated as possible
warming of coastal water	water used to cool machinery in nuclear power stations	may affect development of larvae of shellfish	return water further out to sea
warming of air in cities	heating systems in homes and in industry	increased growth of plants and some animals	more efficient insulation and better dispersal

polymer: a large molecule which is made from many, similar smaller molecules.
- *Starch* is a polymer of glucose molecules.
- *Cellulose* is a polymer of glucose molecules.
- *Proteins* are polymers of amino acids.

polysaccharide: a *carbohydrate* made from many sugar molecules joined together.
(See also *carbohydrate*.)

population: all the organisms of the same *species* living in a certain area.
The size of a population depends on:
- births
- deaths
- migration (animals only).

The numbers of a species surviving in an area may be influenced by *biotic* and *abiotic* factors.
Biotic factors include:
- *competition* for food between individuals of the population
- competition for food between members of different species

- predation by another species (see *predator/prey relationships*)
- *parasitism.*

Abiotic factors include:

- climate and weather
- soil pH
- availability of nutrients in the soil.

population growth curve: a graph showing how the numbers in a *population* vary with time.

The graph shows the growth curve you would expect when a *species* enters a new environment.

- Stage A – the species has just been introduced into the area, some will die, others will not reproduce to their full capacity. The population as a whole is adapting to the new environment. (See *adaptation*.)
- Stage B – the species has adapted, resources are plentiful for the small numbers and so population growth is rapid.
- Stage C – the population has reached the carrying capacity of the environment: space and food resources for the large numbers are limited, predation probably has a larger effect. Some individuals will leave the environment if they can. (See *predatory/prey relationships*.)

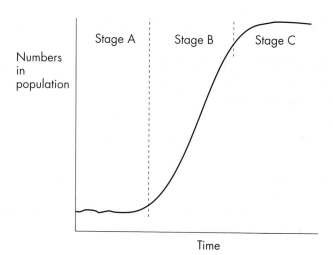

Once the carrying capacity has been reached, the population will remain at this level if there are no significant changes. A new disease could virtually wipe out the population, whereas if more food or space became available, it may be able to increase further.

potable water: water which is fit to drink.

All seawater is unfit to drink because of the high salt (sodium chloride) content. This would causes serious problems of *osmosis* in the body.

Water in rivers, ponds and lakes is also unfit to drink as it may contain:

- *pathogenic bacteria*
- excretory products from animals
- nitrates and phosphates.

All these materials are effectively removed in water treatment plants, and the water we receive in our houses has undergone *chlorination* to ensure it is safe to drink. But water may still be safe to drink even if it has not been treated. Rainwater falls on the earth and:

- percolates through soil and some types of rock
- is filtered as it percolates through the rock and all bacteria and suspended matter are removed
- can safely be taken from deep wells is as it nearly always free from pathogenic bacteria and quite safe to drink.

potometer: a piece of apparatus which can be used to measure water uptake by plants.

Potometers work on the principle that:

- water taken up by the cut end of the stem draws an air bubble along a piece of capillary tubing
- the water is taken up because water is pulled up the stem to replace water lost from the leaves
- the amount of water taken up is roughly equal to that lost from the leaves.

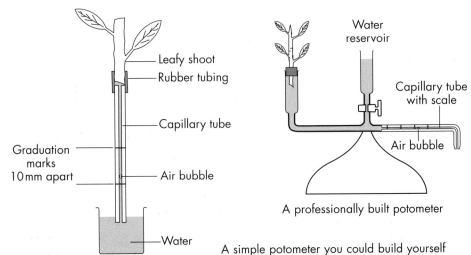

A professionally built potometer

A simple potometer you could build yourself

The distance moved by the air bubble in a given time period is a measure of the rate of water uptake. It can therefore give a measure of the rate of water loss – the rate of *transpiration*.

predator: a *carnivore* which hunts and kills its *prey*.
Some predators hunt collectively: killer whales often hunt in packs and herd salmon or tuna into coves so that they can catch them more effectively. Some attract their prey: deepsea angler fish have a luminous lure in their open mouths which attracts their prey.

predator/prey relationship: the way in which numbers of a *predator* and its *prey* depend upon each other.
The relationship between a predator and its prey is a very close one, and the changes in the *population* of each follow similar, cyclical patterns. This is because the numbers of predators depend on how much prey there is as a food source and the numbers of the prey are influenced by how many predators are killing them and eating them. So:
- as the numbers of prey increase, there will be more food for the predators
- the numbers of predators will increase
- the increased number of predators will eat more prey
- the population of prey will decrease
- there will be less food for the predators so their numbers will decrease
- they will eat less prey so the numbers of prey will increase…
- …and so on!

The graph shows the changes in numbers of lynx (a predator like a large cat) and hares (prey) in an environment in Canada.

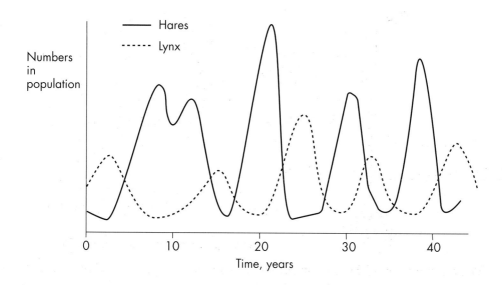

pregnancy: in a *mammal*, the time between *fertilisation* and *birth* when the *embryo* is developing in the *uterus*.

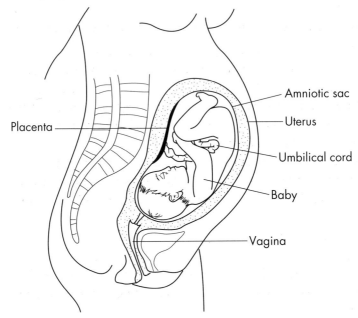

The time spent in the uterus varies enormously between different species. It is only two weeks in mice but nearly two years in elephants. In humans, a woman is pregnant for about thirty nine weeks.

During human pregnancy:
- the embryo is anchored in the uterus by the *placenta* which supplies it with food and oxygen
- all the embryo's major organs form and begin to develop
- the embryo grows more rapidly than at any other time in its life
- the embryo is surrounded by the *amniotic fluid* which cushions it from jolts
- the uterus grows to accommodate the developing embryo and displaces many of the mother's internal organs – including her heart
- the mother often stores fat which will be used after birth to produce her milk.

prey: the organism which is killed and eaten by a *predator*.
Prey are usually more numerous than the predators which kill and eat them because they are lower in the *food chain*. They are often, but not necessarily, *herbivores*.
(See *predator/prey relationships*.)

primary consumer: an organism which feeds from a *producer*.
Primary consumers are *herbivores* as they feed from plants or plant-like

organisms such as *algae*. They include animals such as sheep, rabbits and animals of the *zooplankton*. They are eaten by *secondary consumers* which are *carnivores*.

You can see the position of primary consumers in the following food chain.

grass ⟶ rabbit ⟶ fox
(producer)   (primary consumer)   (secondary consumer)

primary feathers: the feathers on a bird's wing furthest away from the body. The primary feathers are attached to bones in the bird's wing which are the equivalent of our hand and finger bones.

All the feathers on the wing push down on the air as the wing moves down. This is what creates the upthrust and keeps the bird in the air. The primary feathers also create a forward thrust by curling up and back on the down-stroke.

(See also *secondary feathers, wing*.)

primates: *mammals* with four fingers and an opposable thumb (i.e. thumb can be moved to face the fingers) and eyes facing forwards to give stereoscopic vision.

Primates evolved to live in trees, where these two features are clearly advantageous.

● The opposable thumb allows primates to grasp branches securely.
● Stereoscopic vision allows primates to judge distance accurately: an error in judging distance in trees could lead to a fatal fall.

In addition, primates have slender, freely movable limbs which allows them to climb and search for food. They also have large brains and complex social behaviour.

The group includes lemurs, monkeys, apes and humans.

producer: an organism which can make complex *organic substances* from simple molecules.

Producers produce their own food; they are the only organisms which can do this. Nearly all producers can *photosynthesise* and so use light energy to drive the reactions which make *carbohydrates*. All other organisms must ingest organic molecules and are either *consumers* or *decomposers*. Producers are at the beginning of all *food chains*.

progesterone: one of the female sex *hormones*.
Progesterone is produced by the *corpus luteum* in the ovary and, during pregnancy, by the *placenta*. The main function of progesterone is to maintain the lining of the *uterus*. This is essential so that an embryo can implant into the uterus lining and continue to develop. If *implantation* does not take place:
● the corpus luteum degenerates and stops secreting progesterone
● the low level of progesterone causes the blood supply to the uterus lining to be reduced
● cells in the uterus lining die and are lost with blood in *menstruation*.
The high levels of progesterone released during pregnancy inhibit the release of *FSH* and *LH* by the *pituitary gland*. This ensures that no other *follicles* start to develop in the *ovaries* during a pregnancy.

prokaryotes: organisms whose *cells* do not have true nuclei.
The cells of animals, plants and most other organisms have a nucleus which is contained in a nuclear *membrane*. Other *organelles*, such as mitochondria and chloroplasts also have a membrane surrounding them.
Prokaryotes lack mitochondria and chloroplasts. They do not have a true nucleus as their genetic material is not surrounded by a membrane.
The only prokaryotes you need know about are *bacteria*.

prolactin: a *hormone* released by the *pituitary gland*.
Prolactin causes glands in the breasts (alveoli) to produce milk (*lactation*). Another hormone (oxytocin) causes the alveoli to release the milk into ducts in the breast so that the young can obtain it by suckling.

protease: an *enzyme* which digests proteins, or parts of proteins, into smaller molecules.
In humans protease enzymes are secreted by the *stomach*, *pancreas* and *small intestine*. They have the following effects:
● gastric protease – digests protein molecules into shorter chains of *amino acids*
● pancreatic and intestinal proteases – digest proteins and parts of proteins into individual amino acids.

Biological washing powders often contain proteases to remove stains like blood by digesting the proteins in them. Proteases are also used in the brewing industry to reduce the cloudiness of beer by digesting any remaining yeast cells.

protein: a large molecule made of many *amino acids*.

Proteins are needed by all living things to make new *cell membranes* and *enzymes*. They are therefore needed for *growth* and also for repair of damaged *tissue* – anywhere that new cells must be produced. The *antibodies* and some of the *hormones* found in animals are also proteins.

Good sources of protein in our diet include:

- meats – including chicken, beef, lamb and pork
- fish
- eggs
- cheese
- bread
- peas, beans and nuts
- *mycoprotein* products.

Proteins are the only nutrients which contain nitrogen, which organisms need to manufacture *DNA* as well as their own proteins.

protein synthesis: the process by which *DNA* controls the manufacture of *proteins* in a cell.

DNA in the *nucleus* of the cell carries the genetic code which can specify which protein is to be made. The proteins are actually assembled from *amino acids* in the *ribosomes* which are in the *cytoplasm*. Somehow the code must be carried from the DNA to the ribosomes and then decoded.

The code is carried by a messenger – a molecule called messenger RNA (m-RNA). This is made in the nucleus using DNA as the basis. Each triplet of bases on a strand of a DNA molecule codes for an amino acid.

The DNA strands separate and one of them makes a new strand using spare bases which line up according to the base pairing rule.

This new strand is the m-RNA. It is much smaller than DNA, has only one strand and the base thymine in DNA is replaced by uracil (see page 234).

The triplets of bases on the m-RNA now carry the code for the amino acids.

The m-RNA now moves away from the DNA and out of the nucleus.

When the m-RNA reaches a ribosome, it threads itself through the ribosome which 'reads' the code. As each triplet is decoded a different RNA molecule (called transfer RNA or t-RNA) brings the appropriate amino acid. As more and more amino acids are brought, they are assembled in the order specified by the m-RNA.

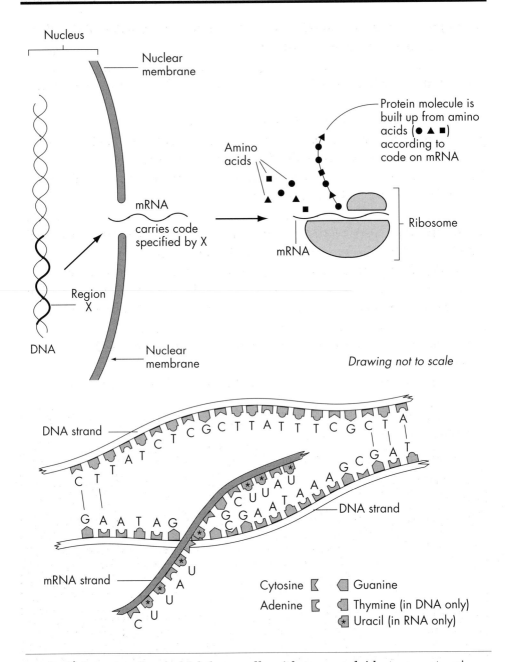

Nucleus

Nuclear membrane

Protein molecule is built up from amino acids (● ▲ ■) according to code on mRNA

Amino acids

mRNA carries code specified by X

Ribosome

mRNA

Region X

DNA

Nuclear membrane

Drawing not to scale

DNA strand

C T C G C T T A T T T C G C T A

A T T A T C A G A T

C T T G

G A A T A G

C U U A U

C U A A A G C G

G G A A T A A A

DNA strand

mRNA strand

U A U C

Cytosine | Guanine
Adenine | Thymine (in DNA only)
Uracil (in RNA only)

protoctista: organisms which have cells with true nuclei but are not *animals, plants* or *fungi.*

Many protoctistans are unicellular, but the group also includes all the *algae*, including the multicellular seaweeds.

protozoa: unicellular members of the *protoctista* which show some animal-like features.
● Most can move using *cilia*, *flagella* or *pseudopodia*.
● None can *photosynthesise*. They must all ingest materials made by other organisms. They feed like animals or animal *parasites*.
The protozoa used to be included in the animal kingdom, but animals are now defined as multicellular organisms.

pseudopodium (plural pseudopodia): a temporary extension from a cell which is used for feeding or locomotion. (See *phagocyte*.)
A pseudopodium is formed when cytoplasm flows into part of a cell and enlarges it. This results in movement of the cell in that direction. Pseudopodia are formed by *protozoa* like *Amoeba* and some types of *white blood cell*.

puberty: the stage of development when sex organs mature and reproduction becomes possible.
The main features of puberty in boys and girls are shown in the table.

Feature of puberty	Boys	Girls
age of onset	12–13 (average)	10–11 (average)
hormone released from sex organs	testosterone	oestrogen
changes in sex organs	● penis enlarges ● testes begin to make sperm ● glands near to the penis develop and begin to secrete fluids	● follicles begin to mature in ovary ● uterus becomes larger and begins to develop linings in preparation for implantation ● *menstruation* begins
secondary sex characteristics	● shoulders broaden ● pubic, facial and other body hair appears ● voice deepens	● breasts develop ● pubic and underarm hair appears ● pelvis becomes wider

It is the name for the physical changes which are the cause of many of the emotional changes of *adolescence*. The age at which puberty begins varies considerably and is getting younger. Girls typically enter puberty at 10–11 whereas in boys the age is usually 12–13. This is, on average, four years younger than it was 100 years ago.

The changes which take place are triggered when the *pituitary gland* signifi-cantly increases its secretion of *FSH*. This hormone affects the ovaries in females, causing follicles to begin to develop and to produce *oestrogen*. In males, FSH targets the testes which produce *testosterone* in response. The sex hormones, (oestrogen and testosterone), bring about the changes of puberty. Biologists are still unsure as to what triggers the pituitary gland to increase the output of FSH.

pulmonary artery: the *artery* which carries *blood* from the *heart* to the *lungs*.

The pulmonary artery carries deoxygenated blood from the right ventricle of the heart. Like all arteries, it has a thick wall to withstand the pressure gen-erated by the contraction of the right ventricle. The wall is not as thick as that of the *aorta* because the right ventricle does not generate as high a pressure as the left ventricle.

The pulmonary artery is the only artery in the body which carries deoxy-genated blood.

pulmonary tuberculosis (TB): a disease which affects the *lungs* and is caused by a *bacterium*.

The bacterium is normally spread by airborne droplets which are breathed in. Inside the lungs, the bacteria multiply and form small lumps or masses called tubercles which give the disease its name. The tubercles are semi-transparent and show up as opaque patches on chest X-rays.

In most cases, the body's own *immune system* can combat the infection at this stage and the person feels no major symptoms except a dry cough. Occasionally, the person may cough up blood from lung tissue damaged by the bacterium.

In about 5% of cases, the infection is not halted by the immune system, may spread to other parts of the body and can be fatal. The bacteria may become dormant and then become active again many years later – often in old age. This secondary stage of TB is called consumption and is often much more serious than the initial infection.

A different strain of the TB bacterium can infect cattle and be spread to humans through the milk. In Britain, this is not a problem because:

- herds of cattle are inspected regularly and if any animal is infected, the herd is slaughtered
- milk is *pasteurised* which kills the TB bacteria.

TB used to be one of the major killer diseases in many countries in the world and still kills millions worldwide. An effective *vaccine* is available and has significantly reduced TB in Europe. It is, however on the increase again in some communities.

pulmonary vein: the *vein* which returns *blood* from the *lungs* to the *heart*. The pulmonary vein carries blood which has been oxygenated in the lungs back to the left atrium of the heart. Like all veins, it has a wide lumen (central space) to reduce resistance to the flow of the blood which is under low pressure. It also has a thin wall.

The pulmonary vein is the only vein in the body which carries oxygenated blood.

pulse: the expansion and recoil of an *artery*.

When the left ventricle of the *heart* contracts, it pumps blood into the *aorta*. The high pressure of the blood stretches the aorta. When the ventricle stops contracting, the valve at the base of the aorta closes and the aorta recoils to its original size.

The increase in pressure due to the contraction of the left ventricle is transmitted through all the arteries as a pressure wave. As the pressure wave arrives at a particular point, the artery is stretched and then it recoils as the wave passes. We feel the stretching and recoil as a pulse.

Do not confuse the pressure of the blood with its movement. Find your pulse at your wrist or your neck. You can feel a pulse about once every second. This is the pressure wave passing through the blood at this point and it corresponds with the contraction of the left ventricle. Blood is moving under your finger all the time – not just when you can feel the pulse.

pulse rate: the number of *pulses* which can be felt in one minute.

Pulse rate varies considerably between individuals. It is affected by a number of factors.

- Age – newborn babies may have a resting pulse rate of 150 bpm, in preschool children it may be 120 bpm whereas in adults it is typically 60–70 bpm.
- Exercise – when we *exercise*, the heart beats faster to deliver more oxygen and glucose to the muscles.
- Health – when we are ill, particularly when we have a fever, heart rate increases.
- Stress – when we are stressed, the *adrenal glands* secrete *adrenaline* which increases heart rate.

pupil: the hole in the *iris* which allows light into the *eye*.

Contraction and relaxation of muscles in the iris can alter the size of the pupil.

The pupil is enlarged when:
- it is dark and we need to allow more light into the eye to see clearly
- when we are in shock.

The pupil is constricted when it is bright and too much light may damage sense cells in the *retina*.

purine: one of the types of bases which make up the *DNA* molecule. Adenine and guanine are the purine bases. Each purine always pairs with a *pyrimidine* base.

putrefying bacteria: the *bacteria* which bring about *decay*. (See *decomposers* and *decay* for details.)

pyramid of biomass: a *food chain* drawn as a pyramid in sequence in which the blocks represent the total *biomass* of each member in the chain. For example, consider these two food chains and their pyramids of biomass. Compare them with their *pyramids of numbers*.

grass ⟶ grasshoppers ⟶ frogs ⟶ birds
oak tree ⟶ aphids ⟶ ladybirds ⟶ birds

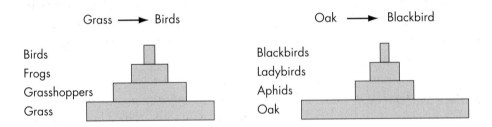

Energy is needed to build biomass and so the total biomass decreases with each link in the food chain. The grasshopper uses some of the energy it receives from the grass for movement, excretion and other body processes. Less energy is passed on to the frogs than the grasshoppers received and so there is less biomass of frogs.

Now look at this food chain and its pyramid of biomass on page 239.

phytoplankton ⟶ zooplankton ⟶ seal ⟶ killer whale

In this case, the biomass of the *phytoplankton* appears less than that of the *zooplankton*. This is true for that moment in time but, over a year, the phytoplankton will make much more biomass than the zooplankton. This is not shown in a pyramid of biomass.

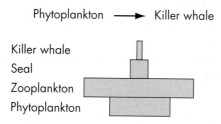

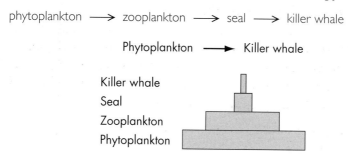

pyramid of energy: a *food chain* drawn as a pyramid in sequence in which the blocks represent the total energy per year of each member in the chain. Look at the food chain based on the *phytoplankton* and its pyramid of energy.

phytoplankton ⟶ zooplankton ⟶ seal ⟶ killer whale

Compare this with the *pyramid of biomass* for the same food chain. The size of the bottom two links in the chain is now as we would expect. Over a year, the phytoplankton absorb and use more energy than they pass on to the zooplankton. This is true of all links in all food chains and so pyramids of energy always look like pyramids!

pyramid of numbers: a *food chain* drawn in sequence as a pyramid in which the blocks represent the total numbers of each member in the chain. Look at these two food chains and their pyramids of numbers.

grass ⟶ grasshoppers ⟶ frogs ⟶ birds
oak tree ⟶ aphids ⟶ ladybirds ⟶ birds

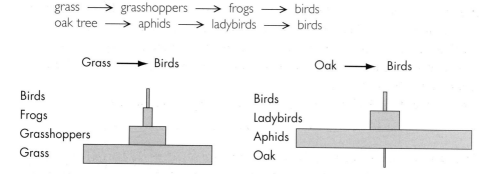

Although the first food chain is represented by a true pyramid, the second one is not. The blocks representing the first two links in the chain are reversed in size. This is because a pyramid of numbers takes no account of size. Obviously one oak tree will provide much more energy for the aphids than one grass plant will provide for the grasshoppers.

Compare these diagrams with the *pyramids of biomass* for the same food chains. This does take account of the size of the organisms and we see a true pyramid for both food chains.

pyrimidine: one of the types of bases which make up the *DNA* molecule. Cytosine and thymine are the pyrimidine bases. Each pyrimidine always pairs with a *purine* base.

quadrat: a square metal frame used in ecological investigations to estimate numbers of organisms in an area.

You can use quadrats in two main ways:
- to estimate the total number of organisms in an area
- to estimate the changes in numbers of organisms across an area.

ESTIMATING THE TOTAL NUMBER OF BUTTERCUPS IN A FIELD

Before you start, you need to know the area of the quadrat and that of the area you are investigating. Once you know these two areas:
- throw the quadrat a number of times (say 50) at random
- count the number of buttercups in each quadrat
- find the average number of buttercups in a quadrat.

You can now estimate the number of buttercups in the field using the formula:

$$\frac{\text{average number of buttercups} \times \text{area of field}}{\text{area of quadrat}}$$

Suppose:
- the field measured 110 m by 50 m, so its area is $110 \times 50 = 5500$ m^2
- the quadrat measured 25 cm by 25 cm, so its area (in square metres) is $0.25 \times 0.25 = 0.0625$ m^2
- the average number of buttercups per quadrat was 6.

The number of buttercups in the field would be:

$$\frac{6 \times 5500}{0.0625} = 528\,000 \text{ (over half a million buttercups!)}$$

ESTIMATING THE CHANGES IN THE NUMBERS IN BUTTERCUPS ACROSS AN AREA

To do this we carry out a transect.
- Lay out a tape measure 100 m long (or longer if necessary) across the area.
- At regular intervals (say every 5 m), place five quadrats next to the tape measure.
- Count the number of buttercups in each quadrat and find the average for each point along the tape measure.

The results can be shown in a diagram which shows how the numbers vary across the area. This can then be related to environmental factors such as changes in soil pH or changes in light intensity.

radicle: the root of the *embryo* in a *seed*.

When a seed *germinates*, the first structure to emerge is the radicle which grows downwards in response to gravity. As it grows, roots hairs appear just behind the tip and it develops lateral branches. It is now called a *root*.

radiocarbon dating: a method used for determining the age of *fossils*.

All sources of *carbon* contain some radioactive carbon – or radiocarbon. Like any other radioactive substance, radiocarbon decays over time. It has a half-life of 5770 years. This means that every 5770 years half of whatever radiocarbon there is decays.

The proportion of radiocarbon to normal carbon is constant in all living things. Once an organism dies and is fossilised, the proportion begins to change. This is because the radiocarbon decays and is not replaced whereas the normal carbon is unchanged.

The proportion of radiocarbon to normal carbon will halve every 5770 years. So by comparing the normal proportion with the proportion in a fossil, we can work out the age of the fossil.

EXAMPLE

Suppose:
- the normal proportions are 1 part radiocarbon to 100 parts normal carbon
- the proportions in a fossil are 1 part radiocarbon to 400 parts normal carbon.

The proportion in the fossil is ¼ of the normal proportion. There is ¼ of the radiocarbon, so the radiocarbon must have halved then halved again. This will have taken two half-lives.

So, the age of the fossil is 2 × 5770 years = 11 540 years.

Because of its relatively short half-life, radiocarbon is not suitable for estimating the age of fossils more than 70, 000 years old.

rate of reaction: the number of molecules of *reactants* which react, or molecules of products which are formed, in a given time (usually a second).

In some biological experiments, we measure how long a reaction takes under different conditions. For example, we might measure how long it takes *lipase* to digest milk fat at different temperatures.

But we are not really measuring rate of reaction. To do this we would need to know how many molecules of fat were digested by the lipase in the time. We could then calculate how many molecules were digested per minute (or per second).

Clearly we do not know how much fat was digested. But, if we keep the amount of the substance the same in each experiment:

● we know that the number of molecules of fat (whatever it really is) will be the same each time

● we can 'pretend' that the number of molecules digested each time is 100 (or any other number)

● the rate of reaction is then:

$$\frac{100}{\text{time taken}}$$

The rates of biological reactions are affected by a number of factors, some of which are shown in the table.

Factor	Effect of changing the factor	Reason for effect
temperature	● increasing temperature up to an optimum increases rate ● further increase in temperature decreases the rate	● reactant molecules have more kinetic energy and so collide more often ● *enzymes* controlling reaction are being denatured
concentration of reactants	increasing the concentration increases the rate of reaction	there are more molecules in the same volume and so more collisions occur
pH of solution	if pH is too far from an optimum, rate will decrease	enzymes are adapted to function within a narrow pH range, usually around pH 7
surface area of a solid reactant	increasing the surface area increases the rate of reaction	reaction can only take place at the surface, so the more surface there is, the greater the number of collisions

reactants: chemicals which react together.

For example, when two glucose molecules react together, they form a molecule of maltose and a molecule of water.

$$C_6H_{12}O_6 + C_6H_{12}O_6 \longrightarrow C_{12}H_{22}O_{11} + H_2O$$

glucose　　　glucose　　　　maltose　　water

REACTANTS　　　　　　　　PRODUCTS

reaction time: the time between a *stimulus* being detected and the first observable *response*.

Reaction times depend on the nature of the coordinating system. As a result, they vary enormously both between organisms and within an organism.

- The time between sense cells in the *retina* detecting a very bright light and the *iris* muscles contracting to make the pupil smaller is less than a second.
- The time between the islet cells in the *pancreas* detecting a rise in blood glucose and cells in the *liver* beginning to absorb the excess glucose is several seconds.
- The time between a shoot tip detecting light from one side and the shoot beginning to grow towards the light is several minutes.

receptor: any structure which can detect a *stimulus*.

Receptors in larger animals are usually specialised sense cells, often in sense organs such as the eye, ear and nose. An earthworm, however, does not have any of these sense organs, but it still has receptors. Plants also do not have sense organs, but structures in cells in the root and shoot act as receptors.

A receptor is essential for any biological response to occur. Biological behaviour always follows the following sequence.

stimulus	→	receptor	→	coordinating system	→	effector	→	response
a trigger		detects the trigger		links receptor and effector		makes something happen		something happens!

Clearly, without a receptor, the chain is incomplete and no response is possible.

recessive: refers to an *allele* which is only expressed when the corresponding *dominant* allele is absent.

For example, dwarfness in pea plants is recessive. A pea plant will only be a dwarf plant if it inherits two dwarf alleles. If it inherits just one tall allele with a dwarf allele, it will be tall because tall is dominant.

Let **T** = tall allele (dominant) and **t** = dwarf allele (recessive):

- **TT** and **Tt** will be tall plants – the tall allele is dominant and so is always expressed.
- **tt** will be dwarf – both alleles are recessive, there is no dominant allele to be expressed.

recovery period: the time taken after *exercise* for pulse rate and breathing rate to return to pre-exercise levels.

During vigorous exercise, our *muscles* generate a lot of energy through *anaerobic respiration* and produce *lactic acid*. After the exercise:

- the lactic acid must be oxidised
- this requires extra oxygen over and above that normally required when we are at rest
- we continue to breathe faster to obtain the extra oxygen
- our heart continues to beat faster to deliver the extra oxygen to muscles and liver to oxidise the lactic acid.

As more and more lactic acid is oxidised, we need less extra oxygen and so breathing rate and pulse rate slow down until they reach the pre-exercise levels.

rectum: the region of the *large intestine* immediately before the anus. The rectum stores *faeces* until they are egested by the anus.

red blood cell: a *blood cell* found in *vertebrates* specialised for carrying oxygen.

Red blood cells are red because they contain the protein *haemoglobin* which can combine with oxygen to form *oxyhaemoglobin*. Oxyhaemoglobin gives blood in arteries its bright red colour. Blood in veins is darker in colour because the haemoglobin has lost some of the oxygen which was bound to it. In humans and most other mammals, the red blood cells are disc-like and do not have a nucleus. Red blood cells in other vertebrates are oval and have a nucleus.

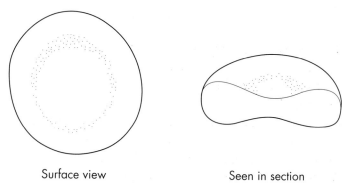

Surface view   Seen in section

There is a huge turnover of red blood cells in humans.
- They live for about 120 days.
- They are manufactured in the *bone marrow* of long bones.
- Worn-out red blood cells are destroyed by *phagocytes* in the spleen and liver.
- Some of the materials in red blood cells are recycled, others are excreted in *bile*.

One estimate is that we make approximately 100 million red blood cells every minute!

Sometimes we do not make enough red blood cells. This condition is known as *anaemia*.

reducing sugar: any sugar which will give a positive result when heated with Benedict's reagent. (See *Food tests*.)
Glucose, maltose and lactose (milk sugar) are all reducing sugars.
Sucrose (the sugar we put in tea and coffee) is a non-reducing sugar.

reduction: a chemical reaction in which the substance reduced gains electrons.

reflection: a wave bouncing off an object instead of passing through it.
Examples of reflection include:
- the greenhouse gases reflecting longwave radiation back towards the earth (see *greenhouse effect*)
- 'green' wavelengths of light being reflected off a leaf – this is why it looks green
- bats using high-pitched sounds to judge the distance of objects – the reflections are detected and decoded by the bat.

reflex action: an automatic, predictable *response* to a *stimulus* brought about by a *nervous system*.
If you touch a hot object:
- you pull your hand away – you don't drum your fingers on the object
- you do it without thinking about how hot it is and whether it might burn you.

This is typical of reflexes: they are automatic and the same stimulus always produces the same response. This is because the same *receptors* are stimulated and they send impulses along the same pathway of *neurones* to the same *effector*. These pathways are called *reflex arcs*.
The sequence of events in a reflex action is:

stimulus	→	receptor	→	sensory neurone	→	central nervous system	→	motor neurone	→	effector	→	response
		detects stimulus		carries impulses from receptor to CNS		transfers impulses from sensory nerve cell to motor nerve cell		carries impulses from CNS to effector		brings about response		

Reflex actions can be:
- protective – the blinking reflex helps to prevent bright light damaging cells in the *retina*

- homeostatic – the reflex increase in breathing rate following an increase in carbon dioxide levels in the blood helps to restore the carbon dioxide level to normal.

Although reflex actions are automatic, we can sometimes override them temporarily. You can keep hold of a hot object if you really decide you are going to – but usually not for long. The reflex response nearly always reasserts itself.

The word 'reflex' is often used incorrectly by sports commentators who describe 'reflex saves' or 'reflex catches'. Of course, there are no such things. Goalkeepers don't have to save goal-bound shots – they choose to. Having decided to save a shot, the goalkeeper must then decide how to save it – a different set of movements is needed for each save. So, it fails the definition of reflex on both counts: it isn't automatic and doesn't always produce the same response.

reflex arc: a pathway of *neurones* which allows a particular *reflex action* to occur.

The diagram shows the reflex arc for the withdrawal reflex (removing your hand from a hot object).

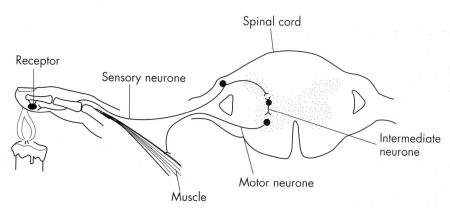

When you put your hand over a flame (you don't have to try it!), the following events occur.

- Sense cells in the skin detect the heat.
- They generate an impulse in the sensory neurone.
- The impulse travels along the neurone which runs in a nerve up the arm to the spinal cord inside the spine in the neck.
- At the end of the sensory neurone, the impulse is transmitted across a *synapse* by chemicals to the intermediate neurone.
- The impulse passes along the intermediate neurone.
- It crosses the synapse between the intermediate and motor neurones.

- The impulse travels along the motor neurone from the spinal cord in the neck, down the arm to the muscles in the hand and arm.
- The muscles contract and move the hand away from the heat.

Each time these sense cells are stimulated, they will send impulses along this reflex arc and the same response will result.

refraction: the change in direction of a wave when it moves to a medium of different density.

The most important example of refraction you need to know is the refraction which occurs as light waves enter the *eye*. The light will change direction when it moves from one medium to another. There are, therefore, four places where refraction will occur:

- as the light enters the cornea from the air
- as the light leaves the cornea and enters the aqueous humour
- as the light leaves the aqueous humour and enters the lens
- as the light leaves the lens and enters the vitreous humour.

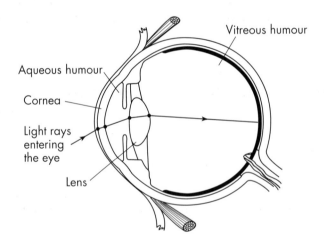

rejection: an *immune response* to a transplanted *organ* or transplanted *tissue*.

The cells of a transplanted organ will not have the same *antigens* as the recipient's own cells. These 'foreign' or 'non-self' antigens are detected by the *immune system* which mounts an immune response to destroy them. This means that the transplant is unlikely to survive.

There are two main techniques which are used to overcome this.

- Tissue typing – this matches donor and recipient as closely as possible. Good tissue typing will give a transplant with antigens which are very similar to those of the recipient. Members of the same family usually have very similar antigen sets. Identical twins match perfectly as they have identical antigens.

● *Immunosuppressive drugs* – these reduce the ability of the immune system to produce an immune response.

rennin: an *enzyme* found in the stomach of young mammals which curdles (clots) milk.

Milk is the only food of young mammals for some time. It is essential that the milk, particularly the protein in the milk, is digested properly. Rennin curdles milk protein which, because it is solid, is retained in the stomach longer and digested more effectively.

Rennet (an impure form of rennin) is used in cheesemaking. After the milk has been soured (made acidic) by bacteria, rennet is added to curdle the milk protein. The solids formed are called 'curds' and these curds are pressed to form immature cheese.

Because vegetarians will not eat cheese made using extracts from the stomachs of young animals, other enzymes have been developed to do the same job. Cheese made with 'vegetarian rennet' is often made using a fungal enzyme.

reproduction: producing offspring of the same *species*.

There are two main types of reproduction: *sexual reproduction* and *asexual reproduction*. Nearly all species can reproduce sexually, and most animals can only reproduce sexually. Most plants and simpler organisms can reproduce both ways.

The table compares sexual and asexual reproduction.

Feature of the process	Sexual reproduction	Asexual reproduction
number of parents	usually two, only one needed in hermaphrodite organisms	one
gametes formed	yes	no
fertilisation occurs	yes	no
offspring vary	fertilisation ensures genetic *variation* of offspring	offspring are genetically identical

reproductive hormones: *hormones* which help to control the processes of *reproduction*.

The table on the next page shows the sources and effects of the main human reproductive hormones.

Hormone	Secreted by	Target	Effect
FSH (follicle stimulating hormone)	pituitary gland	• follicles in ovary (female) • testis (male)	• stimulates development of follicles and secretion of oestrogen by follicles • stimulates development of sperm
LH (luteinising hormone)	pituitary gland	• follicles in ovary • testes	• stimulates ovulation and formation of corpus luteum • stimulates secretion of testosterone
oestrogen	ovary (cells in follicle)	• uterus • pituitary gland • general	• stimulates production of uterus lining • inhibits production of FSH • secondary sex characteristics
progesterone	ovary (follicle/corpus luteum)	• uterus • pituitary gland	• maintains uterus lining • inhibits production of FSH and LH
testosterone	testis	• testis • general	• sperm production • secondary sex characteristics

reproductive system, human: the organs which produce the sex cells (*gametes*), allow intercourse and, in females, allow *fertilisation* and development of the embryo/fetus.

The diagrams show the male and female reproductive systems, and the tables summarise the functions of the parts of the two systems.

MALE

Part	Main function
testis	produces sperm
scrotum	holds testes outside body to maintain ideal temperature for sperm production
sperm duct	carries sperm to urethra
urethra	carries sperm through penis
penis	becomes erect to allow intercourse
seminal vesicles/prostate gland	produce the fluid for sperm to swim in

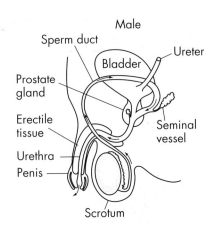

FEMALE

Part	Main function
ovary	produces follicles containing ova
oviduct	carries ova/embryo to uterus
uterus	embryo develops in uterus until birth
cervix	holds the baby in the uterus until ready to be born
vagina	allows intercourse and passage of baby from uterus to outside

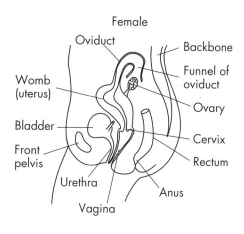

Female

Oviduct
Backbone
Womb (uterus)
Funnel of oviduct
Bladder
Ovary
Front pelvis
Cervix
Urethra
Rectum
Vagina
Anus

reproductive system, plant: the structures in a plant which make and assist with the transfer of the sex cells (*gametes*) and allow fertilisation and formation of the *seed*.

All the reproductive structures of a plant are found within the *flower*.

reptiles: *vertebrates* with dry, scaly skin which hatch from *eggs* with soft shells.

Reptiles are terrestrial (land-dwelling) animals which do not need to return to water to reproduce. *Fertilisation* is internal and the female secretes a leathery shell around the eggs before they are laid.

Other features of reptiles include:
- gas exchange in *lungs*, not through skin like *amphibians*
- a three-chambered *heart* (two atria, but only one ventricle)
- being ectothermic – their temperature changes with the environmental temperature.

resistance: the ability of an organism to be unaffected by a chemical intended to kill it.

Examples of resistance include bacteria becoming resistant to *antibiotics*, insects becoming resistant to insecticides and weeds becoming resistant to *herbicides*.

Resistance usually appears as a result of a chance *mutation* in the *genes* of the organism. Those with the new mutant *allele* for resistance:
- survive the treatment where others are killed
- reproduce and pass on the mutant allele to the next generation
- these individuals also survive the treatment and reproduce and pass on the allele
- the allele for resistance becomes widespread in the population and the treatment becomes largely ineffective.

This is an example of *natural selection* in action. Those best adapted to their surroundings survive to reproduce while others die out. In the examples above, the key feature in the environment is the chemical used to try to kill the organisms. Those that can withstand this have a huge advantage.

respiration: the release of energy from organic molecules.
Respiration occurs in all living things. The energy released in respiration is used to drive all the other reactions and processes which take place in living things.
(See *aerobic respiration, anaerobic respiration* and *fermentation* for details.)

response: what an organism does when it reacts to a *stimulus*.
If you shine light on plant stems from one side only, they respond by growing towards the light.
If you touch a hot object, you respond by taking your hand away.

restriction endonucleases: *enzymes* used in *genetic engineering*.
Restriction endonucleases are used to cut *DNA* into small fragments.
Different endonucleases cut DNA in different places. By choosing the correct endonuclease, scientists can cut out just the part of a DNA molecule they want to work with.

retina: the innermost, light sensitive layer of the wall of the *eye*.
In humans, the retina contains two kinds of sense cells: *rods* and *cones*. Rods are sensitive to low light intensities and allow us to see at night; they do not allow colour vision. Cones are only active in bright light, but allow us to see in greater detail and to perceive colours.

ribcage: the structure which supports and protects the *thorax*.
The ribcage (more correctly known as the thoracic cage) consists of the ribs, the vertebral column (*spine*) and the sternum (breastbone). The *intercostal muscles* lie between the ribs and move the ribcage when we breathe.

ribonucleic acid: see *RNA*.

ribosome: the cell *organelle* responsible for *protein synthesis*.
Ribosomes are found in the cytoplasm of *cells* and decode the 'message' carried by *messenger RNA* (m-RNA) from the *DNA* in the nucleus.
(See *protein synthesis*.)

RNA: ribonucleic acid, a nucleic acid similar in some ways to *DNA*.
There are two main types of RNA: *messenger RNA* (m-RNA) and *transfer RNA* (t-RNA). Both differ from DNA in a number of important ways.
● RNA molecules are single-stranded molecules whereas DNA is double-stranded.
● RNA molecules are much smaller than DNA molecules.
● RNA molecules do not contain the base thymine. It is replace by uracil.
The functions of the two types of RNA are different. Messenger RNA brings the code for a protein from the DNA in the nucleus to the *ribosomes* in the cytoplasm. Transfer RNA brings the individual amino acids to the ribosomes to be assembled into proteins.
(See *protein synthesis* for details.)

rod: a sense cell found in the *retina* of the *eye* of a *vertebrate*.
Rods are sensitive to dim light and allow mammals to see when it is almost dark. They do not allow perception of colour: just black and white and shades of grey.
The rods are found throughout the retina (except at the *fovea*, where there are none), but the highest concentrations are towards the outside of the retina. If you wish to see an object in more detail in dim light, you should look slightly away from it so the rays of light from the object fall on the edge of the retina, where there are more rods. This is why the constellation of

stars called the pleiades (seven sisters) looks brighter in the night sky if you look slightly away from it.

root: the plant organ which anchors the plant in the *soil* and absorbs water and *mineral ions* from the soil.

Roots usually develop from the *radicle* which emerges from the germinating *seed*. Sometimes they develop from stems: in this case they are called adventitious roots.

The region of a root just behind the tip of the root (the apex) is the main region where new cells are formed by *mitosis*. These new cells then elongate to make the root longer. This type of growth is called *apical growth*.

Behind this region of cell division and elongation is a region where there are many *root hairs*. These greatly increase the area available for absorbing water and mineral ions.

Besides the functions described above, roots sometimes act as storage organs. The familiar carrot is a root which contains much stored *carbohydrate*.

root hair: an extension of an epidermal cell of a *root*.
Root hairs are found mainly in the region just behind the tip of the root.

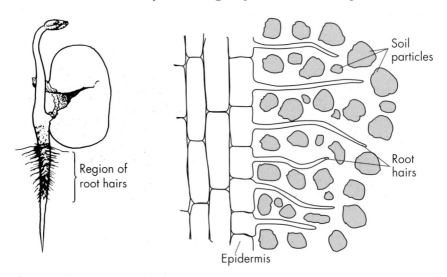

Region of root hairs

Soil particles

Root hairs

Epidermis

They greatly increase the surface area available for *absorption* of water and *mineral ions* from the soil. Root hairs live for only a few days before collapsing. However, as they die, new ones are formed in the same region as the root elongates.

Water enters the root hair cell by *osmosis*. This happens because the solution inside the root hair cell contains more dissolved substances than the solution between the soil particles.

The *cell membrane* of the root hair cell is a *partially permeable membrane*, like all cell membranes, and so water enters by osmosis.

Most mineral ions enter the root hair cell by *active transport*. Energy from *respiration* is needed to move the ions from the soil across the cell membrane into the root hair cell against a *concentration gradient*.

root nodule: a swelling on the root of a *leguminous plant* which contains *nitrogen fixing bacteria*.

The bacteria can convert nitrogen gas into ammonia. They release some of the ammonia they make to the plant cells which use it to synthesise amino acids (and, from them, proteins). The bacteria receive glucose from the plants which they use for *respiration*. So both bacteria and plant benefit from their association – an example of *symbiosis*.

root system: the way *roots* grow.

There are two main root systems.

● The tap root system where a main root develops from the *radicle* and lateral roots grow off this main root.
● The fibrous root system in which the radicle dies soon after emerging from the seed and many roots develop from the base of stems.

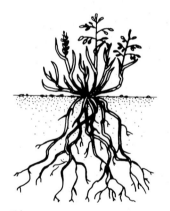

Fibrous root system – grasses

Tap root system – dandelion

Grasses, cereals and members of the onion family have fibrous root systems. Deciduous trees have tap roots when they are young, but lose the central root and retain many of the shallow lateral roots.

Most herbaceous plants and conifers have taproots. The root system of a dandelion is a good example of a tap root system.

rooting powder: a powder which contains one or more plant hormones which is used to help *cuttings* develop *roots*.

Most rooting powder contain *auxins* and other plant growth regulators which stimulate cell division and cell elongation. When bases of stem cuttings are dipped in the rooting powder, cell division is encouraged and the new cells elongate. These two processes lead to root formation.

rumen: the large chamber which is the first part of the stomach of a *ruminant*.

The rumen contains billions of microorganisms: a mixture of *bacteria*, *protoctistans* and *fungi*. These microorganisms secrete *enzymes* which can digest the *cellulose* fibres in plant cell walls. The simple sugars formed from cellulose digestion undergo *fermentation* to release energy for the microorganisms. The also produce organic acids and vitamins which are absorbed through the wall of the rumen. They also produce their own *amino acids* and *proteins*. Eventually, the microorganisms themselves will be digested by the ruminant which will receive an extra supply of protein.

Because both microorganisms and the ruminant benefit, this association is an example of *symbiosis*.

ruminant: a *herbivore*, such as a cow, with a four-chambered stomach.

They feed largely on grass which they chew and swallow and pass to the *rumen* – the first of the four chambers of their large stomach.

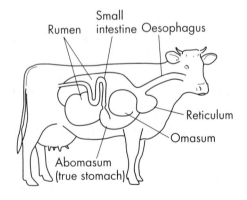

- In the rumen, billions of microorganisms digest the cellulose in the cell walls of the grass and then ferment the simple sugars formed. Some of the products are absorbed through the rumen wall into the blood.
- The animal then regurgitates the food to chew it again (this is called 'chewing the cud' and helps the next stages of digestion).
- The food is swallowed again, but this time bypasses the rumen and enters the other chambers of the stomach. The fourth chamber (the abomasum) is the true stomach and protein digestion proper begins here.

The microorganisms in the rumen produce methane when they ferment the sugars formed by digesting cellulose. Ruminants get rid of this excess gas by belching. The millions of ruminants in the world thus contribute to the levels of methane in the atmosphere and so to the *greenhouse effect*.

saliva: the secretion produced by the *salivary glands*.
Saliva contains:
- *mucus* to lubricate the food when it is swallowed
- water
- an *amylase* to begin the digestion of starch
- sodium hydrogencarbonate to make the solution less acidic for optimum amylase activity.

Saliva is produced whenever we see, smell or taste food.

salivary amylase: the *enzyme* found in *saliva*.
Salivary amylase is the first enzyme to begin to digest food. It digests the polysaccharide *starch* into maltose.

salivary glands: glands found near to the mouth which secrete *saliva*.
The salivary glands are *exocrine glands* as they secrete saliva into a duct which carries it to the mouth.
When we see, smell or taste food, *neurones* carry impulses to the salivary glands which cause them to secrete saliva.

salmonella: the name for a group of bacteria; also used to describe a type of food poisoning caused by the bacteria.
The correct name for the type of food poisoning caused by *Salmonella* bacteria is salmonellosis. The main symptom of salmonella food poisoning is diarrhoea, usually accompanied by vomiting and fever. Other symptoms include headache and abdominal pain.
The diagram on the next page shows the main transmission routes.
Salmonella food poisoning is usually a relatively mild condition and bed rest with regular fluid intake is normally the only treatment required. In more severe cases doctors may prescribe antibiotics, but this is not always effective as strains of salmonella bacteria with *resistance* to many antibiotics have recently emerged.
Transmission can be prevented by a number of measures.
- Good hygiene in the food trade – shops, restaurants and kitchens are inspected regularly to ensure that there is minimum risk of cross-

contamination via utensils and work surfaces. Cooked and raw meats should be stored separately.

- Good hygiene in the home – again, cooked and raw meats should be stored separately. Meat should be cooked thoroughly. Surfaces and utensils should be kept clean. One of the greatest risks comes from not thawing frozen food properly – especially poultry.
- Proper sewage disposal.
- Purification of water.

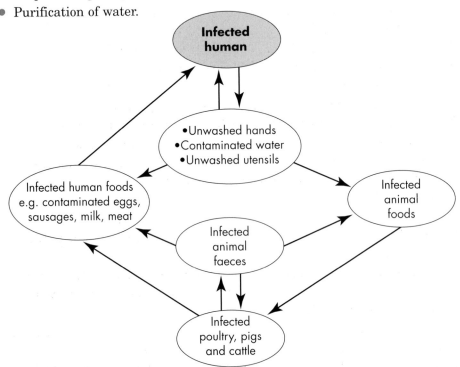

sampling: studying parts of an area to gain an overall picture of the area. It is nearly always impossible to study an entire area systematically because of time limitations. It would take a long time to study every square metre of seashore, for example – and by the time you had finished, some of it would have changed! By studying several small sections of the area, you can make reasonable deductions about the nature of the area as a whole.

Two techniques which can be used to sample an area are *quadrat* sampling and volume sampling.

- Quadrat sampling can be used to estimate the numbers of plants and animals living on the soil surface in the area.
- In volume sampling, samples of water of known volume are taken and examined. These can be used to estimate the numbers and kinds of organisms in a pond or lake.

It is important to take enough samples in order to obtain a reasonable picture of the whole area.

It is also important that the samples are not biased. Do not throw the quadrat in a particular place – samples should be taken at random.

saprobiont (saprophyte): an organism which feeds on dead and decaying material.

Saprobionts are important in bringing about decay and so recycling *nutrients*. Many *bacteria* and *fungi* are saprobionts.

- They release *enzymes* for *digestion* onto the dead material.
- The enzymes digest proteins, carbohydrates and other complex *organic substances* into small, soluble molecules.
- These small molecules enter the saprobionts by *diffusion*.
- The saprobionts use some of the carbohydrate for *respiration*, releasing carbon dioxide into the air. This is important in recycling carbon.
- When they digest and metabolise protein, they release ammonia into the environment. This is important in recycling nitrogen.

(See *carbon cycle* and *nitrogen cycle*.)

saturated fat: fat which contains *fatty acids* with no double bonds in the hydrocarbon chain.

Saturated fats are usually hard, like butter and lard, and of animal origin. They are more likely to cause *atherosclerosis* than soft fats which contain more unsaturated fatty acids.

sclera: the tough, white outer layer of the wall of the *eye*.

The main function of the sclera is to contain and protect the delicate and sensitive tissues inside the eye. At the front of the eye the sclera is continuous with the transparent cornea.

sebaceous glands: glands found in the *skin* of mammals next to hair follicles.

The sebaceous glands secrete sebum (an oily substance) onto the surface of the hair and skin.

Sebum has a number of functions.

- It keeps the hair supple.
- It waterproofs the hair and skin. This is particularly important in aquatic mammals.
- In humans, it has antibacterial and antifungal properties which help to reduce skin infections.

Production of sebum increases at *puberty* and sometimes blocks the ducts of the sebaceous glands. The sebum in these blocked ducts leads to the formation of blackheads.

secondary consumers: *carnivores* which feed on *herbivores* in a *food chain.* (See *primary consumers.*)

secondary feathers: the feathers in a bird's wing nearest to its body. The secondary feathers provide most of the lift when a bird is flying, but contribute little to any forward motion.
(See also *primary feathers, wing.*)

secondary sex characteristics: features which result from the action of *reproductive hormones* and which indicate that the organism is sexually mature.
We usually think of secondary sex characteristics in human terms, but they are present in other animals also. They serve to distinguish between males and females.
In humans, secondary sex characteristics develop at *puberty*. They result from *FSH* secreted by the pituitary gland stimulating the production of *oestrogen* in females and *testosterone* in males.
In females, at puberty:
● the breasts grow
● the pubic and under-arm hair grows
● the pelvis becomes broader
● body fat is redistributed to give a more curved shape.
In males, at puberty:
● facial, pubic and body hair grows
● the shoulders broaden
● the body becomes more muscular
● the voice 'breaks' (the *larynx* broadens causing a drop in pitch of the voice).

secretion: the process by which a substance is released to the outside of a cell.
Secreting substances from cells is usually an active process, requiring energy. This is because the molecules are usually too large to pass through the cell membrane by simple *diffusion*.
Substances secreted by cells usually have a specific function in the organism. So, for example, we talk about:
● *FSH* being secreted by cells in the pituitary gland
● *insulin* being secreted by islet cells in the pancreas

- *auxin* being secreted by cells at the growing points of plant stems
- *hydrochloric acid* being secreted by cells in the stomach lining.

It would be wrong, however, to talk of cells, secreting carbon dioxide.

---

seed: the structure formed when an ovule is fertilised. (See *flower*.)

A seed contains:

- one or two cotyledons which, in many species, contain stored food which is used when the seed germinates
- a radicle which will become the root of the plant
- a plumule which will become the shoot of the plant.

These structures are contained within a testa or seed coat. The testa forms from the wall of the ovule.

Seeds are contained within a structure called fruits. The fruit wall develops from the wall of the ovary after *fertilisation* has taken place.

Once formed, seeds are dispersed from the plant before they germinate.

(See *seed dispersal* and *germination*.)

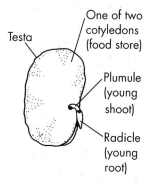

Section through a bean seed

---

seed dispersal: the process by which *seeds* are carried away from the plant which produced them.

Seeds can be dispersed in a number of ways. The fruits which contain them are usually modified in some way to suit their method of dispersal.

Method of dispersal	Example of seed	Adaptation(s)
wind	dandelion	• parachute on stalk gives increased air resistance • seed is very light
animals (eaten)	hawthorn	• fruit is fleshy and nutritious for birds • seed inside is indigestible – will pass through bird's gut undamaged
animals (in fur)	burdock	fruit wall has hooks which attach to the animal's fur
water	coconut	fruit has air spaces and is corky to give buoyancy
self-dispersal	sweet pea (and other plants with small pods)	the wall of the pod (fruit) dries unevenly as it ripens and twists and bursts, shooting the seeds out

Seed dispersal has two main advantages.

- The new plants which grow do not compete with each other, or the parent plant, for carbon dioxide, water, light and mineral ions.
- The seeds colonise new environments: if one of the environments is changed significantly, the species will still survive in the others.

You must not confuse *pollination* with seed dispersal.

---

selective breeding: allowing breeding between only those individuals of a species which would produce offspring with specific, desirable *characteristics*. For example, humans decide:

- which cattle to breed to produce cows with a higher milk yield
- which wheat plants to breed to produce plants with a high yield or plants that are resistant to fungal diseases
- which dogs to breed to produce a 'pedigree' dog of a specific type.

They breed the chosen individuals and then:

- look among the offspring for those with the best combination of the desired features
- use only these individuals for breeding the next generation
- repeat this selection generation after generation.

When breeding is done for specific features in this way, often large numbers of the natural population of, say, cattle are excluded from the breeding programme. Some of the *alleles* which these 'excluded' animals contain may not be present in the individuals used in the breeding programme. They will therefore be lost from the *gene pool* of the species.

The techniques of *genetic engineering* and other advances have made selective breeding a more precise process. All the desired changes can sometimes be achieved within a single generation by genetically engineering organisms. Techniques available to the breeder now include:

- actually breeding the chosen individual plants or animals
- *artificial insemination*
- *embryo transplantation*
- embryo *cloning*
- *micropropagation*
- genetic engineering – introducing new genes for specific features into animals and plants.

---

self-fertilisation: fusion of male and female sex cells (*gametes*) which come from the same individual.

Most plants but few animals are *hermaphrodite* (possess male and female sex organs). Examples of hermaphrodite animals include tapeworms, earthworms and *Hydra*.

Although hermaphrodites have both male and female sex organs, most do not self-fertilise. Earthworms mate and each fertilises the other.

Tapeworms, which are *parasites*, self-fertilise. It is clearly an advantage to such animals: there may be only one tapeworm living in the intestines of an animal. *Cross-fertilisation* would be impossible in these circumsatnces.

Plants also tend not to self-fertilise. There are often barriers to self-fertilisation. These include:

- male and female organs maturing at different times
- *pollen grains* being incompatible with the *stigma* in the same individual.

semen: the liquid ejaculated from the *penis* during intercourse.
Semen contains:

- *sperm* – produced in the testes and carried along the sperm ducts to the urethra
- secretions from the prostate gland and seminal vesicle – these provide nutrients for the sperm and increase their mobility.

(See *reproductive system, human*.)

semi-conservative replication: the type of replication shown by *DNA* molecules.
When DNA replicates (or copies itself):

- the double helix unwinds
- each strand makes a complementary strand from spare bases according to the base pairing rule
- eventually two new molecules of DNA are formed
- each contains one of the original strands of DNA conserved in the new molecule and one new strand
- because one of the two strands of DNA is conserved in each new molecule when it replicates, it is called semi-conservative replication.

semi-lunar valve: the type of valve found in the aorta and pulmonary artery where they leave the ventricles of the *heart*.
(See *aortic valve* for details.)

sensitivity: the ability of an organism to detect, and respond to, changes in its surroundings.
A change in the internal or external surroundings of an organism is called a *stimulus*. This change is detected by the organism and brings about a *response*.

Some organisms have specialised sense cells which detect the stimulus; some even have specialised sense organs, like the *eye*, *ear* and *nose*. Others have no

obvious sense organs yet still respond to stimuli. Plant roots have no specialised sense organs, but they can detect and grow towards gravity.
Some *unicellular* organisms retreat from bright light. The single cell which is their body must be able to detect the light and organise the response.

sensory neurone: a nerve cell which carries *impulses* into the *central nervous system*.

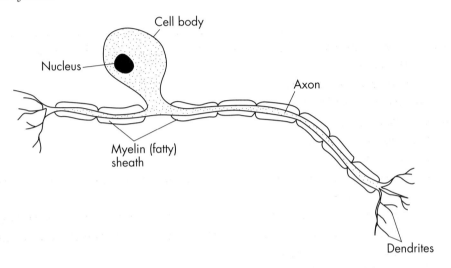

Sense cells detect a *stimulus*. They then trigger an impulse in a sensory neurone which carries the impulse to the central nervous system – either the brain or spinal cord.

sepal: a leaf-like part of a *flower* which protects the flower while it is in bud. Sepals usually have no further function once the flower is open, although some become brightly coloured and, like petals, attract insects.

serum: *blood plasma* from which the proteins involved in *blood clotting* have been removed.
Serum is sometimes prepared from the blood of a person or animal which has been infected with a particular microorganism. This preparation will contain *antibodies* against the microorganism and can be injected into another person. When used in this way it is called antiserum and forms the basis of *passive immunity*.

sessile: permanently attached to one location.
Plants are sessile, but most animals move. Some however are not: the animals of the coral reef are sessile.

sewage treatment: procedures used for making sewage fit to discharge into waterways.

Untreated sewage contains:

- suspended *organic substances*
- dissolved organic substances
- inorganic substances
- a lot of water.

If sewage is released untreated into waterways, it can damage the *ecosystem* in the following ways.

- The suspended organic substances make the water cloudy and block out light. This limits *photosynthesis* which in turn reduces the amount of oxygen released into the water.
- The dissolved organic substances provide a food source for *bacteria* in the water which multiply and use up much of the oxygen in the water in *respiration*. Ammonia released by these bacteria can be converted to nitrates, which may cause *eutrophication*.
- *Pathogenic* bacteria can cause disease in animals living in the water. Sewage treatment removes nearly all of the suspended and dissolved organic substances. In this country the two main methods used are the *activated sludge method* and the *percolating filter* method.

sex cell: see *gamete*.

sex chromosomes: chromosomes which determine the gender (sex) of an individual.

Human cells contain 46 chromosomes arranged in 23 pairs, of which 22 pairs do not influence gender. These are called autosomes. The 23rd pair is the pair of sex chromosomes.

There are two sex chromosomes: X and Y. Males have one X and one Y chromosome in each cell. Females have two X chromosomes in each cell.

The ratio of males to females expected in human families can easily be predicted:

The *genotype* of the male parent is **XY**.

The genotype of the female parent is **XX**.

When any couple has children, the genetic cross is:

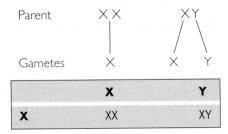

So, we would expect 50% of the offspring to be male and 50% to be female. In any one family, this may not be the case, but the overall ratio for male and female births is very nearly 1:1.

sex hormones: see *reproductive hormones*.

sex-linked inheritance: characteristics controlled by *genes* found on the *sex chromosomes* are said to be sex linked.

In humans, the Y chromosome carries only genes concerned with gender determination. The X chromosome is larger and carries the genes which determine gender and genes which determine other characteristics as well. These are the sex-linked characteristics.

Two examples of conditions in humans which are sex linked are red–green colour blindness and *haemophilia*. Both are determined by *recessive alleles*. The allele for the normal condition is *dominant* in both.

Because the X chromosome carries the allele for red–green colour blindness, the pattern of inheritance is different in men and women. Men inherit only one X chromosome (and a Y chromosome) and so inherit only one allele which affects colour vision. Women inherit two X chromosomes and therefore two alleles which affect colour vision.

If a man inherits an X chromosome carrying the recessive red–green colour blind allele, then he will be red–green colour blind. There will be no dominant normal allele on his Y chromosome to counter the effect.

A woman must inherit two X chromosomes each carrying the recessive allele for her to be red–green colour blind. If she inherits just one, she will have normal vision. The normal allele on the other X chromosome will counter the effect.

If X^C = an X chromosome carrying the dominant normal allele

X^c = an X chromosome carrying the recessive red–green colour blind allele

Possible genotypes and phenotypes are:

FEMALES

X^CX^C – normal vision (has two dominant normal alleles)

X^CX^c – normal vision (has one dominant normal and one recessive red–green colour blind allele)

X^cX^c – red–green colour blind (has two recessive red–green colour blind alleles)

MALES

X^CY – normal vision (has one dominant normal allele)

X^cY – red–green colour blind (has one recessive red–green colour blind allele)

Women with the genotype X^CX^c are called carriers because they have normal colour vision, but can still pass on the red–green colour blind allele to their children.

If a normal man and a carrier woman have children, their possible genotypes will be as follows.

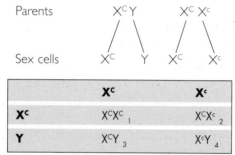

	X^c	X^c
X^c	X^CX^C ₁	X^CX^c ₂
Y	X^CY ₃	X^cY ₄

The offspring would be: 1 – normal female   2 – carrier female

3 – normal male   4 – red–green colour blind male

---

sexual reproduction: reproduction which involves the fusion of two sex cells (*gametes*).

Sexual reproduction involves some or all of the following:

- production of sex cells
- mating behaviour and intercourse
- transfer of sex cells from one individual to another
- fusion of the sex cells to form a *zygote*
- development of the zygote into an *embryo*.

Sexual reproduction is important because, when the sex cells fuse in *fertilisation*, two different sets of *alleles* are mixed. This brings about *variation* in the offspring. Sexual reproduction usually involves two different individuals although many plants and some animals are capable of self-fertilisation. (See also *reproduction, asexual reproduction, reproductive systems.*)

sexually transmitted disease (STD): any disease transmitted through sexual intercourse or other sexual activity.

These diseases used to be called venereal diseases (after Venus: the goddess of love). They are more common in people with many sexual partners. Until recently, people thought of syphilis and gonorrhoea as being the only STDs, but these now make up less than 10% of cases.

AIDS is a relatively new sexually transmitted disease, and a range of infections of the *urethra* (collectively called nonspecific urethritis) is the most common STD worldwide.

The risk of transmission of most STDs can be reduced significantly if the man wears a condom during intercourse.

shivering: involuntary, rapid contraction and relaxation of muscles.

We shiver when we are cold. Temperature-sensitive cells in the brain detect a drop in blood temperature and initiate corrective mechanisms. These can include shivering. When the muscles contract, they release heat energy which helps to return the body temperature to normal.

We also sometimes shiver when we have a fever – we are too hot and yet we still shiver! This is because the 'thermostat' in the brain has been 'reset' to a higher value to help to destroy invading microorganisms. Now any temperature below this can initiate shivering.

shoot system: the parts of a *plant* which grow above ground.

The shoot system usually consists of:
● a *stem* – to support and hold up other parts
● *leaves* – the *organs* where *photosynthesis* takes place
● *flowers* – the organs where *reproduction* takes place.

(See also *root system*.)

sickle cell anaemia: an inherited form of *anaemia*, common in parts of Africa.

The *allele* which causes sickle cell anaemia is *recessive*. So, to inherit the condition, a person must inherit one sickle cell allele from each parent.

The allele causes the body to make an abnormal form of *haemoglobin*. When the *red blood cells* pass through *capillaries* and lose oxygen, the abnormal haemoglobin forms crystals which alter the shape of the red cells. Instead of being discs, they become shaped like a sickle or crescent. These sickle-shaped cells can block small blood vessels and cause tissue damage. They also have a shorter life span than normal red blood cells, which leads to the anaemia.

If a person inherits one allele for sickle cell anaemia and one normal allele, some of the haemoglobin is affected, but the majority is normal. Such people show few symptoms of sickle cell anaemia and lead a normal life. They do however have one important advantage. They have some resistance to *malaria*. The malarial parasite finds it difficult to enter the cells and so cannot reproduce and cause the symptoms of malaria.

single circulation: a *circulatory system* in which the blood passes through the heart only once in a complete circuit of the body.

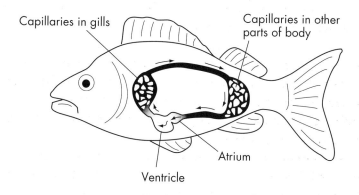

Capillaries in gills

Capillaries in other parts of body

Atrium

Ventricle

skeletal muscle: voluntary muscle which contracts to move all or part of the body.

Besides producing movement, skeletal muscle helps us to maintain our posture. When we are standing still, many skeletal muscles contract partially to hold us in a stable position. Without these partial contractions, we would not be able to stand.

(See *muscle (1)*.)

skeleton: a structure which supports a body; skeletons may also provide protection and allow movement.

We usually think of skeletons in animals, but plants too have structures which support them. The *xylem* (wood) is made of long, tubular, empty cells with very thick cell walls. The arrangement of xylem in a stem helps it to withstand bending stresses.

Animal skeletons are often obvious structures: the hard *exoskeleton* of an *arthropod* or the bony *endoskeleton* of *vertebrates*. Less obviously, the fluid inside an earthworm is a skeleton – the pressure of the fluid provides support for the earthworm and is called a hydrostatic skeleton.

The human endoskeleton has several functions including:

● support – provides a framework for attachment of body parts

- movement – provides a framework for muscle attachment; some joints allow bones to move relative to each other
- protection – parts of the skeleton protect organs from physical damage (e.g. the *skull* protects the brain, the ribcage protects heart and lungs)
- producing red blood cells – the bone marrow of long *bones* produces red and white blood cells.

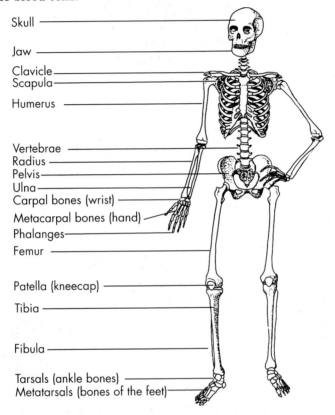

Skull
Jaw
Clavicle
Scapula
Humerus
Vertebrae
Radius
Pelvis
Ulna
Carpal bones (wrist)
Metacarpal bones (hand)
Phalanges
Femur
Patella (kneecap)
Tibia
Fibula
Tarsals (ankle bones)
Metatarsals (bones of the feet)

The skeletons of men and women differ in only a few minor ways.

- Men's bones are often larger and heavier than corresponding bones in women.
- The pelvis is wider in women with a larger cavity to aid childbirth.

The bones of the skeleton are held together at joints, which are either fixed joints (immovable) or *synovial joints* (movable).

---

skin: the organ which covers the body of some animals.

Human skin has a number of functions.

- It protects the inner organs from physical damage.
- It provides a barrier to the entry of microorganisms.
- Skin cells make vitamin D from fatty substances when ultraviolet rays from the sun strike them.

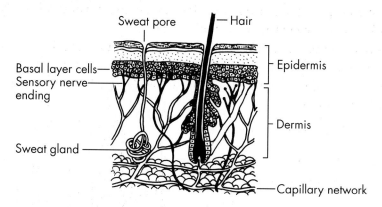

- A film of liquid (a mixture of *sebum* and *sweat*) on the surface has antibacterial and antifungal properties.
- It is a sense organ, with cells sensitive to temperature, touch and pressure.
- *Sweat glands* and *arterioles* in the skin play an important part in temperature regulation.

skull: the part of the *skeleton* found in the head of *vertebrates*.

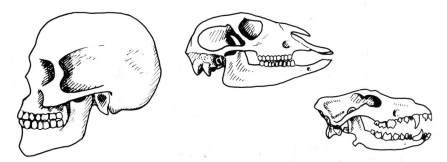

A skull is made of a number of *bones* organised into two main areas:
- the cranium – the part which protects the brain
- facial bones – the part which makes up the face, including the jaws.

The shape of a skull is influenced by a number of factors: brain size and diet are important ones.

sliding filament hypothesis: the hypothesis which explains how *muscles* contract.

Muscle myofibrils contain filaments of two proteins called actin and myosin. The diagram on the following page shows how the two are arranged in a myofibril which has not contracted.

When the muscle contracts *ATP* makes the filaments of actin and myosin slide into each other. This shortens the length of each section of a muscle and so shortens the entire muscle.

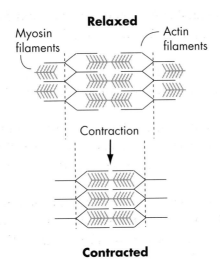

Relaxed

Myosin filaments

Actin filaments

Contraction

Contracted

slipped disc: a condition of the *spine* in which part of a disc between two vertebrae presses on one of the spinal nerves.

The intervertebral discs are made from *cartilage* and, with age, the tough outer layer can degenerate. This allows the softer inner part to protrude and press on a nerve. Slipped discs can sometimes be caused by a sudden force on the spine.

Most slipped discs occur in the lower spine: they are slightly more common in men than in women. They are also more common in people aged between 30 and 40. In older people, the outer layer becomes more fibrous and tougher again.

small intestine: the region of the *alimentary canal* (gut) between the stomach and the caecum (the first part of the large intestine).

The small intestine is where most *digestion* and *absorption* of food takes place. It is divided into two regions, the duodenum and the ileum.

In humans, digestion in the small intestine is the result of three secretions:
- *bile* (from the *gall bladder*) emulsifies fats
- pancreatic juice contains *digestive enzymes* which break down proteins, fats and starch
- intestinal juice (from cells lining the small intestine) contains digestive enzymes which complete the digestion of starch and proteins.

Absorption takes place mainly in the ileum. The ileum is efficient at absorbing digested food because:
- it is long
- the internal wall is folded
- the folds have *villi* on them

these features all increase the surface area for absorption

- the lining is thin, so soluble food molecules can pass through more easily
- each villus is well supplied with blood vessels to absorb the soluble food molecules.

smell: the sense which allows animals to distinguish between molecules of vapours.

The *nose* is the sense organ which allows us to detect smells. Special sense cells in the lining of the nose detect molecules of gases. The gas molecules bind to special receptor sites on the surface of the cells and trigger *nerve impulses* to the brain.

When we have a cold we sometimes say that we cannot taste our food. This is not true: we can still taste our food perfectly well. Taste, however, only tells us whether our food is sweet, sour, salty or bitter. The flavour of food comes from the associated smells.

Humans have a limited sense of smell compared to some other animals. Even so, some people can distinguish several thousand different smells.

smooth muscle: involuntary muscle found in the walls of the *uterus, blood vessels, stomach, intestine* and also in the *iris* of the eye.

Where smooth muscle is found in the walls of organs, it produces wave-like contractions called *peristalsis*. Peristaltic contractions can perform a number of different functions. They:

- mix the contents of the stomach into a milky liquid called chyme
- move food along the intestine
- during labour, move the baby out of the uterus and along the vagina to be born.

Because peristaltic contractions are relatively slow, smooth muscle does not suffer *fatigue*.

soil: a complex material formed from rocks by physical, chemical and biological erosion.

Soils usually contain the following components:

- a mineral skeleton – made from tiny fragments of the original rock
- *humus* – a mixture of the remains of dead animals and plants in various states of *decomposition*, together with excretory products
- a soil solution – soils contain water (held between the mineral particles) which contains dissolved *mineral ions*; the amount of the soil solution varies between types of soils and with weather conditions
- air – the spaces between the particles not occupied by the soil solution contain air; this is the source of oxygen for respiration of the root cells

- a soil population – *bacteria*, *fungi*, small animals, *algae* and *protozoa* all live in the soil. Earthworms are some of the most important soil organisms. Their tunnels aerate the soil and the animals pass soil through their gut which helps to mix the layers of the soil.

Soil provides anchorage for plants as well as the mineral ions they need for healthy growth.

soil erosion: the loss of *soil* from the land due to agents such as the wind and rain.

Soil can be eroded by:

- wind – blows away loose particles of soil from exposed surfaces, especially if it is dry
- running water – loosens and carries away soil particles
- rain – can loosen soil particles
- freezing/thawing of water in the soil – loosens soil particles.

All the above are natural processes and soil erosion occurs in all soils. Its effects are usually minimal because the roots of plants growing in the soil bind the particles together and hold the soil in place. When land is farmed or trees are felled, the plant cover is removed and the bare soil is much more easily eroded. This is particularly true for soils with little *humus*,which helps to bind small soil particles together.

If not corrected, soil erosion can quickly leave an area without any mineral-rich top soil and incapable of supporting plant growth.

One estimate suggests that in the United States alone, 3 billion tonnes of soil are eroded every year.

solvent: a liquid which dissolves a substance to form a solution.

The substance which dissolves in the solvent is called the solute. So:

solute + solvent = solution.

Water is a good solvent: it will dissolve many organic and inorganic molecules. It will not, however, dissolve fats and oils. These will not mix with water and two layers form: the oil (or fat) floats on the water.

Organic liquids like *ethanol* and propanone (acetone) are better solvents for fatty substances.

Organic solvents, such as those found in hairspray canisters, some glues and paint, are sometimes used as drugs. They can produce hallucinations or make the person dreamy for a period of up to 45 minutes. They have been known to cause instant death.

species: organisms which can interbreed and produce viable, fertile off-spring.

Members of the same species can reproduce and produce offspring which are viable (capable of normal, healthy growth) and are also fertile (capable of reproduction).

Sometimes, members of closely related species reproduce and produce viable offspring. Such individuals are called *hybrids* and are nearly always infertile. The mule, produced when a female horse and a male donkey reproduce, is an example of a viable but infertile hybrid.

sperm (spermatozoa): the male sex cells (*gametes*) of animals.

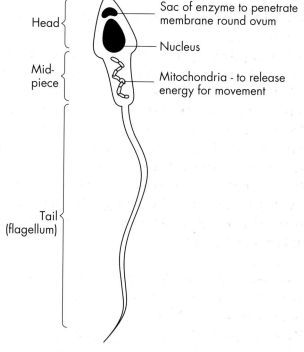

- Sperm are usually much smaller than the female sex cell (the ovum).
- They are motile: they swim using a whip-like flagellum.
- The nucleus of the sperm fuses with the nucleus of the ovum in *fertilisation*.
- They are produced in the *testes* by *meiosis*.
- They have half the normal number of chromosomes (one from each pair).

Sperm need to swim to the ovum so fertilisation must occur either outside the body in water (external fertilisation) or inside a female's body (internal fertilisation).

When frogs mate, the female carries the male for some time and as she lays her egg cells in the water, he immediately sheds his sperm. They swim in the water and enough reach the egg cells to fertilise most of them.

In mammals the sperm are introduced in *semen* into the fem~~a~~ ing intercourse. The female produces liquids in which the spe~~~~ the egg cell.

sperm bank: a place where *sperm* are frozen and stored.
Sperm which have been frozen can survive for long periods o~~~~

therefore possible for sperm from an animal with very desirable features to be used in *artificial insemination* long after the animal has become infertile: even after it has died.

The same technique can be used to store human sperm. This allows a man to father children at any age during his adult life. It also allows him to father children after *sterilisation* should he regret the decision.

Little is known yet of the long-term effects of storage of sperm. It may give rise to more genetic defects than would be normal. Sperm storage is, however, more successful at the moment than storage of egg cells and *embryos*.

sperm duct (vas deferens): the tube which carries *sperm* from the testis to the urethra.
(See *reproductive system, human* for details.)

sphincter muscle: a circular muscle which controls the size of an aperture (a hole or opening).
When a sphincter muscle contracts, it closes the aperture. When it relaxes, the aperture is opened again. Sphincter muscles are found:
- at the junction of the *stomach* and *small intestine*, controlling the flow of food from one to the other
- at the *anus* controlling the egestion of *faeces*.

spinal cord: the cord of nervous tissue in the *spine* which runs through cavities in the *vertebrae*: spinal nerves branching off the spinal cord connect it to all parts of the body below the head.

The spinal cord contains sensory, motor and intermediate neurones. Different neurones in the spinal cord carry out different functions.

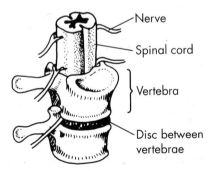

Nerve

Spinal cord

Vertebra

Disc between vertebrae

- *Sensory neurones* in the spinal cord relay *nerve impulses* to the *brain*. These impulses originated in sense cells and were passed to the spinal cord along sensory neurones in nerves.
- *Motor neurones* relay nerve impulses from the brain to other motor neurones which lead to *muscles* or *glands*.
- Intermediate neurones form parts of *reflex arcs*. The sensory and motor neurones of a reflex arc are linked by intermediate neurones.

spine: the column of *bones* and *cartilage* which runs through the *skeleton* of *vertebrates*. In vertebrates with four limbs, the spine extends from the pelvis to the skull.

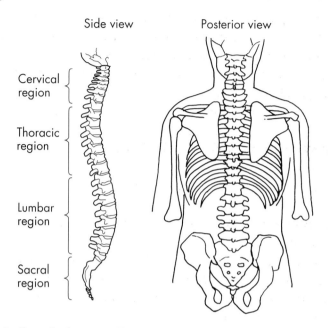

The pelvis, skull and ribs are all attached to the spine.

In humans, the spine is made up of 33 *vertebrae*. Adjacent vertebrae are separated by a cartilage disc which absorbs shock and prevents damage to the vertebrae.

The spine encloses the *spinal cord* and nerves branch off the spinal cord between the vertebrae. These are called spinal nerves.

Adjacent vertebrae are held together by *ligaments*. The vertebrae can slide slightly closer to or further away from each other. This movement allows the spine as a whole to bend and straighten.

spiracles: openings on an *insect's* body which allow air into and out of the breathing system.

There are usually two spiracles on each body segment. Spiracles can be opened or closed according to the needs of the insect. If they remained open all the time, the insect would lose too much water through evaporation. Spiracles open when the level of carbon dioxide in the *tracheae* of the insect builds up.

spirilla (singular spirillum): spiral shaped *bacteria*.
The bacterium which causes syphilis is a spirillum.

spongy mesophyll: the layer of a *leaf* above the lower epidermis which is made up of irregularly shaped cells with many air spaces between them.

The cells of the spongy layer contain chloroplasts, although not as many as the cells of the palisade mesophyll. The main functions of the spongy layer are:

- to allow carbon dioxide entering through the *stomata* on the lower epidermis to diffuse quickly to the cells in the palisade layer
- to allow oxygen produced in *photosynthesis* to diffuse out quickly.

Because of the many air spaces, water vapour can also diffuse quickly to the stomata.

spore: a reproductive structure which can give rise directly to another individual.

Spores are usually single cells which develop into new organisms. All *fungi* reproduce by producing spores which grow into *hyphae*.

Some *bacteria* and *algae* also produce spores.

sprain: damage to the *ligaments* which hold a *joint* together.

Sprains are usually caused by sudden movements which stretch or tear the ligaments. The movement may also damage the joint capsule and the synovial membrane. There is nearly always a painful swelling which limits movement of the joint. Blood vessels may be damaged.

Sprains are treated with an ice pack to reduce swelling and *analgesic* may be necessary. Once the joint is no longer painful, it should be exercised gently.

stamen: the male reproductive structure of flowering plants.

The stamen is made of an *anther* and a filament. The anther produces *pollen grains* by *meiosis*. The filament supports the anther and supplies water and nutrients to it.

When the anthers are mature, they split and release the pollen which is then dispersed by either wind or insects.

starch: a storage *polysaccharide* found in plants.

Starch is a polymer of *glucose* molecules. It is formed in leaves and in special storage organs from surplus glucose made during *photosynthesis*.

The benefits to the plant of converting glucose to starch are:

- the starch is insoluble and so will not move around the plant
- because it is insoluble it cannot produce any osmotic effects (a build up of glucose in a region would cause water to be drawn to that region from another by *osmosis*).

stem: the part of a plant which normally grows above ground and bears *leaves*, *buds* and *flowers*.

Some stems, like the rhizomes of some grasses, grow horizontally underground. They can always be distinguished from *roots* in two ways:

- they have leaves – simple scale leaves, but roots never have leaves
- they have buds.

Stems often have branches which hold the leaves in the best position for *photosynthesis* and hold the flowers in the best position for *pollination*.

Stems also:

- transport water and mineral ions in the *xylem* from the roots to the leaves and flowers
- transport glucose and other organic substances in the *phloem* to and from storage organs
- form storage organs in some plants.

sterile (1): incapable of reproducing sexually because sex cells (*gametes*) are not being produced.

In humans, male sterility occurs when the sperm count drops below 35 million per cm^3 of *semen*. The normal level is near to 100 million per cm^3 of semen.

Female sterility is often not due to lack of production of ova but to blocked *Fallopian tubes*, which means that the ova cannot reach the *uterus*. (See *sterilisation (1)*.)

sterile (2): completely free from microorganisms. (See *sterilisation (2)*.)

sterilisation (1): a procedure which makes an organism incapable of *sexual reproduction*.

In humans, sterilisation is an option for couples who do not wish to have any children, or who do not want any more children. The man or the woman may be sterilised, but male sterilisation is a simpler procedure. (See *reproductive system, human*.)

MALE STERILISATION (VASECTOMY)

- small incisions are made on each side of the scrotum
- the sperm duct (vas deferens) from each testis is cut
- the cut ends are closed with ligatures
- the incisions are closed with stitches.

The male can still make sperm, but they cannot pass to the penis and be ejaculated during intercourse.

FEMALE STERILISATION

- small incisions are made in the body wall above each ovary
- a viewing tube (laparoscope) and operating instruments are passed through the incisions
- the Fallopian tubes are cut and tied or clipped
- the incisions are closed with stitches.

The woman can still ovulate normally, and her *menstrual cycle* is unaffected, but the ova cannot be fertilised by sperm and cannot reach the uterus.

Both male and female sterilisation are effective methods of *contraception* with a success rate of close to 100%.

sterilisation (2): any procedure which removes all living things from an object.
Sterilisation is almost always aimed at ensuring that potentially harmful *microorganisms* are removed. Techniques which sterilise substances or objects include:

- irradiation with ultraviolet light, X-rays or gamma rays
- autoclaving (steaming at high pressures and temperatures)
- using strong *disinfectants* like bleach.

Sometimes, more than one technique is used. For example, in hospitals, bed linen is often disinfected and then autoclaved.
Sterilising food products by using high temperatures can alter the flavour of the food.

steroids: a group of modified *lipids* which includes *cholesterol*, vitamin D (see *vitamins*) and the male and female *sex hormones*.
Some synthetic drugs are steroids. The most well known of these are the *anabolic steroids*. These are drugs which are similar to the male sex hormone testosterone and which mimic its body building effects.

stigma: the receptive surface at the top of the style in a *flower*, which receives *pollen grains*.
Stigmas are adapted to the type of *pollination* which is used by the plant.

- Stigmas of wind pollinated plants are often feathery. This presents a large surface area for the wind to trap as much pollen as possible.
- Stigmas of insect pollinated plants often have sticky surfaces which remove the pollen from the insect and ensure it stays in place.

The stigma often secretes a sugary liquid which stimulates the pollen grain to produce a tube which grows through the style to the ovule.

stimulant drug: a drug which increases activity of the *nervous system*, especially the *brain*.

There are two main types of stimulant drugs.

- Some increase alertness by allowing more nerve impulses to reach the brain. Amphetamines work in this way.
- Some act on the area of the brain which controls breathing and increase our breathing rate. These are called respiratory stimulants.

stimulus (plural stimuli): any change in the environment which produces a *response* by an organism.

When house plants grow towards the window, the stimulus is the higher light intensity on the window side of the plant.

When you withdraw your hand from a hot object, the heat is the stimulus.

The structures which detect stimuli are called *receptors*.

stoma (plural stomata): an opening in the epidermis of a *leaf* surrounded by two guard cells.

The stomata are opened and closed by the guard cells which surround them. They are usually opened when it is light and closed when dark. Changes in light intensity cause the guard cells to change shape which opens or closes the stomata.

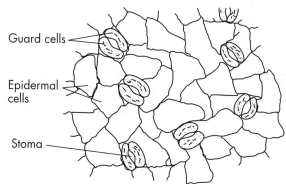

The stomata allow:

- *diffusion* of carbon dioxide from the air into the leaf, to be used in *photosynthesis*
- oxygen produced in photosynthesis to diffuse out of the leaf
- water vapour to diffuse out of the leaf.

Most stomata are found in the lower epidermis. This results in a greater diffusion distance for carbon dioxide than if they had been in the upper epidermis. However, it also results in less water loss by evaporation as the sun does not directly affect the stomata on the lower epidermis.

stomach: the region of the *alimentary canal* (gut) between the *oesophagus* and the *small intestine*.

When food enters the stomach, gastric juice is released by cells in the stomach lining. This contains *hydrochloric acid* and the enzyme *pepsin*. Smooth *muscle* in the wall of the stomach produces waves of contraction which mix the food with the gastric juice. When fully mixed, the resulting liquid is called chyme.

While food is being mixed with the gastric juice, pepsin begins the digestion of *proteins* into smaller molecules called peptides. Pepsin is unique among our *digestive enzymes* in being adapted to work in an acidic environment. The acidic environment of the stomach kills many microorganisms which enter with our food.

Ruminants have a four-chambered stomach. The first of these chambers, the *rumen*, is the largest and contains billions of microorganisms which digest the cellulose in the plant cell walls. This makes it easier for the animal to obtain nutrients from the vegetation being eaten.

stroke (cerebro-vascular incident): damage to part of the *brain* through either an interruption to its blood supply or by leakage of blood from blood vessels.

There are three main causes of strokes:
- a blood clot forming on the inside of an artery in the brain
- a blood clot forming elsewhere and travelling to the brain
- a blood vessel in the brain bursting and leaking blood over the surface of the brain.

Atherosclerosis makes it more likely that a blood clot will build up and block an artery, interrupting the blood supply.

High blood pressure increases the risk of blood clots blocking arteries. It also increases the risk of a blood vessel bursting.

stroke volume: the amount of blood pumped by each ventricle of the *heart* in one beat.

The stroke volume of a typical adult is about 80 cm³ blood per heart beat.

The cardiac output is the amount of blood pumped per ventricle per minute. If the heart rate were 60 beats per minute, then the out put would be $60 \times 80 = 4800$ cm³ blood per ventricle per minute.

The stroke volume is increased when *adrenaline* is released. When you are angry or afraid and release adrenaline, you can feel your heart beating not just faster, but stronger as well. The stroke volume is larger.

style: the structure in a *flower* which connects the stigma and ovary.
The style holds up the stigma so that it can collect *pollen grains* from either the wind or insects.
Pollen grains which land on the stigma produce a tube which grows down the style towards the ovule in the ovary.

substrate (1): the substance on which an *enzyme* acts.
Amylase digests starch into maltose. Its substrate is starch.
Lipase digests lipids into fatty acids and glycerol. Its substrate is the lipid.

substrate (2): the surface or substance on which *cells* are growing.
Bacteria growing in a petri dish are usually growing on an *agar* substrate.
The nutrient solution or gel used in *micropropagation* is the substrate for the plantlets which are growing.

sugars: simple, soluble, sweet tasting *carbohydrates*.
Most sugars are either monosaccharides (single sugars) or disaccharides (double sugars – two monosaccharides joined together).
Two monosaccharide sugars are:
● *glucose* – found in almost all living things, it is the sugar normally used in *respiration* and is used to make *starch*, *cellulose* and *glycogen*
● fructose – found in honey, fruit juices and generally in plants.
Two disaccharide sugars are:
● sucrose – the sugar from sugar beet and sugar cane which we put in tea and coffee and use in baking
● lactose – the sugar found in milk.

sulphuric acid: a strong acid with the formula H_2SO_4 produced when sulphur trioxide (SO_3) dissolves in water.
Sulphuric acid is one of the acids in *acid rain*. In the *atmosphere*, sulphur dioxide (SO_2), produced by burning *fossil fuels*, is oxidised to sulphur trioxide. This then dissolves in water in the air to form sulphuric acid.

surface area: quite literally, the area of any surface.
Surface area is important in living things where exchange between two media occurs. If a substance, or a form of energy, is lost or absorbed through a surface, then the amount of surface will be important in determining how efficient the exchange is.
Examples of surface area being important in exchange in living things include:
● a *leaf* having a large surface area to absorb as much light as possible

- elephants having large external ears to lose as much heat as possible
- the small intestine having millions of *villi* to increase the area for absorption of soluble food molecules
- the *gills* of a fish having many gill filaments with a large surface area for exchange of gases between blood and water.

surface area to volume ratio: the ratio of the surface area of an organism to its volume.

This ratio is important in living things as it is a measure of how efficient exchange is likely to be. Think of a simple, one-celled organism and its oxygen requirements. Assume that it obtains its oxygen by *diffusion* through its *cell membrane* – its cell surface membrane.

- The amount of oxygen the organism needs is determined by how much of the organism there is – its volume.
- The amount of oxygen it can actually get is determined by the surface area.

So the ratio of surface area to volume is crucial in supplying the oxygen to any organism which obtains it through its surface. For unicellular organisms, this is not a problem: there is ample surface compared to the volume.

For larger organisms which obtain their oxygen in this way there is potentially a problem as, when organisms get bigger:

- volume increases proportionately more than surface area
- the rate of supply (by the increased surface area) may not match the increased demand (by the even more increased volume).

To overcome this, larger organisms have evolved either:

- body shapes with a large surface area to volume ratio (such as the cylindrical shape of an earthworm)
- specialised gas exchange structures (such as *lungs* and *gills*) with very large surface areas.

surrogate mother: a female who carries and gives birth to an *embryo* which is not her own.

In cattle, surrogacy has been used for some time. A female with desirable features is made to undergo multiple ovulation and is inseminated with semen from a prize bull. The resulting embryos are recovered and implanted into other cattle, which then carry them and give birth. This allows one cow to produce many more calves than would normally be possible.

In humans, surrogacy is a relatively new phenomenon and has brought legal and moral problems. A woman may carry someone else's baby, but become so emotionally attached that she does not want to give it up once born. Whose baby is it? The couple who supplied the egg and sperm? Or the woman who carried it and whose body produced most of the tissue of the baby?

Surrogacy for financial reward has been banned in some countries, including the UK.

survival of the fittest: one of the key ideas in *Charles Darwin's* theory of *natural selection*.

Darwin's logic was as follows.

- Because living things over-reproduce, not all of their offspring can survive.
- Because the offspring vary, some will be better adapted to their environment than others.
- Those which are better adapted will survive and pass on their genes to the next generation. This is Darwin's idea of the 'survival of the fittest'.
  Darwin didn't use the word 'fittest' in a physical sense: he simply meant those which were best adapted to their environments.

suspensory ligaments: the ligaments which attach the *lens* to the *ciliary muscles* in the *eye* of a mammal.

The tension in the suspensory ligaments determines the shape of the lens. (See *accommodation*.)

sweat: the liquid produced by the *sweat glands*.

Sweat is made up of salts, *urea*, ammonia and uric acid dissolved in water. Evaporation of sweat from the surface of the *skin* requires heat which is taken from the body. This cools the body and is the main reason we sweat.

sweat glands: coiled tubular glands which are found in, or just below, the dermis of the *skin*, in the subcutaneous layer.

Sweat glands are found all over the skin, but are especially numerous in the palms of the hands, soles of the feet, forehead and upper body. They have a good supply of blood *capillaries* from which water and the other substances which make up sweat are absorbed.

There are two kinds of sweat glands.

- Eccrine sweat glands – these are by far the most numerous. The sweat produced by these glands is a transparent watery liquid. They function throughout life.
- Apocrine sweat glands – these are found only in the armpits, around the nipple and around the anus. The sweat they produce is more coloured and viscous. Apocrine glands only begin to function at *puberty*.

swim bladder: a gas-filled structure found in most bony *fish* which can alter the buoyancy of the fish.

By increasing or decreasing the amount of air in the swim bladder, the fish can alter its overall density to match that of the surrounding water. This enables it to maintain a 'neutral buoyancy'. What this means is that because the fish has the same density as the surrounding water, it will not tend to rise or sink in the water.

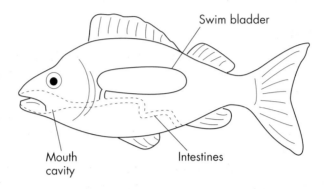

symbiont: one of the organisms involved in a symbiotic association. (See *symbiosis*.)

For example, a clover plant has a symbiotic association with the *nitrogen fixing bacteria* in the nodules on its roots. The clover and the nitrogen fixing bacteria are symbionts.

symbiosis: any intimate, long-term association between organisms of two or more *species*.

The term symbiosis is nearly always used to describe an association in which both organisms benefit. However, the term does cover any association. There are three main kinds of symbiotic associations.

- Mutualism – this type of association is usually called symbiosis. Both organisms benefit from the association. *Nitrogen fixing bacteria* in root nodules of *leguminous plants* like clover obtain sugars from the plant and pass nitrogenous compounds to the plant.
- *Parasitism* – in this type of association, one organism (the *parasite*) benefits, while the other (the host) is harmed. A tape worm living in the small intestine of a mammal absorbs much of the digested food in the gut and so deprives the host of some of its nutrients.
- Commensalism – in this type of association, only one partner benefits but the other is not harmed. Some tropical trees have smaller plants called epiphytes growing on them. Living on the tree enables the epiphytes to obtain sufficient light, water (from rainfall dripping from leaves) and minerals (which are washed from the leaves). The tree is not harmed in any way.

synapse: the small gap between *neurones* (nerve cells).

Nerve cells do not actually touch each other: there is always a synapse between them. When a *nerve impulse* reaches the end of one nerve cell, it must somehow cross the synapse before it can be passed along the next. When an impulse reaches the end of a nerve cell:

- it causes the nerve *cell membrane* to secrete a chemical called a neurotransmitter
- the neurotransmitter diffuses across the synapse to the next nerve cell
- when the neurotransmitter reaches the next nerve cell, it initiates a new nerve impulse.

syndrome: a collection of symptoms which occur together and characterise a particular disorder.

AIDS – Acquired Immune Deficiency Syndrome – is not a simple condition, although it is caused by one virus. A collection of symptoms, which may include some skin and brain cancers as well as a range of infectious diseases, constitute the syndrome known as AIDS.

synovial fluid: the fluid secreted by the *synovial membrane.*

Synovial fluid is a clear, sticky liquid which resembles the liquid white of an egg. Its function is to separate and reduce friction between the surfaces of the bones at a *synovial joint.* The bones would rub against each other if they were not separated by the synovial fluid. This would damage the bones as well as making movement of the joint very painful.

synovial joint: any movable joint.

There are different types of synovial joints, but all have the same basic structure (see diagram on page 288). Two important types of synovial joints are:

- ball and socket joints – found at the hip and shoulder, these joints allow the limbs to rotate freely
- hinge joints – found at the elbow and knee, these allow the limbs to bend and straighten.

synovial membrane: the thin membrane which lines the capsule of a *synovial joint.*

The synovial membrane secretes the *synovial fluid* and encases the joint so that fluid cannot escape.

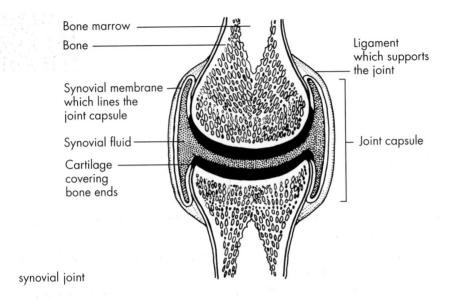

Bone marrow

Bone

Synovial membrane
which lines the
joint capsule

Synovial fluid

Cartilage
covering
bone ends

Ligament
which supports
the joint

Joint capsule

synovial joint

systole: contraction of a chamber of the *heart*.

- During atrial systole, the atria contract and force blood through the atrio-ventricular valves into the ventricles.
- During ventricular systole, the ventricles contract and force blood into the main arteries leading from the heart. The left ventricle pumps blood into the *aorta* and the right ventricle pumps blood into the pulmonary artery.

T cell: a type of *lymphocyte*.

T cells are produced in the *bone marrow* like other blood cells, but then migrate to the thymus gland in the chest to mature. The T denotes that they mature in the thymus.

T cells form an important part of our *immune system*. They target, in particular, cells which have been infected with *viruses*. They do not release antibodies into the blood plasma like B cells, but release chemicals which kill directly the cells containing the viruses.

Some T cells become *memory cells*. They remain in our system for years and can help to mount a quicker response if cells should become re-infected with the same virus.

---

tapeworm: a ribbon-like parasitic worm which lives in the *intestines* of many *mammals*.

Each adult worm is made from hundreds of sections (called proglottides), each of which contains thousands of eggs.

Human tapeworms have life cycles which involve other animals also. There are three main types of human tapeworms:

- the beef tapeworm – the eggs released from the tapeworm develop into larvae in cattle
- the pork tapeworm – the eggs released from the tapeworm develop into larvae in pigs
- the fish tapeworm – the eggs released from the tapeworm develop into larvae in fish.

The diagram on page 290 shows the life cycle of the beef tapeworm.

The adult beef, pork and fish tapeworms may grow up to lengths of 9 metres in the human intestine. Despite this size, they rarely cause major symptoms. Because of regular meat inspection and effective sewage treatment, tapeworm infestations are rare in developed countries. Most cases result from infection in developing countries.

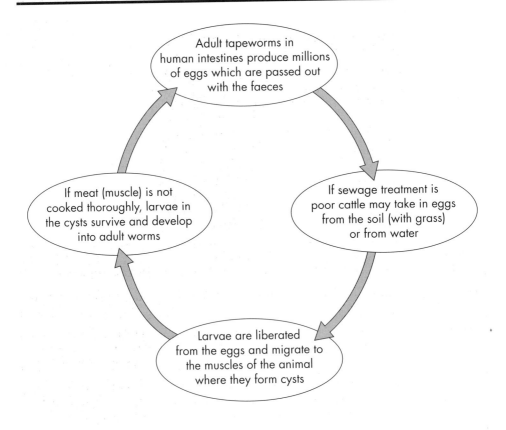

taste: the sense which allows us to distinguish whether a substance is sweet, sour, salty or bitter.

Taste buds on the tongue can distinguish only these four basic tastes. All the flavour of food comes from the interaction between taste and *smell*.

taxonomy: placing living things into groups of related organisms.

teeth: structures in the mouths of *vertebrates* adapted to cut, grind, slice or crush food.

All teeth have the same basic structure: this is shown in the diagram. *Enamel* is the hardest substance in the body and protects the teeth from physical damage when chewing. It is also more resistant to decay than the softer dentine which makes up the bulk of the tooth.

Different types of teeth have different functions In general, the incisors and canines are for biting and holding food and the premolars and molars process the food into smaller pieces. The functions of the different teeth in different *mammals* are shown in the table opposite.

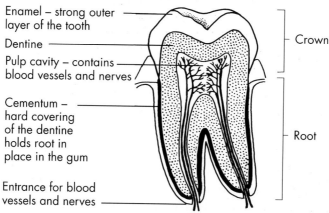

Enamel – strong outer layer of the tooth

Dentine

Pulp cavity – contains blood vessels and nerves

Cementum – hard covering of the dentine holds root in place in the gum

Entrance for blood vessels and nerves

Crown

Root

Type of tooth	Function in:		
	Sheep (herbivore)	Dog (carnivore)	Human (omnivore)
incisor	chisel shaped to cut vegetation	pointed to rip flesh	chisel shaped for cutting food
canine	chisel shaped to cut vegetation	large and pointed to rip flesh and grip prey	slightly pointed, and stronger than incisors: cut and tear food
premolar	flat topped with ridges for grinding vegetation	pointed: points on upper and lower jaws interlock to slice flesh	slightly pointed with two ridges: used to cut and grind food
molar	flat topped with ridges for grinding vegetation	pointed: points on upper and lower jaws interlock to slice flesh	flat topped with small ridges for grinding food

temperature control: see *thermoregulation*.

tendon: a fibrous, inelastic structure which joins *muscle* to *bone*. Tendons are made largely from the fibrous protein collagen. It is essential that tendons are inelastic so that they transmit the pulling force from the muscle to the bone. If tendons were elastic, part of the force from the muscle would be wasted in stretching the tendon.

test tube baby: see *in vitro fertilisation*.

test cross: see *backcross*.

testa: the outer covering of a *seed*, formed from the wall of the *ovule*. The testa protects the embryo and cotyledons from infection by microorganisms and, to a certain extent, from physical damage. When the seed

germinates, the intake of water splits the testa.
(See *germination*.)

testis (plural testes): the male reproductive organ in animals which produces sperm.
- The testes in humans are contained in a pouch of skin called the scrotum. The reason for the testes being outside the body cavity is that sperm production proceeds best at 35°C. This is two degrees lower than the body temperature.
- Sperm are produced in the testes by *meiosis*, which halves the chromosome number from the usual 46 to 23. Each sperm has one chromosome from each pair present in ordinary body cells.

(See also *reproductive system, human*.)

testosterone: the male sex hormone produced in the *testes*.
Testosterone is a *steroid* hormone responsible for:
- promoting muscle and bone growth
- the development of the male *secondary sex characteristics*.

thermoregulation: the ability of an organism to control its body temperature. Temperature regulation is really a feature shown only by animals. The benefit of being able to maintain a more or less constant body temperature is that all *enzyme* systems are always working at their optimum. This means that the *metabolism* is at its most efficient.
There are two main ways in which animals control their body temperatures.

BEHAVIOURAL METHODS

Reptiles such as lizards cannot control their body temperatures in the same way as *mammals*. They can, however, warm themselves up and cool themselves down by alternately moving into the sun and shade.

INTERNAL METHODS

These are shown in the table on page 293.

thermoregulatory centre: part of a region of the *brain* called the hypothalamus.
The thermoregulatory centre can detect and respond to very small increases or decreases in the temperature of the blood passing through it. As a result of maintaining a relatively constant body temperature:
- the *enzyme* systems work at their optimum (most effective) level all the time

● the organism can be more independent of its environment.

The sequence of events by which the thermoregulatory centre maintains a constant body temperature is shown in the flow chart. It is an example of *negative feedback* control and an important example of a homeostatic mechanism (see *homeostasis*.)

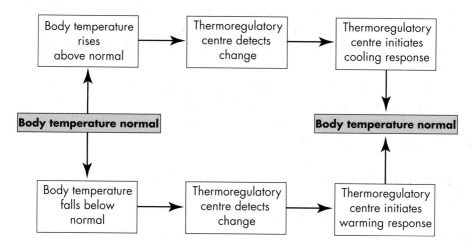

thermoregulation

Mechanism	Change when too hot	Change when too cold
sweat production	increases: extra evaporation of sweat carries away more body heat	decreases: decreased evaporation minimises heat loss
arterioles in skin	dilate: extra blood flow near skin surface allows more radiation of heat	constrict: reduced blood flow to surface reduces radiation
hairs on *skin*	lie flat	stand erect: trap a thicker layer of warm air near skin
shivering	does not happen	shivering increases: rapid muscle contractions generate heat
metabolic rate	decreases: decreased metabolic rate decreases heat production	increases: increased metabolic rate increases heat production

thorax: the region of the body of between the head and *abdomen.*
In humans, the thorax extends from the neck to the diaphragm. It is surrounded by the *ribcage* and contains:

● the *heart* and associated major *blood vessels*
● the *lungs* and most of the other parts of the breathing system
● the *oesophagus*
● part of the *spinal cord.*

thrombosis: formation of a blood *clot* inside a *blood vessel*.

Blood clots usually form when a blood vessel has been damaged. The clot helps to prevent the loss of blood.

A blood clot which forms inside an artery may grow and eventually block the artery, cutting off the blood supply. If this happens in a *coronary artery*, it is called *coronary thrombosis* and can cause a heart attack.

Blood clots can form in other arteries and sometimes in veins. Blood clots in veins may dislodge and be carried to another part of the body where they may block an artery. A clot which breaks away like this is called an embolus and the process of blocking another artery is called embolism.

thymine: one of the bases which makes up the *DNA* molecule.

Thymine on one strand of the DNA molecule is always paired with adenine on the other strand. This is because of the base pairing rule.

thyroid gland: an *endocrine gland* which secretes the hormone *thyroxine*.

In humans, the thyroid gland is found at the base of the neck, just in front of the trachea or windpipe (see *breathing system*). It is shaped rather like a bow-tie.

It secretes the hormone thyroxine which increases *metabolic rate* (the rate at which the body releases and uses energy).

In *amphibians*, hormones from the thyroid gland control *metamorphosis* from larva to adult. A tadpole would not change to a frog without these hormones.

thyroxine: the main hormone produced by the *thyroid gland*.

(See also *hormone, animal.*)

tidal volume: the amount of air breathed in (or out) in one breath.

The tidal volume depends on a number of factors, but the average human tidal volume at rest is about 500 cm^3. This volume increases greatly during exercise (to supply the extra oxygen needed for increased *aerobic respiration*) and immediately after exercise (to oxidise *lactic acid*).

tissue: a group of *cells* arranged together and adapted to perform the same function.

Examples of tissues include:

- *smooth muscle* – all smooth muscle cells are more or less the same shape and have one function which is to contract
- nervous tissue – all nerve cells (*neurones*) are adapted to carry *nerve*

impulses: they are organised into nerves which carry all the impulses to and from a particular part of the body
- *xylem* in plants – all xylem cells are tubular and empty to carry water through the plant: they are connected end to end in long tubes and many of these long tubes lie next to each other, which gives support to the plant.

tissue culture: growing *cells* or *tissues* in a special growth medium under sterile conditions.
The growth medium must contain all the *nutrients* needed for healthy growth, and may also contain *hormones* to encourage growth.
Examples of the use of tissue culture include:
- *micropropagation* of many genetically identical plants from a single plant
- production of *skin* grafts from a few healthy skin cells
- initial testing of new drugs
- research into how cells grow and develop into different types of cells (including cancerous cells).

tissue fluid: the liquid which escapes from the blood as it passes through the *capillaries*.
Tissue fluid escapes from the capillaries because:
- the blood entering the capillaries is under high pressure (due to the force from the *ventricles*)
- the capillary walls are leaky (the single layer of cells in capillary walls do not fit perfectly).
The tissue fluid flows around the cells near the capillary and carries to them dissolved oxygen and nutrients. It collects carbon dioxide and other waste products from the cells.
Of the tissue fluid lost from the capillaries, 90% of it is later drawn back by *osmosis*. The remaining 10% drains into the *lymphatics*.

tissue typing: a procedure used in *transplantation* which matches as closely as possible the *tissues* of a donor with those of the patient.
A transplant will be rejected if its *antigens* do not match those which are normally found on the body cells of the patient. It is impossible to get a perfect match (except with identical twins), but some antigens are more important than others. If these can be matched, or very nearly matched, then *rejection* is unlikely.
A simple example of tissue typing is used in *blood transfusion*, ensuring that the blood given to a patient is of the same group as the patient.

tongue: the muscular organ found in the mouth of most *vertebrates*. The human tongue is the sense organ which gives us our sense of *taste*. It also helps us to chew food, swallow and speak.

The taste buds are structures which are sunk in little pits in the surface of the tongue. They are sensitive to substances in solution, but can only distinguish salty, bitter, sour and sweet tastes. All the flavour of food comes from an interaction of taste and *smell*. When dissolved substances stimulate sense cells in a taste bud, they trigger *nerve impulse*s which pass to the brain.

tooth decay: the gradual erosion of the *enamel* of *teeth* and subsequently, the dentine.

The main cause of tooth decay is *plaque* which builds up on teeth if they are not cleaned regularly. Within the plaque, bacteria multiply using the food debris present and produce acids. The acids erode the enamel covering of the tooth and, if not treated, then erode the dentine.

The main stages in tooth decay are described below.

- Erosion of the enamel – if this is only slight, and the teeth are cleaned regularly, the dentine will be replaced and the decay will go no further.
- Erosion of the dentine – if this occurs, then the only treatment is to drill out the infected area and fill the tooth.
- Infection of the pulp cavity – if this occurs, then you will have quite serious pain. A filling may be sufficient to save the tooth.
- Death of the pulp cavity – by this stage, there is usually no way of saving the tooth and it must be extracted.

Remember:

- brush your teeth regularly – this will remove the plaque and other food debris
- avoid too many sweet foods – bacteria make the acids mainly from sugars.

toxic shock syndrome: a rare but serious illness caused by rapid growth of certain bacteria in the *vagina*.

The bacteria produce a toxin which causes:

- sickness and diarrhoea
- high fever
- muscular aches and pains
- dizziness and disorientation
- a skin rash resembling sunburn.

There may be complications such as *liver* and/or *kidney* failure, dangerously low *blood pressure* and *shock*. It is occasionally fatal.

Toxic shock syndrome has been associated with:

- prolonged use of some tampons (now taken off the market)
- use of a contraceptive cap
- infection of skin wounds.

It is normally successfully treated with *antibiotics*.

toxin: a poisonous substance produced by a living organism.

Toxins are produced by some bacteria (such as the bacterium which causes tetanus), venomous snakes (such as cobras and vipers) and some fungi (such as the death cap mushroom).

Toxins are often *proteins* and are broken down in the *liver*.

trachea (insect): tubes which run the length of an insect's body: one on each side.

Each trachea has tubes to the outside which lead to the *spiracles*. Other tubes lead inside to a network of finer and finer tubes called tracheoles. The smallest tracheoles carry oxygen directly to the cells. Blood is not involved in carrying oxygen in insects.

trachea (mammal): the main breathing tube which carries air from the throat to the bronchi. (See *breathing systems*.)

The trachea is supported by rings of *cartilage* which prevent it from collapsing when we breathe in. The lower end of the trachea divides into two bronchi which carry air into the lungs.

Some cells in the lining of the trachea secrete *mucus* and others have *cilia*. The mucus traps dust and bacteria and the cilia waft this upwards towards the larynx. From there the mixture of mucus and bacteria enters the *oesophagus* and is swallowed. Acid in the *stomach* kills the bacteria.

In humans and other air-breathing vertebrates, the trachea is also known as the windpipe.

transamination: a process which manufactures one kind of *amino acid* from another.

In humans, transamination takes place in the *liver*.

All amino acids contain a group of three atoms called the amino group. This group contains one nitrogen atom and two hydrogen atoms ($-NH_2$). In transamination, the amino group is split off an amino acid and joined to another kind of acid, converting it into an amino acid.

We can make many amino acids in this way, but not all of the ones we need. Those we cannot make by transamination we must obtain from our food. These are called the essential amino acids.

transcription: the process by which *DNA* makes a copy of part of the genetic code in a molecule of *messenger RNA* (m-RNA).

The m-RNA carries the code for the synthesis of a particular *protein*. Each triplet of bases in the m-RNA codes for an amino acid.

(See *protein synthesis* for details.)

transfer RNA (t-RNA): the *RNA* molecule which carries *amino acids* to the *ribosomes* to be assembled into proteins.

Each t-RNA molecule can carry only one type of amino acid.

(See *protein synthesis* for details.)

transgenic: an organism which has had a *gene* or genes from another individual added to its normal genetic make-up.

Due to advances in *genetic engineering*, it is now possible to transfer genes from one organism to another. Examples of transgenic organisms include:

- tomato plants with an extra gene which prolongs shelf-life
- crop plants with a gene which gives resistance to *pesticides*
- sheep with a gene which produces human blood clotting protein in their milk.

translation: the decoding of a code carried by *messenger RNA* (m-RNA).

Ribosomes decode the m-RNA message and build the protein which is specified by that code.

(See *protein synthesis* for details.)

translocation: the movement of *organic substances* through the *phloem* of a plant.

Sugars are made only in the leaves of a plant, but are needed by all living cells. They are moved from one location to another in the phloem (hence the name translocation).

The phloem cells carry sugars and other organic substances from the leaves to:

- storage organs (such as underground stems, bulbs and large roots)
- growing points – the tips of stems (and branches) and roots are actively growing and so need sugars for *respiration* and amino acids to make proteins
- flowers – flowers need the organic substances to make pollen and nectar and, following fertilisation, to make *seeds*.

The mechanism by which phloem cells move organic substances is not well understood.

transmitter substance: see *neurotransmitter*.

transpiration: the loss of water vapour from the *shoot system* of a plant; mainly from the leaves.

Transpiration is a continuous process, but it is helpful to think of it occurring in stages.

1 Water vapour moves through the open *stomata* of a *leaf* by a combination of *diffusion* and being blown by the wind.
2 Water evaporates from the surface of cells in the spongy mesophyll into the air spaces.
3 The spongy mesophyll cells draw water from neighbouring *xylem* cells in the veins by *osmosis*.
4 This loss of water from the xylem cells pulls more water through the xylem in the leaves and in the stem.

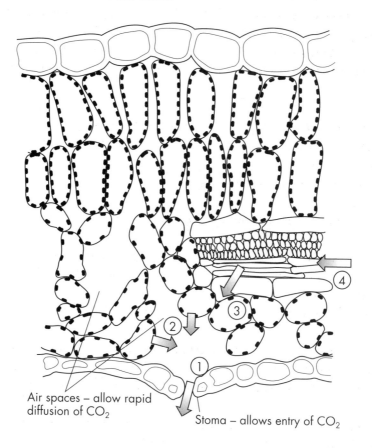

Air spaces – allow rapid diffusion of CO_2

Stoma – allows entry of CO_2

The rate of transpiration is affected by a number of factors. These are explained in the table on the following page.

You can measure the rate of transpiration with a *potometer*.

Factor	Effect on rate of transpiration	Reason for effect
humidity of air around leaf	• dry air increases rate of transpiration	• increases the difference in concentration between air and air spaces in leaf – diffusion is faster
	• humid air decreases rate of transpiration	• decreases the difference in concentration – diffusion is slower
temperature of air around leaf	• warm air increases rate of transpiration	• molecules of water vapour have more energy and so move faster – diffusion is faster
	• cold air decreases rate of transpiration	• molecules have less energy and move slower – diffusion is slower
movement of air around leaf	• moving air increases rate of transpiration	• molecules of water vapour are blown away, increasing concentration difference – diffusion is faster
	• still air decreases rate of transpiration	• molecules of water vapour build up outside leaf, decreasing concentration difference – diffusion is slower
light intensity	• bright light increases rate of transpiration	• stomata open to the full
	• darkness decreases rate	• stomata closed

transplantation: transferring a *tissue* or an *organ* from one individual to another.

In human transplant surgery, one of the main problems which must be overcome is *rejection*. To minimise this problem careful *tissue typing* is carried out. *Immunosuppressive drugs* are also frequently used.

Examples of human transplants now possible include corneal grafts (replacing a diseased or damaged cornea to restore sight is the oldest transplant procedure), bone marrow, heart, lung, liver and kidney.

Sometimes, combined transplants are carried out, for example a heart-lung transplant.

tricuspid valve: the *atrio-ventricular valve* between the right atrium and right ventricle of the *heart*.

It is called tricuspid because it is made from three flaps of tissue.

trophic level: the position occupied by an organism in a *food chain*.

Look at the food chain below:

rose plant ⟶ aphid ⟶ ladybird ⟶ bluetit

There are four trophic levels which fall into the following categories:

producer → primary consumer → secondary consumer → tertiary consumer
(photo-   (herbivore)   (carnivore)   (top carnivore)
synthetic
organism)

You should remember that *omnivores* can be both primary consumers and secondary consumers.

The number of trophic levels in a food chain depends on how much energy is available in the producers. Energy is lost at each stage of the food chain. As a guide, only about 10% of the energy in one trophic level is passed on to the next.

---

tropism: a growth response made by plants to some external *stimulus*.
If the growth is towards the stimulus we say it is a positive tropism. If the growth is away from the stimulus, we call it a negative tropism. Plant *stems* are positively phototropic (they grow towards light) but negatively geotropic (they grow away from gravity).
The main tropic responses of plants are described in the table.

Stimulus	Name of tropism	Response by stems	Response by roots
light	phototropism	grow towards light (positive phototropism)	no response
gravity	geotropism (gravitropism)	grow away from gravity (negative geotropism)	grow towards gravity (positive geotropism)
water	hydrotropism	no response	grow towards water (positive hydrotropism)

---

trypsin: a *protease* enzyme released from the *pancreas* of *vertebrates*.
Trypsin is released when food from the *stomach* enters the *small intestine*. It is released in an inactive form and only becomes active when it reaches the small intestine. There, it continues the digestion of *proteins* begun in the stomach.
Bacterial trypsins have been used in dissolving *blood clot*s in patients with *thromboses*.

---

tuberculosis, pulmonary: see *pulmonary tuberculosis*.

---

tumour: an uncontrolled overproduction of cells in a specific area of an organism.

In humans, tumours are described as benign or malignant. Malignant tumours are *cancers*.

Benign tumours usually grow more slowly than malignant tumours and do not invade nearby tissue or spread to other parts of the body. Benign tumours can, however, be dangerous. A benign tumour of the brain, if left untreated, would put pressure on the brain and disturb normal brain function. It could be fatal.

The commonest benign tumour is a wart.

turgid: a condition in which a plant *cell* has enough water to make the cytoplasm press against the cell wall.

If a cylinder of potato tissue is placed in distilled water:

- the cells gain water from the solution by *osmosis*
- the cytoplasm of the cells expands with the extra water
- the cytoplasm presses on the cell wall and stretches it – the cells are turgid
- the cells in the potato cylinder press against each other and it becomes very firm and rigid; it cannot be bent easily.

Turgid cells support young *stems* with little xylem (woody tissue). If they lose too much water, their cells become *flaccid* and the stem wilts.

typhoid fever: a serious infectious *disease* of the *digestive system*.

Typhoid fever is caused by one type of *Salmonella* bacterium. It is usually contracted by drinking contaminated water or by eating contaminated food. Once in the intestine, the bacteria pass in the bloodstream to the *liver* and spleen where they multiply.

Seven to fourteen days after infection some, or all, of the following symptoms appear:

- headache and fever
- initially constipation, but later diarrhoea
- delirium
- enlargement of liver and spleen.

If treatment is not given quickly, intestinal bleeding may occur, and the intestine may rupture, infecting the body cavity (peritonitis). Kidney failure sometimes occurs.

ultrafiltration: the process by which small molecules such as amino acids, glucose and water are removed from the blood in the *kidney* of *vertebrates*. (See *nephron* for details.)

---

ultrasound: sound with very high frequencies and inaudible to humans. Ultrasound is used by a number of animals as a navigation aid. Dolphins and bats emit high pitched sounds which bounce off objects in their path. The nature of the echoes allows the animals to judge where the obstacles are.

The same principle of ultrasound waves being reflected is used in the ultrasound scanner. This is a technique which allows images of parts of the body to be obtained without the need for surgery or the risk of high energy X-rays. In this process:

- beams of ultrasound waves are directed at a region of the body (such as an unborn baby)
- some of the waves are absorbed, others are reflected
- the amount of absorption and reflection depends on the type of tissue
- the reflections are analysed by a computer which builds up an image of the internal structure on a monitor or screen.

---

ultraviolet (UV) radiation: high energy electromagnetic radiation with a shorter wavelength than visible light and so invisible to humans.

UV radiation is important biologically. Its effect on human *skin* can be both harmful and beneficial.

- It causes special cells called melanocytes in the skin to increase their production of *melanin* which gives protection against too much UV radiation. It also causes a reaction in which fatty substances in the skin are converted into vitamin D.
- Overexposure to UV radiation can cause sunburn and cancers of the skin including *melanoma* – a particularly serious skin cancer. The cancers are the result of *mutations* in the skin cells caused by the high energy UV rays.
- The energy in UV can be used beneficially for sterilisation of equipment.

The amount and kind of UV radiation reaching the earth from the sun is changing. The *ozone layer* filters out much of the UV which would otherwise reach the earth: particularly the highest energy UV. Damage to the ozone layer is allowing more of this high energy UV radiation to reach the earth.

umbilical cord: in a mammal, the cord which connects the unborn *fetus* with the *placenta*.
The umbilical cord contains one *vein* and two *arteries*. The umbilical vein carries oxygenated *blood* with many nutrients from the placenta to the fetus. The umbilical arteries carry deoxygenated blood from the fetus to the placenta.

unicellular: consisting of only one cell.
Unicellular organisms include:
- most of the *phytoplankton*
- most *bacteria*
- *protozoans*.

uracil: the base used in making *RNA* instead of thymine.

urea: the nitrogenous waste product produced from surplus *amino acids* in *mammals*; chemical formula $CO(NH_2)_2$.
When you eat protein, it is digested to amino acids. If you absorb more amino acids than you can use, the surplus amino acids undergo *deamination* in the *liver*. The urea formed in this process passes from the liver into the blood plasma and is excreted by the *kidneys*.

ureter: the tube which carries *urine* from the *kidney* to the *bladder*.
The walls of the ureters contain *smooth muscle* which produce peristaltic waves of contraction to move the urine towards the bladder.

urethra: the tube in *mammals* which connects the *bladder* to the exterior.
In males, the urethra runs through the *penis* and carries both *urine* and *semen*.
In females, the urethra carries only urine.

uric acid: the nitrogenous excretory product formed from surplus *amino acids* in *reptiles* and *birds*; chemical formula $C_5H_4N_4O_3$.
Like *urea*, uric acid is formed from surplus amino acids but, unlike urea, uric acid is insoluble and non-toxic.
It is formed in land animals which begin their lives in eggs. While in the eggs, they are unable to excrete and must store their excretory product. As uric acid is non-toxic, it is an *adaptation* to the way of life.

It can be excreted from adult animals as a paste with very little water loss, a clear adaptation to life on the land.

Humans also produce a little uric acid. If more than usual is produced it can accumulate in the joints and cause gout, a kind of *arthritis*.

urine: the liquid produced from the blood in the *kidneys* of *vertebrates*. When blood enters the *nephrons* of the kidneys:
- it is filtered at the Bowman's capsules: any molecule small enough is forced out
- useful molecules are later actively reabsorbed.

The liquid which results from filtration and reabsorption is the urine.

uterus: the womb: the place where a mammalian embryo develops until it is born.

In humans, the uterus is a hollow, muscular organ with two *Fallopian tubes* which carry fertilised eggs to it. The lining of the uterus thickens during each *menstrual cycle* in preparation for *implantation* of an embryo. If this does not occur, the extra lining is shed in *menstruation* and the cycle begins again.

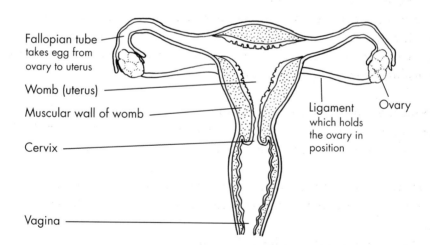

During birth, powerful contractions of the *smooth muscle*, in the wall of the uterus, force the baby to the outside.

(See *reproductive system, human, menstrual cycle, implantation* and *birth* for details.)

vaccine: a preparation containing *antigens* which stimulates an *immune response*.

Vaccines are introduced into the body to produce a specific immune response against the antigens in the vaccine. This will include producing *memory cells* and so give lasting immunity to a disease.

Vaccines are prepared in a number of ways and may contain:

- weakened (attenuated) strains of the *pathogen* (e.g. the polio and *measles* vaccines)
- dead pathogens (e.g. the whooping cough and typhoid fever vaccines)
- modified *toxins* (e.g. the tetanus vaccine)
- only the antigens from the pathogen (e.g. the *influenza* vaccine)
- genetically engineered harmless bacteria (e.g. the hepatitis B vaccine has bacteria which have been genetically engineered to produce the hepatitis antigens).

vaccination: introducing a *vaccine* into an individual.

Vaccination is carried out to give individual long-lasting immunity to a disease. The *antigens* in the vaccine cause an *immune response* by the body. The immune response involves producing antibodies to destroy the antigens and *memory cells* which remain in our bodies for many years. If we are re-infected by *pathogens* with the same antigens as were in the vaccine, the memory cells will produce a much quicker and stronger immune response. The pathogens will be destroyed before they have time to multiply and causes the disease. We are *immune*.

The first vaccination was carried out by *Edward Jenner*.

vacuole: a fluid-filled, membrane-bound cavity inside a *cell*.

Vacuoles vary in size and function. The vacuole found in most plant cells is usually large – up to 90% of the volume of the cell. Vacuoles in animal cells, if present, are usually much smaller. Some *unicellular* organisms have contractile vacuoles which are used for expelling water from the cell.

The vacuoles in plant cells can have several functions:

- storing soluble organic substances (like *sugars*) and *mineral ions*
- storing pigments to give cells in *petals* and other structures their colour

- storing excretory products which may make the plant unpalatable to *herbivores*
- helping to keep the cell *turgid*: they can absorb water by *osmosis* and swell, pushing the cytoplasm against the cell wall.

vagina: the muscular passage in the female reproductive system of a mammal, which connects the uterus with the exterior.
The vagina has two main functions:

- to allow intercourse and therefore sperm to be introduced into the female's body
- to allow the baby to pass from the uterus to the exterior during birth.
The vagina is also known as the birth canal.
(See *reproductive system, human* for details.)

valve: a structure which controls the movement of a fluid.
Vertebrates have valves in their *circulatory systems* which prevent the backflow of *blood*. There are valves between the atria and ventricles of the *heart* and at the base of the large *arteries* leaving the heart. There are also valves in *veins*.

- The valves between the atria and ventricles are called *atrio-ventricular valves*.
- The valves at the base of the large arteries are called *semi-lunar valves*.
- The valves in the veins are called watch pocket valves.

variation: the differences that exist between individuals.
When we talk about variation, we usually mean the differences that exist between individuals of the same *species*.
There are two types of variation.

- *Continuous variation* in which there is a whole range of different values of the feature or *characteristic*. Body mass is an example of this kind of variation in humans. There are extremes of body mass (very heavy and very light) and a range of values in between. Most individuals are about average body mass.
- *Discontinuous variation* in which there are just a few categories with no intermediates. Your earlobes are either attached or not. You are either blood group A, B, AB or O.
Variation has two causes.
- It is partly genetic. Variation in our *genotypes* will make us different.
- It is partly due to the environment. *Clones* of plants grown in different soils appear different. Identical twins, (who are genetically identical),

never look exactly alike, possibly due to different diets and experiences during life.

vascular: anything concerning structures which carry liquids in living things. The vascular tissues in plants are:
- the *xylem*, which carries water through the plant
- the *phloem*, which carries dissolved organic materials through the plants.

In animals, the vascular structures are the *blood vessels* and the *lymph* vessels.

vascular bundles: strands of *xylem* and *phloem* cells in the stem and leaves of a plant.

The vascular bundles are arranged around the edge of a stem to give maximum support and resistance to bending stresses.

vas deferens: see *sperm duct*.

vasoconstriction: the narrowing of *blood vessels*, nearly always *arterioles*. Arterioles lead from the arteries carrying blood into an organ to the capillaries which exchange materials within the organ. They have *smooth muscle* in their walls which can contract or relax.

When the muscle in the wall of an arteriole contracts:
- the lumen (internal space) gets narrower
- less blood can pass through the arterioles
- the blood supply to the organ is reduced.

Vasoconstriction can divert blood away from an organ when it is not needed there.
- Vasoconstriction of arterioles in the *skin* when we are cold reduces blood flow to the surface of the skin and so reduces heat loss by radiation.
- Vasoconstriction of arterioles leading to the gut when we exercise allows more blood to be delivered to the muscles.

vasodilation: the widening of *blood vessels*, usually *arterioles*. To dilate an arteriole, the *smooth muscle* in its wall relaxes. When this happens:
- the lumen (internal space) becomes larger
- more blood can pass through the arteriole
- the blood supply to the organ is increased.

This allows the blood supply to an organ to be increased as necessary.
- Vasodilation of arterioles in the *skin* when we are hot increases the blood flow to the surface of the skin and allows more heat to be lost by radiation.

- Vasodilation of arterioles leading to muscles during exercise allows more oxygenated blood to be delivered to them.

vector (genetic engineering): the structure which is used to carry *DNA* into the cell of another organism.

The commonest vectors are plasmids and *viruses*.

(See *genetic engineering* for details.)

vector (disease): an organism which transmits *pathogens* (disease causing organisms).

The female *Anopheles* mosquito transmits the *parasite* causing *malaria* from one human to another.

Houseflies transmit bacteria from one place to another (e.g. onto food).

vein (leaf): the *vascular bundles* (strands of *phloem* and *xylem*) in a *leaf* which connect to those in the *stem*.

The xylem in the vein brings water to the leaf, some of which is used in *photosynthesis*. Any water not used by the leaf cells is lost through the *stomata* in *transpiration*.

The phloem transports soluble organic molecules (like *glucose* and *amino acids*) into and out of the leaf, depending on needs.

Glucose is transported out of the leaf when the leaf is actively photosynthesising and there is a surplus.

vein (mammal): a blood vessel which carries blood away from organs, back to the heart.

Veins have the following features.

- They are thin walled. The blood they carry is under very little pressure and a thick wall is not necessary.
- They have a wide lumen (internal space). This reduces friction against the wall and the low-pressure blood can flow more easily.
- They have *valves* to prevent backflow of blood.

Nearly all veins carry deoxygenated blood. The exceptions are the pulmonary veins (from the lungs) and, before birth, the umbilical veins (from the placenta). These both carry oxygenated blood.

Small veins are called venules.

(See *blood vessels* for a comparison with arteries and capillaries.)

vena cava: the main *vein* in the body of a mammal.

There are, in fact, two venae cavae. One collects blood from all the veins above the *heart* (the superior vena cava). The other collects blood from all the veins below the heart (the inferior vena cava).

ventilation: another name for *breathing*.
It is the process which moves the oxygen-carrying medium (air or water) past the *gas exchange* surface.
- We ventilate our *alveoli* by breathing air in and out.
- A fish ventilates the filaments in its *gills* by moving water over them.
- An insect ventilates its tracheoles by moving air in and out of them. (See *trachea (insect)*.)

ventricle: a muscular chamber of the heart of *vertebrates* which pumps *blood* out of the heart. (See diagram of *heart*.)
In the cardiac cycle of a mammal, the ventricles receive blood from the atria. When they are full they contract and force blood out of the heart into the *aorta* and *pulmonary artery*. *Atrio-ventricular valves* prevent blood from returning to the atria.
Mammals have a heart with two ventricles. The left ventricle pumps oxygenated blood into the aorta. Branches of the aorta carry blood to all parts of the body except the lungs. The right ventricle pumps deoxygenated blood into the pulmonary arteries which carry it to the lungs.
The wall of the left ventricle is much thicker than that of the right ventricle. This is necessary to generate enough force to pump the blood greater distances against a greater resistance. The right ventricle need only generate enough force to pump blood a few centimetres through the capillaries in the lungs. Too high a pressure would damage these capillaries.

vertebrae (singular vertebra): the bones which make up the vertebral column (*spine*) in *vertebrates*.
Most vertebrae have:
- a space in the middle in which the *spinal cord* is found
- projections at the back and sides for *muscle* attachment

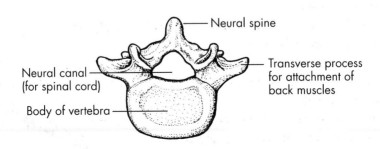

Neural spine

Neural canal
(for spinal cord)

Transverse process
for attachment of
back muscles

Body of vertebra

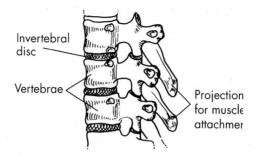

Invertebral disc

Vertebrae

Projection for muscle attachment

- projections (facets) which fit into similar projections on adjacent vertebrae. Adjacent vertebrae are separated by a disc made from *cartilage*. In humans, these discs separate the vertebrae and act as shock absorbers, absorbing the energy of movement.

vertebral column: the column of bones and cartilage discs running through the body of *vertebrates*.
(See *spine* for details.)

vertebrates: animals with a vertebral column (*spine*) and a *skull*.
There are five classes of vertebrates:
- *fish*
- *amphibians*
- *reptiles*
- *birds*
- *mammals.*

vibrio: a comma-shaped bacterium.
The bacterium which causes cholera is a vibrio.

villus (plural villi): a fingerlike projection of the inner surface of the *small intestine*. (See diagram on page 312.)
The millions of villi create a large *surface area* for *absorption* of soluble food molecules into the *blood plasma*. To aid absorption each villus has:
- a good blood supply
- a *lacteal* (lymph vessel) to absorb fatty acids and glycerol
- a thin lining (one cell thick).

virus: a *pathogenic* particle containing only a nucleic acid (*DNA* or *RNA*) inside a protein coat.
Viruses cannot be regarded as living organisms because:
- they are acellular (do not have any cells)

- they cannot carry out any of the characteristics of life outside their *host's* cells.

To reproduce, viruses must enter living cells and there they 'take over' the metabolic machinery of the cell. The DNA or RNA from the virus 'instructs' the cell to make more virus DNA/RNA and more virus protein. These components are then assembled (by the cell) into new viruses which escape and infect other cells.

Because they can only reproduce inside living cells, all viruses are *pathogens*. Human diseases caused by viruses include AIDS, poliomyelitis, chicken pox, *influenza* and the common cold.

Some viruses are used as *vectors* in *genetic engineering*.

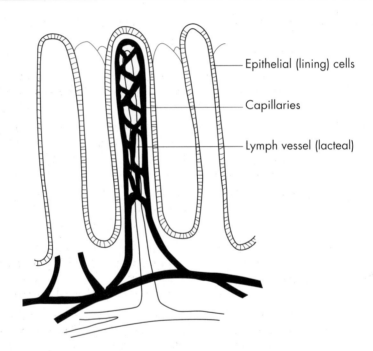

Epithelial (lining) cells

Capillaries

Lymph vessel (lacteal)

villus

vital capacity: the maximum amount of air that you can breathe out after breathing in as deeply as possible.

The vital capacity is not the same as the total lung volume. No matter how hard you try, there is always some air you cannot breathe out. This is called the residual air.

vitamins: *organic substances* needed in small amounts in the diet for normal *metabolism*.

The vitamins are not related to each other. They do not all belong to one group of chemicals and they do not influence our bodies in the same way.

What vitamins do have in common is that a deficiency disease results if we do not get enough of any vitamin in our diet.

The sources, functions and deficiency diseases of the main vitamins are shown in the table.

Vitamin	Source	Function	Effect of deficiency
A	carrots, liver, milk, cheese, yellow and green vegetables	essential for normal vision, normal growth	night blindness, growth retarded
B_1 (thiamine)	liver, yeast, cereals, leafy green vegetables	important in metabolism of carbohydrates and amino acids	beriberi – weakened heart muscle, nervous and digestive disorders
B_2 (riboflavin)	liver, cheese, milk, eggs, leafy green vegetables	essential in aerobic respiration	dermatitis
B_6	liver, meat, cereals, peas, beans and pulses	needed in amino acid metabolism	dermatitis, disorders of digestive system, convulsions
folic acid	liver, cereals, dark green leafy vegetables, intestinal bacteria	essential in the manufacture of red blood cells	one kind of anaemia, increased risk of heart disease
B_{12}	liver, meat, fish	important in metabolism	one kind of anaemia
C	citrus fruits, tomatoes, green leafy vegetables, green peppers, strawberries	needed for manufacture of collagen, amino acid metabolism, bone growth	scurvy – wounds heal slowly, scars split open, capillaries become fragile and bleed easily, bones do not grow or heal properly
D	oily fish, cod liver oil, egg yolk, margarine, action of UV on skin	helps in absorbing calcium from intestine – essential for normal bone growth	bone deformities – known as rickets in children

voluntary muscle: muscle which can be controlled consciously.
The only type of muscle which can normally be controlled in this way is skeletal muscle.

water treatment: the way in which water is made fit for drinking.

In developed countries, water is collected and purified on a large scale at water treatment plants. The rainwater is collected in reservoirs and piped to the treatment plants.

The flow chart describes the main stages in the purification of water.

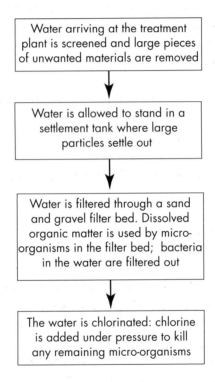

The purified water is then pumped to domestic and industrial users.

Watson, James: an American biologist who, with *Francis Crick*, worked out the structure of the *DNA* molecule.

Watson and Crick worked in a laboratory in Cambridge University and also used information which had been discovered by other scientists. In particular, they used some X-ray images of the DNA molecule first obtained by *Rosalind Franklin* working in a laboratory in London University.

Piecing together all the information, Watson and Crick proposed the now famous double helix structure for DNA.

Understanding the structure of the DNA molecule was crucial to understanding how it copies itself and controls *protein synthesis*. Without this knowledge, *genetic engineering* would be impossible and many of the products of modern *biotechnology* would not exist.

weed: an unwanted plant growing in the wrong place.

Weeds are usually wild plants which are growing in gardens or in fields of crop plants. They often grow vigorously and out-compete the plants which the gardener or farmer wishes to grow.

They can be controlled in three main ways:

- cultivation: the weeds are turned into the soil periodically by ploughing or, on a small scale, hoeing or pulling out the weeds.
- using weedkillers (*herbicides*)
- using *biological control.*

weedkiller: a substance used to kill weeds. (See *herbicide* for details.)

white matter: nervous tissue which consists largely of the axons of *neurones*.

The white matter is found on the outside of the *spinal cord* but inside the *brain*.

white blood cell: see *leucocyte*.

wilting: loss of rigidity in plant stems and leaves, often causing them to droop: it is most obvious in young plants with little woody tissue (*xylem*).

Wilting occurs when young plants lose more water in *transpiration* than they take in by *osmosis* from the soil. When this happens, the cells in the stem and leaves lose water and become plasmolysed, (see *plasmolysis*).

The cells are no longer *turgid* and no longer press strongly against each other and the *epidermis*. It is this pressure which keeps the stem upright so, if it is reduced, the stem will droop or wilt.

wine: an alcoholic drink made from the *fermentation* of fruit pulp.

Most wine is made from grapes which are fermented by *yeasts* occurring naturally on the fruit. To produce red wines, the skins of the grapes are left on longer during fermentation.

The yeasts ferment sugars in the grapes to produce the *alcohol*.

winemaking: producing *wine* by allowing *yeasts* to ferment the sugars in fruits (see *fermentation*).

Wine can be made from most fruits, but nearly all the wine which is sold is produced from grapes.

The flow chart shows the main stages in the commercial production of wines from grapes.

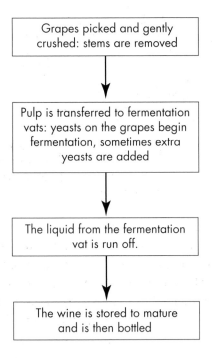

Grapes picked and gently crushed: stems are removed

Pulp is transferred to fermentation vats: yeasts on the grapes begin fermentation, sometimes extra yeasts are added

The liquid from the fermentation vat is run off.

The wine is stored to mature and is then bottled

wing: a structure with a large surface area which allows flight in some animals.

Birds and bats have forelimbs which are modified to form wings. Bird's wings are covered in *feathers* while bat's wing are covered by a thin membrane. Many *insects* also have wings: some have two pairs, some have just one pair.

When a bird is flying, the *primary feathers* provide most of the forward thrust while the *secondary feathers* provide most of the lift.

The shape of a bird's wing is related to the way in which it flies.

- Birds like the albatross which spend a lot of time gliding have long thin wings. These wings have a large surface area to gain maximum lift from air currents. This reduces the amount of energy the bird must use in flying.
- Smaller birds have shorter, fatter wings. This means they cannot glide as the wings do not have sufficient surface area, so the bird must use more

energy in flight. They have less air resistance however, which makes the bird more manouverable.

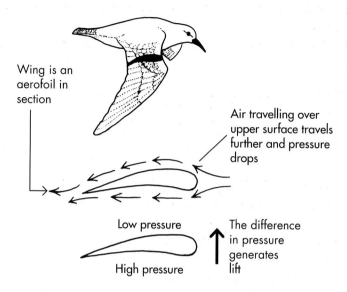

Wing is an aerofoil in section

Air travelling over upper surface travels further and pressure drops

Low pressure

High pressure

The difference in pressure generates lift

A bird's wing provides lift because it has an aerofoil shape in cross section. The upper surface of an aerofoil is longer than the lower surface. Air travelling over the upper surface must travel further than air travelling under the lower surface. The air above the upper surface travels faster and the particles become more spaced out. This reduces the pressure above the upper surface and so the higher pressure underneath forces the wing up.

X chromosome: one of the two *sex chromosomes* present in human cells. The X chromosome is larger than the Y chromosome and has more *genes*. Besides the genes which determine gender, it also carries genes which determine a number of sex-linked characteristics. The Y chromosome does not carry these genes.

Men have the genotype XY; women have the genotype XX.

(See *sex-linked inheritance* for details.)

xerophyte: a plant which is adapted to live in dry conditions.

Plants living in these conditions often have *adaptations* which:

- reduce the amount of water they lose in *transpiration*
- allow them to gain as much water as possible from the soil.

To reduce the amount of transpiration, xerophytes may have:

- *leaves* reduced to spines or scales
- a dense covering of hairs over each leaf to trap moist air next to the leaf
- sunken *stomata* which lose water less readily.

To gain as much water as possible, xerophytes often have extensive *root systems*.

Most *cacti* are xerophytes.

xylem: the empty, tubular cells which carry water throughout a plant.

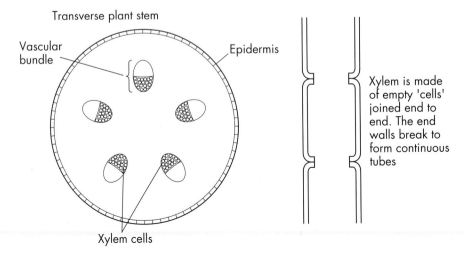

Transverse plant stem

Vascular bundle

Epidermis

Xylem cells

Xylem is made of empty 'cells' joined end to end. The end walls break to form continuous tubes

Xylem cells join end to end to form tubes which are continuous from the root, through the *stem* and into the *leaves*. Water is moved through the xylem by *transpiration*.

The xylem cells are arranged in *vascular bundles* in the stem, along with the *phloem* cells which carry organic materials through the plant.

The *cell walls* of xylem cells are much thicker and stronger than those of ordinary cells. Xylem makes up the wood of a plant and is the tissue which gives the plant most support.

Y chromosome: one of the two human *sex chromosomes*.

Only men have a Y chromosome in their cells. It determines maleness. It carries no other *genes* and so is smaller than the X chromosome which is present in both men and women.

Men have the genotype XY; women have the genotype XX.

(See *sex-linked inheritance* for details.)

---

yeast: a *unicellular fungus* used in baking, *brewing* and *winemaking*.

In all these processes, yeast ferments glucose to form carbon dioxide and alcohol, (see *fermentation*).

In brewing and winemaking, the alcohol is the important product.

In baking, carbon dioxide is the important product as this is what makes the dough rise.

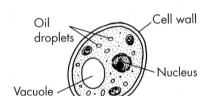

A yeast cell

Yeast can reproduce by budding (a kind of *asexual reproduction*) to form many yeast cells very quickly, under ideal conditions.

---

yellow body: see *corpus luteum*.

---

yoghurt: semi-solid dairy product made by allowing specific *bacteria* to ferment milk (see *fermentation*).

To make yoghurt:

- heat-treated milk is used and two strains of bacteria (*Streptococcus lactis* and *Lactobacillus bulgaricus*) are added
- the bacteria ferment the milk sugar (lactose) into lactic acid
- the lactic acid curdles the milk proteins to form the natural yoghurt
- fruit and flavourings are added as required.

The acid conditions preserve the yoghurt by preventing spoilage by other bacteria.

---

zooplankton: small, often microscopic non-photosynthetic *plankton* which live in the upper layers of freshwater and the oceans.

Most zooplankton are herbivorous and feed on the phytoplankton. Some are carnivorous and eat other zooplankton.

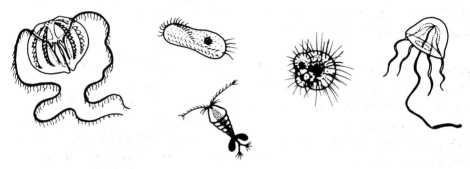

Zooplankton include tiny *crustaceans*, jellyfish, comb jellies, some *protozoans* and larvae of some sea urchins, crabs and worms. They are all weak swimmers and tend to drift with the water currents.

zygote: the single cell formed by fusion of a male and female *gamete* (sex cell) in *fertilisation*.

The gametes have only half the normal number of *chromosomes*, so when they fuse, the zygote has the full number again. It contains all the genetic information to control its development into an adult.

The zygote divides by *mitosis* to form an *embryo* and eventually an adult. As a result, all the cells in the body of the adult (except the sex cells) will contain the normal number of chromosomes.

HINTS FOR EXAM SUCCESS

Every year, many candidates lose marks, and probably grades, in Biology examinations, not because they don't understand the Biology, but because they don't use their time effectively. To obtain the very best grade possible, there are things you should do before the examination and during the examination.

BEFORE THE EXAMINATION

- Remember that the coursework (assessed practicals) count for 25% of all the marks and make sure that you have produced the very best coursework you are capable of producing. A good coursework mark, rather than an average one, may make the difference between a grade D and a grade C – or between a grade B and a grade A. There are a number of hints given in this book in the appendix 'Getting the most out of your coursework'.
- Make sure that you understand terms and ideas as you go along. You don't necessarily have to remember every last detail about photosynthesis as you are being taught it, but you must make sure that you understand the process. If you understand it, it will be easy to revise later. If you don't, you will just be learning a mass of meaningless terms. Look up new terms in this book as you go along, check them with your teacher, talk to your fellow students about them but don't just leave them only half understood.
- When the time comes for your final preparation for the written examination, be quite clear about a number of things.
  - You will need to know how you work best – in short bursts or a long uninterrupted session.
  - You will need to know what sort of activity helps you to learn. There are several things you can do:
    copy your notes
    precis your notes
    write key points on post cards
    talk to your friends about a topic
    make a tape and replay it
    but you must do something as well as just reading your notes through and hoping for the best.
  - You will need to give yourself enough time to learn all your notes – so you must have a plan.
  - You will need to be able to check that you have learned the material, by rewriting notes, reciting sections of notes, trying questions, talking it over with friends/parents.

You should also have a final check on the meaning of the various terms used in examinations.

You also need to be aware that, every year, certain topics are answered badly. If you can be clear about these topics and avoid most of the errors usually made, you will give yourself an advantage.

Marks are most frequently lost in the following ways.

1   The nitrogen cycle. Many candidates are unable to supply any detail about this beyond saying that dead material decays into nitrates. Make sure that you know all the intermediate stages and the names of the bacteria which bring about the conversions.
2   Eutrophication. Often candidates suggest that the rapidly reproducing algae use up the oxygen in the water. Make sure you are clear that it is bacteria which decay the dead algae which use up the oxygen. Eutrophication is also confused with pollution of water by organic materials. Make sure you are clear about each process, particularly as organic pollution can lead (later) to eutrophication.
3   Saprotrophic (saprophytic) nutrition. Candidates often fail to give sufficient detail about how this kind of nutrition takes place. You need to talk about secretion (release) of digestive enzymes, digestion of organic materials and absorption by diffusion or active transport of the soluble products of digestion.
4   Sewage treatment. Again, lack of detail is the usual failing. You need to be quite clear about what is happening at the various stages of the treatment process and what the various microorganisms actually do.
5   Osmosis. Candidates often have the idea that the process involved is osmosis, but get horribly confused about what is moving, where and why. In most questions about osmosis, you will need to identify four elements: the stronger solution, the weaker solution, the partially permeable membrane (usually cell membranes) and the direction of water movement. Remember only water moves across the partially permeable membrane and it moves from the weaker solution to the stronger one.
6   Digestion. In many cases, candidates cannot supply the necessary detail. You should know:
    ● the breakdown products of starch, fat and protein
    ● the enzymes responsible for the digestion of these molecules
    ● the region of the gut in which the digestion takes place.
7   In addition to the lack of detail in answers on the topics above, certain other terms/topics are often confused. These include:
    ● plants produce oxygen in photosynthesis, they do not use it

- diseases are caused by bacteria/viruses/fungi/protozoa – not germs
- the greenhouse effect and destruction of the ozone layer
- glycogen (a storage carbohydrate in animals)and glucagon (a hormone)
- mitosis (cell division producing diploid body cells) and meiosis (cell division producing haploid sex cells)
- respiration releases energy, it does not use it
- muscles need oxygen not air
- respiration (the release of energy from food molecules – usually glucose) and breathing (exchanging gases with the environment)
- gene (a section of DNA which governs a particular feature, e.g. height in pea plants) and allele (the form the gene takes, e.g. the tall allele of the gene for height or the dwarf allele of the gene for height)
- genotype (the type of alleles an organism contains) and phenotype (the feature which results from the genotype).

8 In addition, there are certain errors which almost assume the level of a criminal offence!

- nerve cells carry impulses not messages
- capillaries do not move higher and lower in the skin so that we can lose more/less heat
- animal cells do not have cell walls.

Before you go into the examination, try to clarify these points in your mind.

DURING THE EXAMINATION

Examinations are stressful experiences for most of us, and the examiners know this. They will make some allowances for silly slips if they possibly can. But you must do all you can to minimise the stress on yourself and so you must have a strategy for approaching the examination. The following hints are intended to help you score every mark you possibly can.

- Don't start to write answers the minute you are told to begin. Most Biology examinations have a reasonably generous time allocation and you can afford to spend five minutes or so at the start of the examination 'planning your campaign'.
- Do read through all the questions first and identify those which you think you can do best and do them first. Do them carefully and get as many marks on them as you possibly can. There are three main reasons for this.
  - Writing down answers you are reasonably confident about will help to relax you.
  - As you write these answers it will help to jog your memory about other related topics.

- If you do run out of time at the end of the examination, at least you will not be losing time on a question you know you could have answered well.
- Do read the question carefully and note carefully which of the terms (state, explain, describe, etc.) is being used.
- Do take notice of the mark allocations and the amount of space left for an answer. Don't write reams about your favourite aspect of Biology if the question is only worth two marks. Similarly, a one word answer to a question worth six marks will not get you very far.
- Do try and stick to the point in your answers. This is particularly true where there is scope for you to write at length. Including irrelevant material has two negative effects:
  - it uses up valuable time in the examination
  - it makes it harder for the examiner to find the relevant points in your answer.
- Don't leave a question unanswered. If you have done a reasonable amount of preparation and you are faced with a question to which you don't know the answer, you can:
  - eliminate a lot of areas of the syllabus as being irrelevant
  - focus on one area and try to eliminate parts of that
  - make an educated guess at the right answer.
- Do check your answers as carefully as time permits. It is easy to make silly mistakes (writing 'use' instead of 'produce', for example) and then not spot the mistake because you are reading what you want to see, not what is actually written.
- Do take particular care over drawing graphs and labelling diagrams. Both require a level of precision. Marks are easily lost because a plot is not quite where it should be, or a label line finishes just short of the structure.
- Do write as legibly as possible. The examiner knows that an examination is a stressful experience and he/she will try to make sense of what you have written, but if an answer really is illegible, then you will not score any marks.

GETTING THE MOST FROM YOUR COURSEWORK

Your coursework (practical investigation) is an important part of the course you are following. It develops skills which are important to a biologist other than those of knowledge and understanding of biological facts and ideas.

On a more practical level, the assessment of these skills is worth 25% of all the marks in your Biology GCSE examination. A really good coursework assessment (20+ of the 25%) can mean that you will need less than 50% of the marks in the written examinations to achieve an overall Grade C.

Four skill areas will be assessed, they are:

- Planning
- Obtaining evidence
- Analysing evidence
- Evaluation

The following hints are designed to help you score the highest marks possible.

PLANNING

It is often helpful when you begin to plan an investigation to phrase the title in the form of a question. 'Investigating the effect of temperature on the activity of lipase' is better rephrased as 'How does a change in temperature affect the activity of lipase?'.

Once you have the title as a question ' How does X affect Y?', you have defined the two variables.

> X is the independent variable – it is the one you will change in the investigation
> Y is the dependent variable – it is dependent on the value of X.

Now you need to think about changing the independent variable. Remember that you can usually do three things with the independent variable:

- you can increase it
- you can decrease it
- you can leave it as it is.

Your investigation should aim to take in all three aspects. You can also increase it a little or a lot and decrease it a little or a lot – and you should aim to do both. Try to end up with at least five values for your independent variable.

The way in which you change the independent variable will depend on the nature of the variable itself, but you must take reasonable precautions to ensure that you do not change any other factor at the same time. For example, if you change light intensity, you might also change the temperature – How could you stop this from happening? Make sure that you only change the variable you are investigating and take positive measures to keep constant all the other variables which might also affect the results.

When you have an outline plan in your mind, you should try it out. This is your preliminary work. You might find that things do not work quite as you had expected, or that other factors need to be taken into account. Once you have done this preliminary work you can then make a detailed plan. Refer to your preliminary work in your detailed plan to say how you knew to use such and such concentrations, light intensities or temperatures and not others. Include in your detailed plan all the technical details of your experiment(s) as well as:

- an explanation of the form in which you will record your results – including units;
- how you will identify anomalous results
- any possible errors which might arise (this does not mean recording inaccurately – that is carelessness).

Once you have your detailed plan, you will often be able to predict what you think will happen. Your prediction should say what will happen to the dependent variable as you change the independent variable. There are no marks for a guess. You should have sound biological reasons for your prediction and you should include them in your account.

OBTAINING EVIDENCE

This section essentially assesses how well you gather the information from your investigation. It has two main elements:

- carrying out the investigation carefully and systematically, including making an appropriate number of suitable observations or measurements
- recording the observations accurately and clearly – including appropriate units.

During this stage of the investigation, you are gathering the information which you will use to solve the problem posed in your investigation. You need to be sure that the information is both as accurate and reliable as possible.

To ensure that the information you gather is accurate be aware of the following:

- Take care when taking readings from instruments.
- Be aware of their limitations – a thermometer which reads from 0°C to 300°C in 5° intervals may not be accurate enough if you are dealing with a temperature range of 0°C to 70°C.
- Make sure that you know the actual values of your independent variable – not just the planned values. Just because a water bath is set to be at 50°C, does not mean that it is. Check it. If you move a light source twice as far away you should decrease the light intensity to 25% of its previous value – but, again, use a light meter and check it!

To ensure that the information you gather is reliable, be aware of the following:

- Repeats help you to identify anomalous results. But you must have three repeats. If you have two repeat results for a certain temperature which are very different, you may not be sure which is the anomalous result. If you have three and two are similar and one is different, then this is probably the anomalous value.

ANALYSIS

In this section you will have to do two things.

- You will have to present your results in the most appropriate way so that it is easy to identify any patterns or trends.
- You will have to explain any patterns and trends and justify your explanations.

Convert your results to an appropriate graph or chart where at all possible. This makes it easier to identify any trends. Make sure that you use an appropriate chart or graph.

- Bar charts are used to show how the dependent variable changes among several non-numerical categories. For example you may choose to investigate the effect of different exercises on heart rate. If you jog, cycle, swim and walk, you cannot easily put these activities on a numeric scale and so a bar chart is the best way of representing the data. Remember, the bars should not touch each other.
- Line graphs are appropriate when the values for both variables are numerical and you are not plotting a frequency distribution. Remember to:
  - choose a suitable scale and make sure that your scale does not change along the axis
  - label your axes fully, including your units
  - give your graph a title

- plot your points accurately
- draw a line of best fit through the points, excluding any obviously anomalous results.

When you have identified a trend, you should describe it as accurately as possible. This does not mean restating what happened at every value of your independent variable. It does mean, however, looking for a change in the trend. If your results show (for example) a large increase in rate of reaction over one set of values and then a smaller increase over the next set of values, say so. Don't just say there is an increase.

Once you have described the trend, you should then use it to attempt to draw a general conclusion. For example, the trend may be that 'the nearer the light source, the more bubbles of oxygen are given off by *Elodea*'. A conclusion from this trend would be that 'the rate of photosynthesis increases with increasing light intensity'. You should then try to justify your conclusion using your biological knowledge and understanding. You should also try to relate your results and conclusions to your original prediction and use them to say how far your prediction was proved to be accurate.

EVALUATING

In this section, you should attempt to assess just how dependable your investigation has been. You should include comments about the following:

- the suitability of the procedure itself
- the accuracy of the results you obtained
- the reliability of the results overall
- any way in which you could extend the investigation.

The procedure you chose may only be one of several possible ways of investigating the problem. You should try to find out if:

- there were any other (better) ways of changing the independent variable
- there were any other (better) ways of measuring the dependent variable.

You can then comment as to how suitable your particular procedure was. Don't be afraid of finding out that you could have done it better – research scientists are constantly finding out that they can do things a lot better.

Anomalous results are usually fairly easily identified, but don't fall into the trap of always using the same deviation as a measure of anomaly. For example, suppose you were timing how long it took for amylase to digest starch at different temperatures and you obtained the following results for 35°C and 50°C.

Temperature (°C)	Time taken (seconds)			
	1	2	3	Average
35	25	23	35	24
50	280	294	266	275

Clearly, at 35°C, results 1 and 2 are nearly the same, but result 3 is very different. It took 10 seconds longer than result 1. It is therefore probably anomalous and is not included in the average.

At 50°C, the results all look similar, but, in fact the difference between the middle result and the other two is 14 seconds – more than the 10 seconds which was unacceptable at 35°C.

This is because you should consider the % difference. At 50°C, both other results are just 5% different from the middle result. At 35°C, result 3 is 40% different from the middle result.

Once identified, you should try to think of reasons for your anomalous results. Don't say things like 'I may not have timed properly' or 'I may have spilled some chemicals when I was measuring'. These are admissions of carelessness and you should either not have done it or you should have corrected it.

Once you have completed your investigation, it is often quite easy to think of extra things you could have done to make it a better, more comprehensive investigation. Take care however and look at the title of your investigation. If you were investigating the effect of temperature on enzyme action, suggesting that you also investigate pH does not improve the investigation. Suggesting that you investigate an extended range of temperatures may well be useful. Suggesting that you now investigate a certain narrow range of temperatures where the enzyme appears to be most effective would also take you forward. Both these are still within the context of your original investigation. Whatever you propose, you should be able to say how it will improve the investigation.

EXAMINERS' TERMS

Calculate means calculate – add up, subtract, divide, multiply, do a sum. Remember, there are no marks in a Biology exam for being a genius at mental arithmetic – so show your working. It is easy to press the wrong button on a calculator and get the wrong answer – and if all the examiner sees is the wrong answer, you will get no marks. If the examiner sees that you used a correct method, you may still score a mark even though the actual answer is wrong.

Compare means point out both similarities and differences in the data or structures referred to in the question.

Don't just put one side of the argument and leave it to the examiner to assume you know the other. For example in comparing the left and right ventricles 'the left ventricle has a thick wall' doesn't compare the two ventricles. 'The left ventricle has a thicker wall' does make a comparison.

Complete means that you should insert your answers in spaces left in the question.

Sometimes a list of the missing words will be supplied. In these cases take care to note whether each word can be used once only or more than once.

Describe means list the important features of.

You may be asked to describe:

● structures or processes from memory
● trends in graphs or tables
● structures or adaptations presented in diagrams or photographs.

The term describe does not mean explain, so you don't have to say why a trend or adaptation is the way it is.

Draw/plot a bar chart means you must represent the data as a series of bars.

If a scale is not given, choose one which will allow you to use most of the graph paper supplied. Bars on bar charts should not touch each other.

Draw/plot a line graph means that you must represent the data as a series of points joined by either a line of best fit or a curve through the points. Sometimes you may be asked to join the points with straight lines. Read carefully the instructions in the question.

Graphs are usually worth several marks and you should score all of them if you:

- choose suitable scales which use most of the graph paper supplied
- label your axes clearly, remembering to include the units
- plot the points carefully with a sharp pencil – a blunt pencil will produce plots that cover too much area on the graph paper to be accurate
- remember to plot the experimentally determined variable (the one you are measuring, finding out about in an experiment) on the y (vertical) axis
- draw an appropriate line through the points (read carefully what is required) – there may be an obviously anomalous point so do not draw your line/curve through this point.

Explain means give biological reasons for.

If you are asked to explain why or how something happens, you have no need to describe it as well. 'Explain why heart rate increases with exercise' does not require a detailed description of how much it increases with different exercises. It requires an answer based around the biological reasons – delivering more oxygen to muscles and removing more heat and carbon dioxide. If you are asked to explain why you were late for a lesson, you don't describe the lateness all over again – you try to think of an acceptable reason!

From the graph/table/diagram/photograph means that the answer is to be found in the data supplied and you should not modify it.

Give reasons for means list several, different reasons.

Usually, you will be asked for a certain number of reasons. If you are asked for two, give two not three.

Give/state usually means that you should write short answers, often one word, without attempting an explanation.

List means that you should supply a list of short answers, ideally on separate lines or in the spaces left on the question paper. Very similar to 'give/state'.

Name means you should give the biological name of a structure or process.

The name is all that is required. There is no need to preface your answer by writing 'The name of the structure labelled X is ....'. This just takes up valuable time in the examination without scoring any marks.

Suggest means that you should put forward a plausible explanation based on the evidence you have been given.

You will often find this term being used in a question where you are thinking 'We never did this in Biology lessons'. The examiner is aware also that you never did this in Biology lessons. You are being tested to see if you can use your knowledge to analyse data about unfamiliar situations. There are often several possible answers and you must suggest one of them.

Using information from ... means that you should use the information supplied in a graph/table/ chart as a basis for your answer.

For example you may be given information about the rate of photosynthesis in pondweed in different light intensities. If you just describe, from memory, the effect of light intensity on photosynthesis without relating it to the data, you will not score full marks.

What is meant by means that you should give a brief definition of the term.

Why is used less and less in Biology examinations, but where it is used it means give a biological reason for.

REVISION LISTS

These revision lists have been specifically designed to help you to organise your revision.

Your Biology syllabus contains two major components:

- the core, which is almost the same for all examination boards
- the extension material which is different for the different examination boards.

You will need to know all the terms contained in the core and the terms contained in the extension material for your syllabus. So, to avoid learning terms which you do not need to know, you must find out precisely which syllabus you are following. Some examination boards offer more than one syllabus.

To use the lists effectively, choose, first, the topic you are revising and look up the terms which are listed. You will find that many of these terms refer you to other entries which will help you to get a fuller understanding of the topic. The terms are listed in sections under two main headings:

- core biology
- extension biology.

The extension biology terms are grouped according to syllabus.

You will find that some terms are followed by another in brackets. The terms are alternatives. The first term is the one which will be found in this book: the second may be used by some of the examination syllabuses.

Sometimes a term may be followed by a list of other bullet-pointed terms. For example:

Nitrogen cycle
- Nitrogen fixing bacteria
- Nitrifying bacteria
- Denitrifying bacteria
- Nitrification
- Denitrification

In a case like this, you should look up the first term first. It will contain a brief description of the others. If you feel that you need more detail, you can then look up the other terms.

Some terms are printed in italics: these terms will only be used on the higher tier papers.

CORE BIOLOGY

Life processes and levels of organisation: top 15 revision terms

Abdomen
Excretion
Growth
Nutrition
Organ
Organ system
Reproduction
Respiration
Root
Root system
Sensitivity
Shoot
Shoot system
Thorax
Tissue

Cells: top 25 revision terms

Allele
Amino acid
Cell
Cell membrane
Cell wall
Cellulose
Chloroplast
Chromosome
Concentration gradient
Cytoplasm
Diffusion
DNA
Enzyme
Gene
Meiosis
Mitochondria
Mitosis
m-RNA
Nucleus
Osmosis
Partially permeable membrane
Protein synthesis
Ribosome
t-RNA
Vacuole

Revision lists for GCSE

Human nutrition: top 40 revision terms

Amino acid

Amylase

Balanced diet

Bile

Carbohydrate

Digestion

Digestive enzymes

Digestive system

Emulsify

Faeces

Fat

Fatty acid

Food tests

- Benedict's test
- Biuret test
- Emulsion test
- Iodine test

Gall bladder

Glycerol

Hydrochloric acid.

Large intestine

Lipase

Liver

Minerals

Nutrition

Oesophagus

Pancreas

Peristalsis

Protease

Protein

Saliva

Salivary gland

Small intestine

Smooth muscle

Starch

Stomach

Sugar

Teeth

Villus

Vitamin

Human circulation: top 25 revision terms

Atrio-ventricular valve

Blood

Blood cells

- Platelets
- Red blood cells
- White blood cells

Blood circulation

Blood clotting

Blood plasma

Blood pressure

Blood vessels

- Artery
- Vein

- Capillary
- Aorta
- Pulmonary artery
- Pulmonary vein
- Vena cava

Bone marrow

Circulatory sytem

Haemoglobin

Heart

Pulse

Semi-lunar valve

Ventricle

Human breathing: 15 top revision terms

Alveoli
Breathing
Bronchioles
Bronchus
Cilia
Diaphragm
Diaphragm
Intercostal muscle

Lung
Mucous membrane
Mucus
Rib
Ribcage
Thorax
Trachea

Respiration: top 10 revision terms

Aerobic respiration
Alcohol
anaerobic respiration
ATP
Glucose

Lactic acid
Mitochondria
Oxidation
Oxygen debt
Respiration

Human nervous system: top 40 revision terms

Accommodation
Aqueous humour
Blind spot
Brain
Cerebrum
Ciliary muscles
Cone
Conjunctiva
Coordination
Cornea
Ear
Effector
Eye
Fovea
Grey matter
Iris
Lens
Motor neurone
Nerve
Nerve impulse

Nervous system
Neurone
Neurotransmitter
Optic nerve
Receptor
Reflex action
Reflex arc
Response
Retina
Rod
Sclera
Sensory neurone
Skin
Smell
Spinal cord
Stimulus
Suspensory ligament
Synapse
Taste
White matter

Revision lists for GCSE

Human hormones: top 20 revision terms

Adrenal gland
Adrenaline
Diabetes
Fertility drug
FSH
Gland
Glucagon
Glucose
Glycogen
Hormone

Insulin
Islet cells
LH
Menstrual cycle
Menstruation
Oestrogen
Pancreas
Pituitary gland
Progesterone
Testosterone

Human homeostasis: top 25 revision terms

ADH
Bladder
Deamination
Dialysis
Excretion
Glucagon
Homeostasis
Insulin
Kidney
Kidney transplant
Negative feedback
Nephron
Shivering

Skin
Sweat
Sweat gland
Thermoregulation
Thermoregulatory centre
Ultrafiltration
Urea
Ureter
Urethra
Urine
Vasoconstriction
Vasodilation

Health: top 20 revision terms

Addiction
Alcohol abuse
Antibody
Antigen
Antitoxin
Bacteria
Cilia
Disease transmission
Drug
- Analgesic

- Depressant
- Hallucinogen
- Solvent
- Stimulant

Drug abuse
Immune response
Immunity
Mucus
Protozoa
Viruses

Photosynthesis and mineral nutrition in plants: top 15 revision terms

Active transport
Chlorophyll
Chloroplast
Guard cell
Leaf
Limiting factor
Mineral ions
Mineral salts

Minerals
Palisade mesophyll
Photosynthesis
Spongy mesophyll
Starch
Stomata
Vein (leaf)

Water relations of plants: top 15 revision terms

Diffusion
Evaporation
Flaccid
Leaf
Osmosis
Phloem
Plasmolysis
Potometer

Root hair
Stomata
Translocation
Transpiration
Turgid
Wilting
Xylem

Control of plant growth: top 5 revision terms

Auxins
Cuttings
Geotropism

Phototropism
Tropism

Growth: top 5 revision terms

Chromosome
Growth
Growth hormone

Growth rate (individual)
Mitosis

Reproduction: top 20 revision terms

Asexual reproduction
Chromosome
Down's syndrome
Egg cell
Embryo
Fertilisation

Fetus
Gamete
Identical twins
Meiosis
Ovary (human)
Ovary (plant)

Reproductive system (human)   Sperm
Reproductive system (plant)   Stamen
Seed   Testis
Sexual reproduction   Zygote

Inheritance: top 25 revision terms

Allele   Heterozygous
Autosome   Homozygous
Chromosome   Huntingdon's chorea
Cystic fibrosis   Meiosis
DNA   Mitosis
Dominant   Phenotype
F1   Recessive
F2   Selective breeding
Gene   Sex chromosome
Genetic engineering   Sex determination
Genotype   Sex linked inheritance
Gregor Mendel   Sickle cell anaemia
Haemophilia

Variation and evolution: top 10 revision terms

Charles Darwin   Fossil
Continuous variation   Meiosis
Discontinuous variation   Mutation
Evolution   Natural selection
Extinction   Species

Adaptation and competition: top 5 revision terms

Adaptation   Population growth curve
Competition   Predator prey relationships
Population

Cycles of matter and energy: top 12 revision terms

Carbon cycle   Decomposition (decay)
Consumer   Energy flow diagram
Decomposer   Food chain

Food web

Nitrogen cycle

Producer

Pyramid of biomass

Pyramid of energy

Pyramid of numbers

Humans and the environment: top 15 revision terms

Acid rain

Biological control

Biosphere

DDT

Ecosystem

Eutrophication

Fertiliser

Food chain

Global warming

Greenhouse effect

Ozone layer

Pesticide

Pollution

Soil erosion

Ultraviolet radiation

SOUTHERN EXAMINING GROUP (SEG) – BIOLOGY

Patterns of feeding: top 15 revision terms

Caecum

Carnivore

Decomposer

Ectoparasite

Endoparasite

Filter feeder

Fluid feeder

Herbivore

Parasite

Plankton

Rumen

Ruminant

Saprobiont (saprophyte)

Symbiosis

Teeth

Patterns of support and movement: top 30 revision terms

Skeleton and muscles:

Antagonistic muscle

Bone

Cartilage

Ligament

Muscle

Pectoral girdle

Pelvic girdle

Ribcage

Skeleton

- Exoskeleton
- Hydrostatic skeleton

Skull

Tendon

Vertebral column

Vertebrate

Adaptations for movement:

Carpal

Cilia

Feathers

Fins

Flagella

Metacarpal

Myotomes

Pentadactyl limb

Phalanges

Pseudopodia

Swim bladder

Wing

Plant responses:

Auxin

Geotropism

Phototropism

Revision lists for GCSE

Microorganisms: top 25 revision terms

Anaerobic respiration (in yeast)

Antibiotic

Bacteria

Bacillus

Coccus

Spirillum

Vibrio

Baking

Brewing

Budding (in yeast)

Cell membrane

Cell wall

Cheese

Digestive enzymes

Disease

DNA

Flagella

Fungi

Hyphae

Mycelium

Pathogen

Virus

Wine making

Yeast

Yoghurt

Controlling the spread of disease: top 15 revision terms

Antibodies

Disease

Disease: prevention

Disease: transmission

Immunisation

Incineration (of household rubbish)

Landfill tipping (of household rubbish)

Lymphocytes

Sewage

Sewage treatment
- Activated sludge method
- Percolating (biological) filter method

Vaccination

Vaccine

Water treatment

SOUTHERN EXAMINING GROUP (SEG) – BIOLOGY (HUMAN)

Maintenance of circulation in humans: top 20 revision terms

Angina

Antibody

Antigen

Aorta

Atrio-ventricular valves (cuspid
valves)

Blood clot

Blood group

Blood pressure

Cholesterol

Coronary artery

Fatty acids

Heart

Heart disease

Pulmonary artery

Pulmonary vein

Pulse

Pulse rate

Saturated fat

Stroke

Vena Cava

The human skeleton: top 20 revision terms

Antagonistic muscle

Bone

Cardiac muscle

Cartilage

Dislocation

Fatigue

Ligament

Muscle

Pectoral girdle

Pelvic girdle

Ribcage

Skeletal muscle

Skeleton

Skull

Slipped disc

Smooth muscle

Synovial joint
- Synovial fluid
- Synovial membrane

Vertebral column

Human reproduction and development: top 30 revision terms

Amnion
Birth
Breast
Colostrum
Corpus luteum (Yellow body)
Egg cell (Ovum)
Fertilisation
FSH
Growth rate (individual)
LH
Menstrual cycle
Menstruation
Oestrogen
Ovary
Oviduct (Fallopian tube)
Ovulation
Penis
Pituitary gland
Placenta
Pregnancy
Progesterone
Reproductive system – human
Sperm (Spermatozoon)
Sperm duct (Vas deferens)
Testis
Testosterone
Umbilical cord
Uterus
Vagina
Zygote

Causes and control of disease in humans: top 25 revision terms

Antibody
Asbestosis
Bacteria
Disease
Disease – prevention of
Disease – transmission
Down's syndrome
Farmer's lung
Fungi
Huntingdon's chorea
Immunisation
Incineration (of household rubbish)
Infection
Landfill tipping (of household rubbish)
Lymphocytes
Pathogen
Protozoa
Sewage treatment
- Activated sludge method
- Percolating (biological) filter method
Vaccination
Vaccine
Viruses
Water treatment

LONDON (EDEXCEL) – BIOLOGY

MICROORGANISMS AND DISEASE IN HUMANS

Structure and reproduction of microorganisms: top 20 revision terms

Bacteria
- Bacillus
- Coccus
- Spirillum
- Vibrio

Binary fission
Budding (in yeast)
Cell membrane
Cell wall
Cytoplasm

Fungi
Hyphae
Mycelium
Nucleoid
Parasite
Pathogen
Plasmid
Protozoa
Viruses
Yeast

The spread and control of disease: top 15 revision terms

Antiseptic
Cholera
Disease
Disease – prevention
Disease – transmission
Disease, infectious
Disinfectant
Infection

Joseph Lister
Louis Pasteur
Measles
Pulmonary tuberculosis
Salmonella
Sterilisation
Vector – disease

Safe food and water: top 10 revision terms

Pasteurisation
Potable water
Sewage
Sewage treatment
- Activated sludge method
- Percolating (biological) filter method

Food poisoning
Salmonella
Hygiene
Food preservation

Revision lists for GCSE

Combating infection: top 15 revision terms

Alexander Fleming
Antibiotic
Antibody
Antigen
Bactericidal
B-Lymphocyte
Ernst Chain
Hepatitis B

Howard Florey
Infection
Memory cell
Monoclonal antibodies
Penicillin
Phagocyte
T-lymphocyte

BIOTECHNOLOGY IN FOOD PRODUCTION

Fermentation using yeast and other organisms: top 10 revision terms

Bioreactor (Fermenter)
Brewing
Ethanol
Fermentation
Lactic acid

Mycoprotein
Pasteurisation
Sterile
Wine making
Yoghurt

Manipulating genes and reproduction: top 15 revision terms

Allele
Artificial insemination
DNA
Egg cell (ovum)
Embryo
Embryo transplant
Gene
Genetic engineering

Implantation
In vitro fertilisation (IVF)
Plasmid
Surrogate mother
Transgenic
Vector (genetic)
Zygote

MIDLAND EXAMINING GROUP (MEG) – BIOLOGY SYLLABUS A

Diversity and adaptation: top 40 revision terms

Acid rain
Adaptation
Biological control
Cactus
Deforestation
Classification
- Protoctista
  - Algae
- Bacteria
- Fungi
- Plants
  - Mosses
  - Ferns
  - Angiosperms
- Molluscs
- Annelids
- Arthropods
  - Myriapods

- Crustaceans
- Arachnids
- Insects
• Vertebrates
- Fish
- Amphibians
- Reptiles
- Birds
- Mammals
Competition
Fluid feeder
Greenhouse effect
Metamorphosis (complete)
Pesticides
Predator
Predator – prey relationships
Xerophyte

Microorganisms and food: top 15 revision terms

Active site
Baking
Cheese
Disease – prevention
Enzymes
Food poisoning
Food preservation
Genetic engineering

Hygiene
Lock and key hypothesis
Mycoprotein
Rennin
Wine making
Yeast
Yoghurt

Revision lists for GCSE

Infectious diseases: top 20 revision terms

Alexander Fleming
Antibiotic
Antiseptic
Biological control
Disease – infectious
Disease – prevention
Disease – transmission
Edward Jenner
Ernst Chain
Howard Florey

Immunisastion
Louis Pasteur
Malaria
Mildew
Parasite
Pathogen
Resistance
Selective breeding
Vaccination
Vaccine

MIDLAND EXAMINING GROUP (MEG) – BIOLOGY SYLLABUS C (SALTERS)

Off the blocks: top 35 revision terms

Absorption
Aerobic respiration
Anabolic steroid
Anaerobic respiration
Antagonistic muscles
ATP
Blood groups
Blood vessels
- Artery
- Capillary
- Vein

Bone
Breathing
Diaphragm
Digestion
Drug
Drug abuse
Exercise

Heart
Joint
Lactic acid
Lungs Alveoli
Mitochondrion
Muscle
- Cardiac muscle
- Skeletal muscle
- Smooth muscle
- Involuntary muscle
- Voluntary muscle

Oxygen debt
Ribcage
Skeleton
Small intestine
Synovial joint
Tendon

Revision lists for GCSE

Growing crops: top 25 revision terms

Annual

Biennial

Cereals

Competition

Fertilisation

Fertilizers

Gene pool

Genetic engineering

Genotype

Germination

Herbicide (Weedkiller)

Hydroponics

Inheritance

Mineral ions

Mineral salts

Perennial

Photosynthesis

Pollen tube

Pollination

Resistance

Seed dispersal

Selective breeding

Soil

Soil erosion

Weed

The ploughman's lunch: top 15 revision terms

Bacteria

Baking

Binary fission

Brewing

Cheese

Fermentation

Food preservation

Fungi

Protozoa

Rennin

Sterile

Viruses

Wine making

Yeast

Yoghurt

Industrious microbes: top 10 revision terms

Antibiotic

Bacteria

Bioreactor (Fermenter)

Cloning

Enzymes: commercial applications

Enzymes: immobilised

Genetic engineering

Lipase

Mycoprotein

Protease

MIDLAND EXAMINING BOARD (MEG) – BIOLOGY SYLLABUS D (NUFFIELD)

Helpful organisms: top 10 revision terms

Bacteria
Viruses
Fungi
Amino acid
Baking

Cheese
Wine making
Mycoprotein
Nitrogen fixing bacteria
Decomposers

Harmful organisms: top 15 revision terms

Bronchiole
Disease
Disease – prevention
Disease – transmission
Food poisoning
Food preservation
Fungi
Immune response

Immune system
Phagocytes
Pulmonary tuberculosis (TB)
Skin
Toxic shock syndrome
Trachea
Water treatment

Vaccines and antibiotics: top 10 revision terms

Antibiotic
Antibody
Antigen
Bacteria
Cancer

Colostrum
Immune response
Memory cells
Vaccination
Vaccine

Applied genetics: top 10 revision terms

Cystic fibrosis
Down's syndrome
F1
F2
Haemophilia
Huntingdon's chorea (Huntingdon's
    disease)

Hybrid
Mutation
Pollination
Sex linked inheritance

Genetic engineering: top 10 revision terms

Allele

DNA

Gene

Genetic engineering

Monoclonal antibodies

m-RNA

Mutation

Protein synthesis

Ribosome

t-RNA

Conservation: top 5 revision terms

Conservation

Diversity index

Ecosystem

Habitat

Biosphere

Pollution: top 10 revision terms

Acid rain

Eutrophication

Fertiliser

Indicator species

Pollution – thermal

Pollution – air

Pollution – freshwater

Pollution – land

Sewage

Sewage treatment

WELSH JOINT EDUCATION COMMITTEE – BIOLOGY

Please note: the subdivisions used here do not correspond with any printed in the syllabus. They are included to try to make your revision more manageable.

Making useful products: top 10 revision terms

Antibiotic

Baking

Bioreactor (Fermenter)

Brewing

Fermentation

Lactic acid

Penicillin

Wine making

Yeast

Yoghurt

Major groups of microorganisms: top 10 revision terms

Algae

Bacteria

Cell membrane

Cell wall

Cytoplasm

Fungi

Gene

Moulds

Protozoa

Viruses

Commercial applications of enzymes: top 10 revision terms

Amino acid

Digestive enzymes
- Lipase
- Protease

Enzymes

Enzymes – commercial applications

Fat

Fatty acid

Glycerol

Protein

Sewage treatment: top 5 revision terms

Organic

Sewage

Sewage treatment

- Activated sludge method
- Percolating (biological) filter method

Vaccines and immunity: top 10 revision terms

Antibody
Antigen
B-lymphocyte
Immune response
Immune system

Immunisation
Immunity
Memory cell
Vaccination
Vaccine

Technology in medicine: top 5 revision terms

Dialysis
Immune response
Kidney transplant

Rejection
Transplantation

NORTHERN EXAMINATIONS AND ASSESSMENT BOARD (NEAB) – BIOLOGY

Exercise and health: top 20 revision terms

Antagonistic muscles
Blood pressure
Bone
Dislocation
Exercise
Fitness, physical
Heart
Ligament
Muscle
Pulse rate

Recovery period
Respiration
- Aerobic respiration
- Anaerobic respiration

Sprain
Stroke volume
Synovial joint
- Synovial fluid
- Synovial membrane

Tendon

Biotechnology and disease: top 25 revision terms

Antibiotic
Antibody
Antigen
Arthritis
Bacteria
Blood groups
Blood transfusion
Dialysis
Immune response
Immune system
Immunisation
Immunity
Immunosuppressive drug

Louis Pasteur
Memory cells
Penicillin
Rejection
Tissue typing
Transplantation
Vaccination
Vaccine
Viruses
White blood cells
B-lymphocytes
T-lymphocytes

Using microorganisms to make useful substances: top 10 revision terms

Agar
Algae
Antibiotic
Bacteria
Baking

Bioreactor (Fermenter)
Fermentation (yeast)
Mould
Yeast
Yoghurt

Revision lists for GCSE

Amylase

Lipase

Enzymes – commercial applications

Protease

Enzymes – immobilised

NORTHERN IRELAND CCEA – BIOLOGY

Classification and life cycles: top 25 revision terms

Algae
Annelids
Arthropods
Myriapods
Crustaceans
Insects
Arachnids
Classification
Fungi
Life cycle
Metamorphosis
Molluscs
Moulds

Plants
- Mosses
- Ferns
- Angiosperms

Quadrats
Sampling
Vertebrates
- Fish
- Amphibians
- Reptiles
- Birds
- Mammals

Conservation and pollution: top 15 revision terms

Acid rain
Conservation
Deforestation
Eutrophication
Greenhouse effect
Herbicide
Ozone layer
Pesticide

Pollution – air
Pollution – freshwater
Pollution – land
Pollution – thermal
Population growth curve
Sewage treatment

Genetics: top 10 revision terms

Artificial selection
Cancer
DNA
Genetic engineering
Mutation

Protein synthesis
Selective breeding
Sex linked inheritance
Tumour
UV radiation

Revision lists for GCSE

Microbiology: top 25 revision terms

Antibiotic
Antibody
Antigen
Antiseptic
Bacteria
Baking
Bioreactor
Brewing
Decomposers
Disease
Disease – infectious
Disease – transmission
Food poisoning

Food preservation
Fungi
Immune response
Immune system
Immunity
Pasteurisation
Penicillin
Pulmonary tuberculosis (TB)
Salmonella
Viruses
Wine making
Yoghurt

EXTENSION MATERIAL

NORTHERN IRELAND CCEA – BIOLOGY (HUMAN)

MAN AND THE ENVIRONMENT

Sewage and water treatment : top 7 revision terms

Environment
Sewage
Sewage treatment
  • Activated sludge method

  • Percolating (biological) filter
    method
Potable water
Water treatment

Diseases and disorders: top 25 revision terms

Alcohol abuse
Anaemia
Antibiotic
Antiseptic
Arteriosclerosis
Bacteria
Bronchitis
Disease – infectious
Disease – prevention

Disease – transmission
Drug abuse
Fungi
Kwashiorkor
Malaria
Obesity
Parasite
  • Ectoparasite
  • Endoparasite

Pasteurisation
Protozoa
Salmonella
Sterilisation

Vector (disease)
Viruses
Vitamins

Food and microbes: top 5 revision terms

Cheese
Food poisoning
Food preservation

Mycoprotein
Yoghurt

Human reproduction and development: top 30 revision terms

Amnion
Birth
Colostrum
Corpus luteum (Yellow body)
Egg cell (Ovum)
Fertilisation
FSH
Growth rate (individual)
In vitro fertilisation (IVF)
LH
Menstrual cycle
Menstruation
Oestrogen
Ovary
Oviduct (Fallopian tube)

Ovulation
Pituitary gland
Placenta
Pregnancy
Progesterone
Reproductive system – human
Sexually transmitted disease (STD)
Sperm (Spermatozoon)
Sperm duct (Vas deferens)
Testis
Testosterone
Umbilical cord
Uterus
Vagina
Zygote

The human skeleton: top 15 revision terms

Antagonistic muscle
Bone
Cartilage
Ligament
Muscle
Pectoral girdle
Pelvic girdle
Ribcage

Skeleton
Skull
Slipped disc
Synovial joint
  ● Synovial fluid
  ● Synovial membrane
Vertebral column

The following *GCSE A–Z Handbooks* are available from Hodder & Stoughton. Why not use them to support your other GCSE and Intermediate GNVQs? All the *A–Zs* are written by experienced authors and Chief Examiners.

0 340 73060 9 *GCSE A–Z Double Science* £7.99
0 340 68366 X *GCSE A–Z Business Studies* £7.99
0 340 72447 1 *GCSE A–Z Geography* £7.99

All Hodder & Stoughton *Educational* books are available at your local bookshop, or can be ordered direct from the publisher. Just tick the titles you would like and complete the details below. Prices and availability are subject to change without prior notice.

Buy four books from the selection above and get free postage and packing. Just send a cheque or postal order made payable to *Bookpoint Limited* to the value of the total cover price of the books including postage and packaging. This should be sent to: Hodder & Stoughton *Educational*, 39 Milton Park, Abingdon, Oxon OX14 4TD, UK. EMail address: orders@bookpoint.co.uk. The following postage and packaging costs apply:

UK & BFPO: £4.30 for one book; £6.30 for two books; £8.30 for three books.
Overseas and Eire: £4.80 for one book; £7.10 for 2 or 3 books (surface mail).

If you would like to pay by credit card, our centre team would be delighted to take your order by telephone. Our direct line (44) 01235 827720 (lines open 9.00am - 6.00pm, Monday to Saturday, with a 24 hour answering service). Alternatively you can send a fax to (44) 01235 400454.

Title _____ First name _____ Surname _____

Address _____

Postcode _____ Daytime telephone no. _____

If you would prefer to pay by credit card, please complete:

Please debit my Master Card / Access / Diner's Card / American Express (delete as applicable)

Card number _____ Expiry date _____ Signature _____

If you would not like to receive further information on our products, please tick the box
☐